THE STORY

OF AN

AMERICAN

COMMUNIST

THE
STORY
OF AN
AMERICAN
COMMUNIST

by John Gates

THOMAS NELSON & SONS

Edinburgh NEW YORK *Toronto*

To Lillian

ACKNOWLEDGMENTS

I am especially indebted to Alan Max and Joseph Starobin for their assistance in preparing this book. They studied my manuscript closely, helped edit it and gave a great deal of their time. Joseph Clark also read the manuscript and made many helpful suggestions.

My wife discussed its ideas with me at every stage, gave me unfailing inspiration and kept my nose to the grindstone. It could not have been written without her.

For what may be deemed good in the book a great many people deserve credit. Otherwise the full responsibility for what is contained in it is mine alone.   J. G.

Brooklyn, N.Y.
July 19, 1958

FOREWORD

THE STORY OF JOHNNY GATES IS PART OF THE STORY OF AMERICA. It is a personal story, and therefore unique, different from that of any other person. At the same time, however, it is representative of what happened to a generation of young Americans who approached maturity during the shattering days of 1929 to 1934. This was the period of the Great Economic Crisis, when for the first time in our history America as a whole, not merely a region, lost the perspective and self-confidence transmitted from older generations, and felt impelled to strike out on new paths, toward some goal still but vaguely sensed, if our country was to escape disintegration.

Those days are now but a dim memory to most of those who lived through them—and a bad memory, something like that of a nightmare, to be pushed away from consciousness. The generations that came to maturity later knew nothing, or next to nothing, about that experience. The 1930s that marked a great turn in American history are known today, by and large, only by the net result that emerged; the experience itself has been lost to consciousness. In the national memory the 1930s are today mostly a blank, somewhat analogous to the mind of an individual suffering from amnesia. America has not recovered from the shock of the

Great Economic Crisis. It was much deeper than the shock of the Second World War.

Such a trauma or break in the national consciousness is unhealthy and even dangerous. It was the breeding-ground for McCarthyism, which is the specific American name for a political disease that is international, and that hit Russia even harder than it did America.

The Gates story is a contribution toward the recovery of America from the national amnesia regarding the 1930s, and the conditions that caused the rise of communism as a national political influence for the first, and probably the last, time in American history.

Equally important, Gates gives us an inside view of the decay of the American communist movement after 1945. The book gains much of its significance from the fact that Gates' attachment to that movement was not superficial. He belonged to the "hard core," and he liberated himself from it only as a result of "nuclear fission," the process of the splitting of its fundamental atoms—an explosion of which the Hungarian Revolution of 1956 was the prime example. Thus when Gates left the communist movement, this reflected not some merely personal revulsion, superficial disagreement, or personal emotional upset, but was rather a break in the very foundations of communism, of deep international significance.

Gates himself is still not fully conscious of all the deeper meaning of his own story. He is still too close to his own act of self-liberation from communist dogma to evaluate it with full objectivity. But that his liberation is fundamental, not a mere shifting of allegiances or turning of coats, is satisfactorily demonstrated by the character of the book which reflects the man. It is the character of men, even more than their ideas, which shape their history.

The intelligent reader of the story of Johnny Gates will find its main interest, not in the particular judgments expressed therein, which are transitional, but rather in the direction in which they move.

It is refreshing that Gates gives us nothing of the breast-beating confessions of sin that have made most of the writings of ex-communists so stale and boring to the point of nausea. Even when such outpourings are sincere, the possibility of which must be allowed, they are an offense to human dignity and expose a shallow character and intelligence. Gates does not apologize for his life, he explains it while changing it—and preserves in the process those basic values which always for him made life worth living intensely and with full commitment. And though the reader may disagree with his detailed opinions, he cannot escape the conviction that here he is dealing with an honest and courageous man—a circumstance still rare enough to be marked with high value.

My own long experience in the communist movement began much earlier than that of Gates, but also ended twelve years earlier. I was thrown out without ceremony, whereas Gates left it of his own volition. This difference marks the collapse of all communist morale during that twelve years; in 1945 communist conceit was high, and they thought their dogma was akin to natural law, but in 1958 they already knew their powerless and contemptible position in America, and therefore were afraid to expel Gates even when he openly denounced their most sacred dogmas in the columns of the *Daily Worker*. Now they hardly need expulsions any more, since everyone with the intelligence for revolt has walked out. Gates shows with chapter and verse how that decline was self-inflicted.

The past always merits our study, especially as it may influence the future. Gates shows us that the influence of American communists on the future is now confined to the role of horrible example of what to avoid. But he is not therefore pessimistic about America and the world today. He finds that today's young people, while they have learned to avoid the mistakes that ruined the communist movement, have by no means lost that eternal questing spirit of youth that in an earlier generation led them to communism, but which today will surely find a more reliable channel.

EARL BROWDER

Yonkers, New York
August 1, 1958

CONTENTS

Acknowledgments		vi
Foreword		vii
	PROLOGUE	3
I	EARLY YEARS	7
II	COLLEGE, CRISIS, AND COMMUNISM	14
III	YOUNGSTOWN	28
IV	SPAIN	42
V	THE MARCH TO WORLD WAR	68
VI	FROM THE ALEUTIANS TO GERMANY	84
VII	POSTWAR AND POST-BROWDER	101
VIII	TRIAL	119
IX	PRISON	136
X	THE FIGHT THAT FAILED	157
XI	THE END IS A NEW BEGINNING	192

THE STORY

OF AN

AMERICAN

COMMUNIST

PROLOGUE

UNTIL I RESIGNED FROM THE COMMUNIST PARTY OF THE UNITED
States on January 10, 1958, I had been a member for 27 years.
Every human being has a story. Mine is why I joined the Communist movement at the age of 17, what I did as a Communist
until the age of 44, why I left and what I believe now.

Mine is not only a personal history. It is also a story of important
events and great movements in which we who were members of
the Communist Party participated. These are now part of American and world history. My quarter of a century in the Communist
movement spanned the Great Depression of the thirties, the
Hoover and Roosevelt eras, the rise of Hitler to power, the birth
of the CIO, the Spanish Civil War, the second World War and
the defeat of fascism, the Chinese Revolution, the cold war and
the H-bomb, and the infant age of automation, atomic energy and
space. This book, of course, is not a history of these epoch-making
years—only of their impact upon me.

The Communist Party's relationship to these events of the past
few decades is complicated and had both positive and negative
aspects. Much of the party's story has been obscured, exaggerated
and distorted. Most Americans are largely ignorant of the real
facts, yet it is safe to say that the lives of all Americans have been

3

influenced both for good and for evil by what has been done *by* the Communist Party and by what has been said and done *about* the party. Although it once enjoyed considerable influence, the Communist Party never had more than 75,000 members at one time; never has so much been written, never such a frantic furore aroused about so small a political group.

There have been several reasons for this. The Communist Party here, weak even at its zenith, was identified with world communism which is very substantial and powerful. Because of this identification, political reaction here at home was able to manufacture a grossly inflated Communist menace which it used against the New Deal, the labor movement and liberal causes.

The Communist issue became a political football in the game of partisan politics. Politicians rode to power and influence upon it. Liberals competed with reactionaries to enact "anti-communist" legislation, to drive Communists out of jobs and organizations, to illegalize the Communist Party and make lepers of its members.

Few saw, and still fewer cared, that the constitutional liberties of all Americans were being eroded in the process. Undemocratic concepts alien to the Bill of Rights, such as preventive arrest, guilt by association, character assassination and anti-intellectualism began to flourish, stifling the atmosphere with fear, secrecy manias, censorship and conformity. The Communists were harshly victimized. But America was harmed even more.

In the name of secrecy, we managed only to keep things secret from our own scientists and the public, hampering our own progress more than that of others. In the name of defending freedom, we were losing our own. In the name of beating the Russians, we began to fall behind. In the name of security, we undermined security itself by contributing increased tension to an already overtense world.

At the press conference held when I quit the Communist Party, I made a prediction that the House Committee on Un-American Activities and the FBI would claim the death of the *Daily Worker* and my resignation only meant that the party was stronger than ever. Two months later J. Edgar Hoover published a book making this very claim. To those of us who left the Communist Party in the recent period, this talk about the organization growing stronger, is sheer fantasy. So little still remains of the party and of its influence, that at best it can be called a living corpse.

If J. Edgar Hoover really has the inside information which he claims, then he knows better than what he writes. Why does he persist in perpetuating a myth? Perhaps appropriations for his department have something to do with it. A growing number of Washington correspondents have begun to notice a rash of "communist menace" reports breaks out whenever government agencies are scheduled to request additional funds from Congress. Whereupon a duly frightened legislature proceeds to shell out and no questions asked.

There is a legitimate body of opinion which seeks to counter many of the ideas and methods of communism with what it holds to be superior ideas and practices; but there is also a spurious anticommunist racket which is financially lucrative, politically deceitful and a weapon against progress and freedom. Perhaps this too explains why some persons are so reluctant to give up the ghost of the "communist menace" in this country.

The title of Mr. Hoover's book *Masters of Deceit* is, in my opinion, a misnomer. The Communist Party here never mastered the art of persuading very large numbers of Americans, deceptively or otherwise. The only deception at which it proved adept was self-deception—the basic cause of its demise as an effective political trend. Persecution and prosecutions undoubtedly harmed the Communist Party, but the greatest injury was done to it by the party itself. The party was in some ways a continuation of American radicalism, and in some ways its negation. The party fell apart because it would not think for itself, would not face reality; it tried to ride two horses at one time, refused to change when changes became necessary, and finally insisted on committing suicide.

My chief interest in writing this book is to help create understanding. All our debates will become academic in the event of atomic war. In the present terrible impasse between the capitalist and communist worlds, the greatest single barrier to peace is the lack of understanding by both sides of the other. Just as love can blind us to the evil in the object of our affection, as happened with American Communists in their attitude to the communist world, so can hate blind us to what may be good. Neither is the path to a sound understanding. We need to be as objective as we can. While I am not against partisanship, I am against blind partisanship of any kind which operates at the expense of truth and justice.

The Communist Party in this country has failed. But who among us has succeeded? Who in judging the Communist Party can escape self-judgment, for is not every aspect of American life in crisis? Communists are people, human beings with the same qualities and frailties as everyone else; the American Party, when it had any effectiveness, contained universal aspects as well as its own peculiarities. It was neither all black nor all white, neither all good nor all evil.

Although I have left the Communist Party because of profound disagreements, I do not feel that my 27 years as a member were wasted. While there is much of which I am ashamed, there is also much of which I am proud. One's life is wasted only if one fails to learn from the past in order to become a better human being in the future. I am today trying to learn from my experiences of yesterday.

To the extent that these experiences are shared with the reader, and become part of his own, this book may be worthwhile.

I

EARLY YEARS

ELECTRICITY WAS REPLACING GASLIGHT WHEN I WAS BORN ON MAN-
hattan's East Side in 1913; horses were giving way to the automobile; the Model-T Ford became the symbol of a new age. The
airplane had been invented ten years earlier, and radio was in
its crystal-set infancy. My parents, of Jewish faith, had come
from Poland when they were in their teens, and they met and
married here. It was as a waiter in Ratner's Restaurant on De-
lancey Street that my father and the American economic system
first came together.

From there our family followed the cycle described by Samuel
Lubell in *The Future of American Politics*. When I was four, we
moved out of the slum tenement on East 4th Street and traveled
uptown to 98th Street near Central Park West, where my father
was now owner of the inevitable candy store. Six years later he
bought a large ice-cream parlor on Fordham Road in the Bronx
and once again we moved.

As store-keeper, my father worked from six o'clock in the morning until midnight to support my mother and four children. Rigor-
ously orthodox in his faith, he possessed a strong sense of right
and wrong, and was stern with us and generous too. My mother,
a pretty blond woman, vivacious and fun-loving, had married him
when she was sixteen. She was seventeen when I was born.

7

Of our first home—the East Side tenement—I remember little except the stench of the building, which was already ancient and decrepit. All the tenants on a floor shared a toilet in the hallway. When I visited the area a few years ago I was startled to find the building still standing and, worse, still tenanted.

The lower East Side has been immortalized by Jacob Riis, Abraham Cahan, Michael Gold; by the life-stories of Alfred E. Smith and its many other distinguished citizens. The area was mainly Jewish when I lived there, although there were also large Italian, Irish and Chinese communities. Today the East Side has changed in many ways; in many ways it remains the same.

Puerto Rican and Negro families have arrived in considerable numbers, but many of the old families are still there. Tremendous housing projects now cut the sky-line, but at their feet still squat the crumbling tenements. Transcontinental planes flash overhead in the sun, while down below fires still rage in the factory lofts, taking their toll much as the famous Triangle disaster did half a century ago.

I was a stubborn and opinionated child, it seems. I refused to take my milk straight and my mother had to disguise it with chocolate or coffee. Besides, I would drink only from my own cup —and the contents had to be stirred clockwise. When my grandmother once stirred my milk counter-clockwise, I became furious and called upon God to punish her. My family tells the story with amusement but I am horrified to have been already so self-righteous at such an early age. More understandable was my refusal to take castor oil. Once four people tried to pour the terrible potion into me without success. Years later, in a matter involving castor oil and having nothing to do with medicine, I was, if anything, even more stubborn.

When we moved to the upper West Side, I found to my delight a seemingly endless park only a block away from our new home. We children romped all over Central Park and played ball there. We stole potatoes from vegetable stands and baked them in fires near the curb. We played games suitable to the narrow streets hemmed in on both sides by houses: stickball with a rubber ball and a broomstick for a bat, handball against the walls of the buildings, stoopball against the front stairways of houses. We developed agility in dodging traffic as we ran bases and chased balls under auto and wagon wheels.

During the First World War, we sang a ditty as part of a street game: "Fat, fat, Kaiser rat, fifty bullets in your hat." I recall a block party to sell Liberty bonds—an important occasion for my father because his candy store supplied the pop and confetti, and a shortage of supplies presented him with big problems of procurement and distribution. There were speeches, I am sure, but I remember only the excitement and the good time.

I was a steady patron of the silent movies at the theater on West 99th Street, admission 11 cents (10 cents plus a penny war tax) and an admirer of the pianist who provided the musical accompaniment, his fingers racing tirelessly, his foot pounding mercilessly upon the loud pedal during the westerns. My favorites were Pearl White, harassed heroine of the serials, courageous William S. Hart of the westerns, and Elmo Lincoln, the first of a long line of muscular, tree-swinging Tarzans.

It was the Era of the Flapper (and of post-war breadlines). It was the Age of Jazz (and of the deportation delirium). One of my joys was being sent down to the corner saloon with a tin pail for beer for our supper table. The saloons had swinging half-doors and I was short enough to walk right under them. When Prohibition came, I still walked in under the doors, but I came out with "near-beer."

Ninety-ninth Street, next street to ours, was an all-Negro block, a one-street ghetto surrounded by a White community. From time to time organized street fights broke out between the two blocks. We would rope off the streets and throw rocks and milk bottles at one another. To me it was only a good fight, an exciting game, with no undertones of prejudice. When I first went to school, it was to P.S. 179 on West 101st Street and Amsterdam Avenue, the Negro children from 99th Street attended the school; there was no segregation and it never occurred to me that it could be otherwise.

I was appointed to the color guard at school. Our duty was to carry the American flag down the aisle during the daily assembly and to lead the body in the pledge of allegiance. My experience in the color guard was to be a factor many years later when Congress decided to change the form of the allegiance pledge.

My cousin Jack took me to my first big league ball game. Jack was about seven years older than I, with an artificial leg—result of a street-car accident. That first game was between the Yankees and the Athletics and to complete the day, Babe Ruth hit a home run.

When we moved to the Bronx, we lived on Fulton Avenue facing Crotona Park. I belonged to a club. It was a natural form of organization for recreation, sports and social life. We built clubhouses on empty lots and occasionally engaged in street fights with other clubs or gangs. A gang in itself is not destructive. The youth groups which take part in normal fun and the gangs that engage in sordid, violent activities, are separated by a thin line. The difference lies in the degree of poverty, the stability of family life, housing and school conditions. Our neighborhood—the Claremont Parkway area in the Bronx—was not a well-to-do or even middle-class community. But it was a healthy environment. Settlement houses existed in the area and my club became part of the Young Men's Hebrew Association. While the neighborhood was primarily Jewish, many Negroes, Poles, Italians and Irish also lived side by side here and went to school together.

My school was then P.S. 42 on Claremont Parkway, from which I graduated in 1926, class valedictorian and winner of a gold medal. The principal, a Mr. Garland, asked me in class one day why I planned to go to De Witt Clinton High School. "Because there are no girls there," I replied, as the class laughed. My decision to enroll in an all-boys school was my first big decision which I lived to regret. It was by no means my last.

I began to read a great deal—from pulp magazines and dime novels to serious literature beyond my capacity. Perhaps because I read so much, I found studying easy. I did not read at the expense of play. My reading was done late at night and, to the annoyance of my family, while I ate my meals. I spent as much time as possible out of doors playing ball. My mother persuaded me to take piano lessons. I took *one.*

I read the Merriwell saga, the Rover Boys, Tom Swift, Buffalo Bill, Nick Carter, Horatio Alger. Since I often worked after school in candy stores, I seized the opportunity not only to eat a good part of the stock, but also to read all the magazines on sale— *Argosy All-Story, True Story,* westerns, *Amazing Stories, Weird Tales,* as well as good fiction publications like the *Golden Book.* I read fairy tales, too, and I read *The Brothers Karamazov* by Dostoevsky, although without understanding very much of it. My great passion continued to be the movies which now began to talk. I also became a live vaudeville enthusiast, a fan of Jimmy Durante, Eddie Cantor, W. C. Fields, James Barton and other masters of the gag, sentimental musical phrase and light-hearted dance-step.

At election time, all political parties held street-corner meetings (this was before the day of the sound truck). It was not unusual to have four meetings going simultaneously at the busy intersection of Claremont Parkway and Washington Avenue, with the Democrats, Republicans, Socialists and Communists each occupying a corner.

Oratory was an art in those days and I would circulate from corner to corner. I remember nothing of what was said, however, until the presidential campaign of 1928, when Al Smith became my first political hero. The fact that Smith was the son of immigrants, had been born on the East Side and was now the target of religious bigotry, made him attractive. By this time I had become a foe of Prohibition and an advocate of evolution. (As I followed the Tennessee trial over the advocacy of evolution, it never occurred to me, of course, that one day I would figure in a trial over the right to advocate revolution.)

Radio was used on a wide scale for the first time in that 1928 campaign and I remember the fine scorn with which Smith ridiculed the GOP slogans of "Two Chickens In Every Pot" and "Two Cars in Every Garage," and the way he pronounced "raddio." My disappointment over Smith's defeat was great and I attributed it to bigotry. Undoubtedly this was an important factor, but I didn't understand then that Smith had been defeated mainly by the very prosperity which was the butt of his sarcasm.

De Witt Clinton High School, which I now attended, was an excellent school—even though there were no girls. The building was located at 59th Street and Tenth Avenue, in the area of Manhattan then called Hell's Kitchen. The students came from all over the city and the school reflected the melting pot that was New York.

Most of them were poor but some were of middle-class and even wealthy families. There was no discrimination of which I was aware—Negro students were readily elected to the top student-body posts. Later we moved from the cramped quarters in Hell's Kitchen to the splendid new premises on Moshulu Parkway in the northern part of the Bronx.

At school I was a member of the Printing Squad which set up and printed the school newspaper. We also printed the examination papers. This made membership on the squad a post of trust, but I could not resist taking a peek on occasion. On our own time we printed business cards and invitations, which brought us a bit of spending money.

By now I was an inveterate newspaper reader. I had begun with the tabloids, moved on to the Hearst press, then to the *New York World* and finally reached the *New York Times*. The editorial pages were of special interest as a result of a contest sponsored by the *World*. This was the "Biggest News of the Week" contest, with cash prizes awarded to high school students for the best essays on the developments of a particular week.

I competed for years and while I never won a cash prize, I did collect a considerable number of honorable mentions. In my senior year I took a course in journalism with an instructor who was a socialist and who introduced us to the liberal weeklies, the *Nation* and the *New Republic*. Climax of the course was a visit to the offices and plant of the *New York Times*. We inspected the giant presses and were conducted into a large paneled room where, we were told, the august editorial board held its meetings. This was impressive enough, even though no editor was anywhere in sight. Many years later I entered the field of journalism as a profession, but at a considerable distance from the *New York Times*.

During my high school days I read George Bernard Shaw's *An Intelligent Woman's Guide to Socialism and Capitalism.* Up to that moment I would describe my political point of view as liberal-capitalist, but Shaw made an intellectual socialist out of me. Finding myself with a new set of ideas, I looked around for opportunities to discuss them. Always ready to discuss with me was a student in my history class who impressed me with his serious, analytic mind. His name was Joseph Starobin and he was the first Communist I had ever met. Years later he became the foreign editor of the *Daily Worker.*

De Witt Clinton afforded advantages of an unusual order—for instance, by cutting the late afternoon classes, I could arrive in time for the game at Yankee Stadium and for fifty cents sit in the right field bleachers just behind Babe Ruth. I was well up on batting and fielding averages and could hold my own in an argument on these vital matters.

In January of 1930 I graduated at the age of 16. I won a New York State Regents scholarship which made it easier for me to go to college, and the citywide medal for proficiency in Spanish, the knowledge of which was to make it easier for me in my first experience with war. As a member of the Arista honor society, my name was inscribed in gold letters on the corridor walls along with the names of all the other Clintonites elected to Arista down through the years.

This was my life before I entered college. It strikes me as a happy childhood. Morris Ernst and others have written that the people attracted to communism are usually neurotics and misfits. It is possible, of course, to define neurotic so broadly as to take in all of mankind, and become meaningless. It is also true that the Communist Party, just like any other movement, included some crackpots, strange characters and unbalanced minds. But most of us who joined the party had lived the normal, typical life of our times. No one can understand the nature of communism, and the Americans who believed in it, if he looks for personal abnormalities. The explanation is to be found less in the aberrations of the individual than in the aberrations of our society.

II

COLLEGE, CRISIS, AND COMMUNISM

THREE MONTHS BEFORE I ENTERED THE COLLEGE OF THE CITY OF New York, an event took place which changed the course of my life. More important, it changed the course of America. This was the Wall Street crash of October 1929. Few realized then that the ticker in the brokerage houses was heralding the most severe depression in the history of capitalism, a catastrophe worldwide in scope which would bring in its wake vast human suffering, fascism, wars and revolutions. Within our own country, the crash would result in great new social changes and the introduction of sweeping progressive reforms.

I am always startled these days when college audiences express incredulity at my descriptions of the depression era and of the part played by the Communists. On second thought, of course, there is nothing surprising about the skepticism of these young people.

Edmund Wilson, who calls the 1929 depression the "American Earthquake," writes of "how difficult it is for persons who were born too late to have memories of the depression, to believe that it really occurred, that between 1929 and 1933 the whole structure of American society seemed actually to be going to pieces . . .

14

and, in consequence, [how difficult it is for them] to understand the direction that the interests and activities of American liberals took."

But if the skepticism of present-day youth can be excused on the ground that it did not actually experience the Great Depression, what is to be said for those older persons who knew the depression well but prefer to forget it or to learn nothing from it?

Some months ago I read a speech delivered by Herbert Hoover at Valley Forge. It sounded vaguely familiar. Sure enough this was exactly the same speech delivered 27 years earlier by exactly the same Herbert Hoover in the depths of the depression. Now he was repeating it for the edification of the present generation. The speech, which Mr. Hoover believed so deserving of immortality, had for its theme: sit tight, keep calm, chin up, smile, rugged individualism, rely on private enterprise, everything will work itself out. This is where I came in. This is exactly what made a Communist of me.

Recent economic developments have made it somewhat easier for today's youth to understand the years of the depression. At the outset of 1958, the country was entering the most serious recession since the '30s. If there are new features today, the fact is these are largely a result of the popular struggles of two decades ago in which the Communists took a creditable part. Today we have economic shock absorbers, such as unemployment and social insurance, bank savings insurance, stock market controls. Although these have proved unable to avert serious recessions, they have had an important mitigating effect. The principle of government responsibility and intervention to guarantee full employment and a stable, flourishing economy has been established beyond recall. It has even been enshrined in law, although the Eisenhower Administration has replied to the latest recession by invoking the ancient superstitions of Herbert Hoover. If ever an administration has relied on private enterprise, it has been President Eisenhower's and it is this naive faith that brought the country into the sorry mess of 1958 with its privations for millions of people.

Some time before the 1929 depression, my father had sold his ice cream parlor for a fair profit and like many small business-men of those days, he was drawn into the fever of the stock market. It was possible in that period to buy stocks on a 10% mar-gin—in fact, it was almost your patriotic duty to do so.

When the crash came, my father could not even begin to cover his losses and along with hundreds of thousands of others, was wiped out. It was not only a case of the big operators fleecing the little ones. That took place, but many big timers lost too. Suicides, like the recent one of Robert Young reportedly over financial diffi-culties, were not unusual in the early '30s.

My father went back to work as a waiter. He finally scraped enough money together to buy another candy store and returned to the drudgery of a sixteen-hour day and a seven-day week. I had always worked after school and during the summers to make some spending money, but now I looked for a job out of necessity.

Over the years I had worked on and off as a sales clerk and cashier for my father, as delivery boy for fruit and grocery stores, delivered the *Bronx Home News* (since merged with the *New York Post*) and worked at concession stands in Jersey summer resorts.

One of my best jobs was distributing election posters for Judge Peter J. Schmuck. The work not only paid well but it had the unu-sual feature that we could always manage to ditch the final batch of posters for the day. Fortunately for the judge, he did not rely solely on our conscientiousness to get himself elected. At other times I distributed a trade publication in the buildings in the garment district. I also sold powdered soap house-to-house.

When I began studying at the College of the City of New York, it was without perspective or purpose. Why I was there, I did not know—except that my entering CCNY had always been taken for granted in my family. City College was free, and in addition, my Regents scholarship gave me $100 a year for four years. If the generation after World War I was the Lost Generation, we stu-dents in the first years of the Hoover depression were the Aimless Generation. But our very uncertainty drove many of us to search for answers and for a cause to live by.

The student body at CCNY was in ferment. The old world had been found wanting; ideas and shibboleths of the past were examined, assailed, discarded; new, radical notions became popular. The campus was a hive of political clubs: the Liberal club, led by Lewis Feuer and Joseph P. Lash; a Socialist club led by Winston Dancis and William Gomberg; the pro-Communist Social Problems club, led by Max Weiss, Max Gordon, Adam Lapin, Joseph Starobin; a Catholic Newman club; societies of young Democrats and young Republicans, and many others.

I was mainly interested in the Socialists and the Communists. Already socialist-minded in a hazy, untroubled way, I soon learned that the adherents of socialism were in violent disagreement among themselves. I listened entranced to their fierce debates. Their doctrinal disputations over what Marx and Lenin had really said and really meant, their waging of the Russian Revolution over and over again, led me to the Marxist classics in the college library. A new world began to open up before me.

These writings provided me with what seemed to be the key to the universe. Poring over the pages, I found the answers I had been searching for: the causes of depression, of war, of injustice, oppression and inhumanity, and the solution through the socialist reorganization of society and the creation of a world brotherhood of man.

When it came to the disputes between the followers of socialism, it seemed to me that the Socialists only talked, while the Communists acted. Had not the Communists brought into being the first successful socialist country, the Soviet Union? And wasn't this accomplished over the opposition of the Socialists? Was not the Soviet Union moving forward with its Five Year plans, was it not planning production and abolishing unemployment when the richest country in the world, the United States, was in the throes of terrible depression?

Meanwhile American Communists were doing something about the appalling situation here—they had organized a gigantic coast-to-coast demonstration on March 6, 1930, for relief for the unemployed and for unemployment insurance. The Socialists seemed to oppose mass action. Moreover, they claimed that capitalism could be abolished peacefully; but, the Communists asked, would the capitalists ever permit this to happen when they even used violence against people who merely sought unemployment relief or who went on strike against a wage-cut?

I joined the pro-Communist Social Problems Club, but remained an observer, listening and studying. Toward the end of the year, the most prominent Communist at the school, Max Weiss, was suspended for editing an unauthorized publication, *Frontiers*. Weiss, a serious, studious and precise young man, was a member of the National Committee of the Young Communist League. At that time, ROTC was a voluntary course at the college but there were rumors that it was to be made compulsory. The Communists saw this as preparation for imminent war and *Frontiers* campaigned against making military training obligatory.

Suspension of Weiss from college was the signal for the Social Problems club to spring into action. A campaign was begun for the reinstatement of the young Communist leader, who had almost completed his senior year. When a committee representing all points of view on the campus was organized to defend academic freedom, I was invited to join, and became part of a delegation to President Frederick E. Robinson of the college. We did not manage to get Weiss a reinstatement or a diploma, but it was a good fight. One incidental result was that in March of 1931 I joined the Young Communist League.

By now I knew what I wanted. I lost all interest in my studies and determined to devote myself to my new purpose. I dedicated my life to the Communist movement.

Those were, as Edmund Wilson writes of the Hoover years, "desperate days when nothing worked." There was a vacuum of ideas and of action, which the Communists were trying hard to fill. They alone seemed to have a program. Lincoln Steffens, the crusading journalist and reformer, had written earlier of the Soviet Union: "I have seen the Future and it works"—words which now assumed fresh meaning as the Soviets progressed while capitalism sank into what looked like a bottomless pit.

The Communist movement was the locomotive of the future, capitalism only a convulsive, dying gasp. Only the Communists were able to infuse youth with idealism, missionary zeal and a crusading spirit. And with these, they invoked a willingness to undergo any hardship, to sacrifice life itself if need be, for the cause of the socialist revolution.

I now attended classes only enough to collect my scholarship money. Any conflict between school hours and my political activities was resolved in favor of the latter. As I became filled with the superiority of my new-found faith, I was sure there was nothing that college could teach me. I wrangled with my teachers and developed a contempt for them. I began to experience that disdain for the ideas of others which could only transform Communist theory, supposed to be a philosophy of permanent change, into a closed system of dogmatic thought, blinding its adherents to the complexities of reality.

In the Social Problems club I did plenty of "Jimmy Higgins" work, as it was called after Upton Sinclair's fictional rank-and-filer who did all the unheralded, routine tasks of a political organization. I was on the committee that secured speakers, I helped mimeograph and distribute the throwaways advertising the meetings, and at the meetings I sold pamphlets. I became an expert in the science of the street corner meeting—calling up the police for a permit, carrying the American flag, step-ladder and literature to the meeting spot.

Sometimes I did all these jobs myself, and finally the day was to come when, after setting up the speaker's stand, I also climbed up and proceeded to hold forth. This did not happen right away; it took me almost a year as a Communist to overcome my shyness and reserve, during which time I hardly opened my mouth. In high school there had been only one subject which I had ever flunked. This was public speaking. I had a whistling "s."

A speaker was the last thing I ever expected to become, but become one I did—although I still tend to whistle my "s's." My debut as a speaker came about when the Young Communist club in the Bronx to which I belonged, assigned me one day to chair a street-corner meeting. Although I was terrified, I did not dare to refuse. I carefully wrote out and memorized a speech which would last for all of thirty seconds. When the great evening came,

I mounted the platform, outwardly calm, but trembling inside. I began and for about fifteen seconds did fine—then suddenly I forgot the rest and stood there hopelessly tongue-tied.

Fortunately, the main speaker of the meeting was a veteran at such crises. He yanked my leg and told me to introduce him, which I proceeded to do. That broke the ice and I never had trouble again. I still become nervous whenever I am about to speak, but once I begin I am completely at ease—since I know what I want to say, I manage to forget about myself and to think only of the audience.

A few weeks after I joined the YCL (Young Communist League), nine young Negroes were arrested on a freight train near Scottsboro, Alabama, convicted of raping two white women and sentenced to the electric chair. This was the famous Scottsboro case. It was to have lasting significance for our country and to set off a chain reaction that is still felt throughout the world.

The *Daily Worker* gave banner headlines to the case—this was April, 1931—and the Communist Party rose to the defense of the Scottsboro Boys, as they were called. The Communists charged that the case was a frame-up from start to finish, and, in fact, that is just what it turned out to be. The fight proved to be a prolonged and stormy one. Nothing had so dramatized the issue of civil rights since the Civil War. Finally all the boys were freed, but only after years of national and world protest-campaigns and protracted legal battles, and after the white women in the case confessed to having lied, one of the women, Ruby Bates, even joining the crusade for the freedom of the young Negroes.

Before the case reached its final conclusion, a large part of America was made aware for the first time of the code under which southern Negroes enjoyed no rights, could expect no justice.

The Communists took the initiative in the case, although in later stages the legal defense was taken over by the National Association for the Advancement of Colored People and others, and lawyers like Samuel Leibowitz played a prominent role. It has been charged that the Communists cared less about defending the boys than about dramatizing the larger political issues, but this argument has never impressed me. The Scottsboro frame-up was the product of an outrageous social and legal system in the South (still existing in large part); individual cases could not be separated from the oppressive background which gave rise to them. The Communists deserve credit not only for pioneering in the case, but for focusing the attention of the country on the underlying issues. This campaign opened the way for an assault upon the all-white jury system and the white primary. The trouble has not been that the Communists ever did too much but that white America has done too little, and this is our national shame.

I myself was deeply moved by the terrible injustice that the case revealed. The plight of an entire people was suddenly illumined for me. Besides, some of the Scottsboro Boys themselves were of my own age; they were victims of the same depression which affected all of us in one way or another. The role of the Communists in the case confirmed my conviction that I had been right in joining up with them.

During the Scottsboro crusade I became a member of the International Labor Defense, a civil liberties and civil rights organization sponsored by the Communists, and this now became the center of my activity. My closest friend at the time was Frank Carlson. We had attended high school together, gone to City College and become members of the Young Communist League together, and now we joined a young people's branch of the ILD (International Labor Defense) in the Bronx, called the Young Defenders. Carlson, sharp-featured and blond, was temperamentally quite unlike myself. Ebullient and out-going, he was a witty and eloquent speaker. With Carlson taking the lead, we now proceeded to organize a series of Young Defender branches through the Bronx, established a youth section of the ILD, published our own organ *The Young Defender* and developed our first heresy. We were unorthodox and imaginative, and the adult leaders of the ILD became suspicious.

We were accused of competing with the official publication, *The Labor Defender,* and were ordered to disband the youth branches and discontinue our modest little paper. Unimpressed, we defied our superiors and appealed the matter to national headquarters. Numerous hearings were held, but we lost. Whereupon we appealed to the international defense organization located in Moscow and with which the ILD was affiliated. It seemed altogether logical to do so, as we were "proletarian internationalists," and Moscow was certain to take our views seriously. Only after we lost there too, did we cease and desist. That was the end of the Young Defenders and, for that matter, of youth activity in the ILD.

If life in the Communist movement was exciting, it was also peculiar. We soon came up against the strange jargon copied from the terminology of the Russian Communists, and Carlson and I scoffed at it. Everything Russian was imitated, even to the wearing of leather jackets, and while Carlson and I admired the Soviet Union as much as anyone, we could not understand why admiration had to be carried to ridiculous lengths. We laughed out loud at the mannerisms of our teacher in the Workers School and were put out of the class.

But in most of the movement's strange ways, we joined with enthusiasm. On holidays like May 1st and November 7th, anniversary of the Russian Revolution, we went out at night with buckets of red paint and splashed slogans on walls and streets: Down Tools on May 1, Fight Against Imperialist War, Defend the Soviet Union. It was against the local ordinances and gave us a sense of defying reactionary authority, a feeling of high adventure, and an emotion of oneness with Communists all over the world who were doing the same thing.

During this period, Carlson and I took off three months from college—unofficially—to make an intensive study of Karl Marx's *Capital*, the mastering of which we considered indispensable for becoming able Communist leaders. In the course of this study we wrote out our own synopsis of the first volume of *Capital*. (Long afterwards, in the Smith Act trial, I attempted to introduce this synopsis as evidence of how I understood and discussed Marx, but Judge Medina refused to admit it.) Once again Carlson and I found ourselves in trouble. We were threatened with expulsion from the YCL for neglecting practical work and for the unusual way we went about re-writing Karl Marx. After convincing our accusers that we were not trying to improve on Marx, we were exonerated.

But internal peculiarities and radical romanticism played only a minor part in our lives as Communists. It was the depression which was the overriding fact for most of us. Evictions were an every-day occurrence, with furniture a common sight on the streets. We protested, organized street meetings at the scene of an eviction, enlisted the support of indignant onlookers and carried the furniture back into the house. Carlson and I formed a club of young people to stop evictions, called the Young Hunger Fighters.

The principle of government assistance to the unemployed was not yet established in our country. It was looked upon as a form of charity. The American Federation of Labor—this was before the formation of the CIO—opposed the very idea of unemployment insurance. It was left to the Communists to lead the fight for government responsibility to the unemployed, and for this purpose they sparked the formation of the unemployed council movement. In December of 1931, the Unemployed Councils organized the first National Hunger March to Washington. Carlson and I were designated as delegates to Washington by the Social Problems Club at college.

We rode to the capital in large moving vans, picking up recruits in the cities along the way, fed by friendly people or by agencies like the Salvation Army. Riding in a van in the cold of winter was an ordeal and to keep up our spirits, we sang song after song, one of which went like this:

> Oh, those beans, bacon and gravy,
> They almost drive me crazy,
> I eat them till I see them in my dreams,
> In my dreams.
> When I wake up in the morning
> Another day is dawning
> And I know I'll have another mess of beans.

Carlson and I described our arrival in Washington in an article entitled "From Sea to Shining Sea," which appeared in the Jan.

1932 issue of *Frontiers,* the magazine of the Social Problems Club:

"We were marching down Pennsylvania Avenue to the Capitol," we wrote. "The procession was headed by several hundred ex-servicemen, carrying banners. 'We fought the last war for the capitalists, we will fight the next war for the workers.'

"We were flanked on both sides by cops who marched with us. Thousands of spectators followed us along the sidewalk. When we reached the Capitol grounds, we formed a semi-circle on the Plaza facing the Capitol. Between us and the building was a tightly packed line of motorcycle cops. On the steps and in the windows were policemen with machine guns, sawed-off shotguns, tear gas bombs, etc. Marines were held in readiness in the barracks near by. Detectives from all parts of the country scanned the marchers. Democracy must be guarded. An ex-serviceman growled, 'For the first time, I have looked into the muzzle of my own gun.'

"Scattered shouts swelled into a tremendous roar: 'We—De-mand—Unemployment Insurance,' which echoed back from the Capitol and floated over the city. A delegation of twelve went into the building. 'We Demand the Bonus,' shouted 1600 voices. 'Not War, Bread!'

"The delegation was refused admittance. There were too many. Three delegates were immediately chosen. In a few minutes they returned. One of them, from the shoulders of fellow marchers, shouted through a megaphone: 'The delegation you have elected was refused admission. The entire matter was handled by the police.' The tense silence continued. Then—

> We're here from mine and mill and rail,
> We're here from 'cross the sea.
> From coast to coast we'll make the boast
> Of Solidarity.

"We left the Capitol grounds and marched to the White House. But Hoover was dining with a friend and could not be disturbed. Again we marched—this time to William Green, President of the American Federation of Labor. He told the delegation of A.F.L. members that went in to see him that the A.F.L. is a respectable organization, would have nothing to do with them, and that 'organized labor' was against unemployment insurance.

"Downstairs we responded, 'To hell with Green's hypocrisy.'

"Our experiences in this Hunger March sketched in our minds a perspective of action by embittered and aroused unemployed workers. We came face to face with workers from Seattle, Tucson, Minneapolis, Louisville. Workers grown inured to many hardships, cold, no place to sleep, miserable inadequate food. But workers who had realized that such suffering was not inevitable, that society owed them the necessaries of life, that they were suffering and dying because they had worked too hard and too much. Workers, in short, determined to ACT to save themselves and their families. Charity drives, community chest donations, Salvation Army Santa Clauses, might get the front pages, but among the workers was growing the sense that their welfare was their own concern."

Not until after four more years of activity was unemployment and social insurance enacted. It took a political unheaval, a new president and a new philosophy to get a simple and humane law placed upon the statute books.

Early in 1932 Carlson and I quit college. This time it was official. Carlson became an organizer for the Young Communist League in Trenton, New Jersey, where he helped to organize a union and a successful strike in a doll factory. I obtained a job in a radio parts factory in New York City at 32 cents an hour. The place was unorganized and I joined an independent union which became the Steel and Metal Workers Industrial Union, affiliated to the Trade Union Unity League. This independent labor federation, led by Communists, sought to organize the workers of the mass production industries into industrial unions. In those years the AFL refused to organize the giant industries like steel, auto and rubber, except for some of the highly skilled crafts.

The Republicans renominated Herbert Hoover in 1932 and the Democrats designated Governor Franklin D. Roosevelt of New York. Seeing no difference between the two parties, nor anything new or hopeful in the candidacy of Roosevelt, the Communist Party put forward its own ticket—William Z. Foster for President and James W. Ford, a Negro, for Vice-president. We campaigned vigorously but managed to get on the ballot in only a few states. In several we were arbitrarily ruled off the ballot though we filled all requirements. The official vote for the Communist Party was 75,000, but this did not dishearten us. All big things have little beginnings. Had not Karl Marx begun with a handful of adherents and had not the ideas of communism already triumphed on one-sixth of the earth's surface? Capitalism was in a severe crisis and could find no way out. We had the answers. Our turn would come and, we were certain, soon.

For it was undisputed that we were making important head-way, winning adherents and spreading our influence on all sides. Evidence of this was the galaxy of intellectuals who publicly supported the Foster-and-Ford campaign, among them such prom-inent figures as: Edmund Wilson, John Dos Passos, Sidney How-ard, Sherwood Anderson, Horace Gregory, Alfred Kreymborg, Waldo Frank, Malcolm Cowley, Matthew Josephson, Granville Hicks, Countee Cullen, Langston Hughes, Isador Schneider, Sid-ney Hook, Frederick L. Schuman, Lincoln Steffens.

I was not at all sorry to be laid off at the radio parts factory in the fall of 1932. I had already determined to become a full-time organizer for the Communist cause and here was my opportunity. I went to the national headquarters of the Young Communist League on East 12th Street and volunteered for some heavy-industry area, where, I was convinced, the American socialist revolution would shortly erupt.

It was decided to send me to Warren, Ohio, a steel town. The day before I was to set out, the YCL leaders asked me what my new name would be. I was prepared for this and had chosen a name at random out of some newspaper (not the *Daily Worker*). Until then my name had been Sol Regenstreif; henceforth it was to be John Gates. There was no compelling reason to change the name except that it was the thing to do in those days. Had not Lenin and Stalin and countless other revolutionaries changed their names? It was not only people with foreign-sounding names who changed them to more "native" ones; those with perfectly simple names also made the change. This was not to hide anything but to symbolize a change in a way of life. The new name itself was a trivial matter; the change in my life was very real indeed.

One day in early November, I bid my family goodbye and left home, carrying a small suitcase with a few articles of clothing and two or three books. In my pocket was a bus ticket to Cleveland but not a cent of money—as I told my family, I needed none. I had the address of the Communist headquarters in Cleveland, and that was enough. Where I would live, I had no idea. I had been promised a subsidy of $3 a week but that didn't really interest me. I was not going to Ohio to make money. I was going to make the Revolution.

III

YOUNGSTOWN

AFTER RIDING THE BUS ALL NIGHT, I ARRIVED IN CLEVELAND AND walked from the station to the party headquarters. The office, one flight up in an old building near the center of town, was locked. It was Sunday morning, so I sat down in the hall on my suitcase and waited. Someone would be along any minute to pick me up, I was sure. But no one came.

Without money or acquaintances in the city, there was little I could do about the situation except to remain planted on my suitcase, periodically getting up to stretch my legs and peek down the stairs. Several hours passed this way and finally I heard steps. It was the state organizer of the Young Communist League and he was amazed to find me there. It seems that nobody had bothered to notify him that I was being sent to Ohio to take up an important post in his organization. He told me how lucky I was— if he hadn't left some material by mistake in the office the previous night, he wouldn't have dropped by at all. I was given the address of friends who would put me up for the night. Their place was about two miles away from the office and, tired and hungry as I was, I proceeded there on foot. It was a sunny day, I would be able to see the city this way and, besides, I had no money for bus-fare.

I was given a warm welcome and a good meal and asked if I wanted to rest. "No, thank you," I said, "not at all"—and promptly fell asleep. The next morning, after breakfast, my new-found friends directed me to the point on the outskirts of the city where I would start hitchhiking to Warren. Warren is 53 miles from Cleveland and it seems to me that I hiked more than I hitched. I still carried my suitcase, of course, but none of this bothered me— with every mile I was closer to my goal. I was to spend considerable time in the next four years, walking and hitching rides, this way maintaining a physical fitness which was to stand me in good stead through two wars and a long prison term.

It was already dark when I arrived in Warren, a city of 40,000, and a plant of the Republic Steel Corporation. I had been given an address, and in Warren I found Joe Dallet, the local Communist Party organizer. A delegation was going that very evening to the City Council. Would I go along? A bare two hours later I was addressing the City Council of Warren, Ohio, representing the unemployed workers of that town, none of whom I had even met yet, and demanding of the city fathers, whose names I did not even know, that they immediately raise the weekly relief allotments, then $2.25 for a family of three. It had not taken me long to become a citizen of Warren. Only after the hearing was over did it occur to me to ask Joe Dallet where I would live. It was to be with an Italian-American steel worker who had taken part in an unsuccessful strike at Republic Steel a few weeks earlier and was now on the blacklist.

Joe Dallet himself was from New England, the son of wealthy parents, a Dartmouth graduate. He was in his early twenties, which then seemed to me quite old. Dallet was a highly accomplished pianist, had attended European universities and had lived in the Latin Quarter of Paris. Before joining the Communist Party he had sported a goatee, spats and a cane. But it was many years before I learned all this for Dallet did his best to conceal his background. He was an organizer of steel workers now and he dressed and talked (he thought) just like a worker in the mills. He idealized the working class and affected great contempt for non-workers whom he called "petty-bourgeois intellectuals." Devoted, self-sacrificing and highly intelligent, Dallet was later to go to his death fighting the fascists in Spain.

The whirlwind pace which had marked my debut in Warren that first evening never slackened in the weeks and months to follow. Water was being turned off in many homes and my first leaflet was titled "Every Man, Woman and Child Must Have Water." As in New York City, people were being evicted from their homes. We carried the furniture right back in.

Workers in this steel town had considerable mechanical skill which they now used to devise tools for turning on water, gas and electricity almost as fast as the utility companies turned them off. Everywhere in the country, since the government was refusing to take action, people increasingly felt they had no recourse but to act themselves. Farmers, dispossessed from the property they and their families had worked for generations, attended the sheriff foreclosure sales—sometimes armed with rifles—and proceeded to buy back their mortgages and equipment for next to nothing. No one dared bid against these angry Americans and the sales became known as Penny Auctions. (Judging from the statistics, dispossessions from family-sized farms have been continued right through the recent period of prosperity but with greater subtlety and effectiveness than in the '30s.) These movements of direct action gave people the experience that led in several years to the famous sitdown strikes in the auto and rubber plants which at last cracked the open-shop industries and won recognition for unionism.

We planned a demonstration of the unemployed for the occasion of President Roosevelt's first inauguration on March 4, 1933. At City Hall we asked the mayor for a permit, which he promptly refused. I protested so loudly right in his office that the mayor lost his temper and called me a "young snotnose," which not only made me indignant but humiliated me terribly. Perhaps I gave him some cause.

Naturally we decided to go through with our plans, permit or not, and I was designated to open the demonstration. The newspapers had given the matter considerable publicity and on the day of the demonstration the courthouse square was full of police and curious onlookers, as well as demonstrators.

At the appointed moment, I took my place in front of the court-house and began to speak. Although short in stature, I had a very loud voice, and I opened with the familiar words "Comrades and fellow workers . . ." That was as far as I got. A hand was clapped over my mouth as several cops grabbed me, whisked me into the courthouse, then out again on the opposite side, across the street and right into the county jail. There, behind the bars, my own speech cut short, I sat and listened to FDR make *his*.

He announced the closing of the banks and the inauguration of a New Deal for the American people. Listening to the broadcast there in jail, it did not sound exactly like a New Deal to me. I did not believe the President serious and had no confidence in him. Nor were Communists the only ones to feel this way. Edmund Wilson, in his essay "Washington: Inaugural Parade," written at the time, said of the address: "There is a suggestion, itself rather vague, of a possible dictatorship."

A Communist named Frank Rogers had also been arrested and jailed that day. I was somewhat mortified when, to separate me from Rogers, I was placed in the women's section, in a cell by myself. It turned out there was no law in Warren against making a speech without a permit; so they dug up an ancient ordinance and charged me with "making a loud noise" without a permit.

In line with Communist practice of the time, I refused to have a lawyer and defended myself. My defense would be *political,* not legal, therefore what need was there for a lawyer? Besides, those who labored for the cause of the workers could expect nothing but injustice in a capitalist court. The legal issues, as presented by the prosecutor, were simple and clear: did I or did I not have a permit? did I or did I not make a loud noise?

I tried to make the issue one of free speech, and of Capital vs. Labor, but found it hard going. Whereupon I suddenly introduced a dramatic turn in the trial—I subpoenaed the mayor himself. Despite the disgust of the judge, the mayor had to be called and was placed on the stand, while I proceeded to question him. I could not get any more out of him than his name—the judge ruled out all my other questions. Since the mayor's name was already well-known, it could hardly be said that any new evidence had been introduced. The verdict was "guilty," and the fine $50 and costs. This would mean 30 days in jail since I did not have the money, and would not have paid it anyway, as a matter of principle. Four days later, a friendly farmer put up a property bond of $2,500 and I was let out on bail pending appeal. Eventually the case was dropped and I never served my time.

Every day groups of unemployed would go to see the relief officials and often we got results. The atmosphere was quite different from what I had known in New York. There the main base of the Communist movement had been Jewish; here it was mainly Slavic of various nationalities, as well as Hungarian, Italian, Roumanian, Greek, for this was the origin of the working people of that generation. The towns seemed to melt into the countryside. Everyone had his own garden in which not only flowers but things to eat were grown. Weekends, when it was warm, there was always a picnic; when the weather was cold, an indoor affair of some sort. I loved these gatherings and always liked to be bartender. It was a custom to have a speaker; the older people especially liked me to speak because even when they could not understand me, I spoke with a good loud voice and a youthful passion and fire. Naturally everybody wanted to buy the speaker a drink.

At nearby Newton Falls (pop. 3,000) we used to hold weekly meetings which attracted almost the entire town. One day Israel Amter, a national leader of the Communist Party and head of the Unemployed Councils of America, spoke there and was highly impressed by the turnout. He inquired of Tony Peck, head of the local organization, what made him so successful a leader. Peck, a Slovak in his early 30's, replied simply that since he only did whatever the members told him to do, he got the credit when things turned out well, while when they went badly, the members had only themselves to blame. A little shocked, Amter decided to give Peck a lesson in the responsibilities of leadership. "But what would you do if the members one day told you to blow up the City Hall?" he asked. Without the slightest hesitation Peck replied: "Blow 'er up!"

The national hunger marches had been so successful that it was decided to organize them on a state scale as well; in the Spring of 1933, a march was held on Columbus, state capital of

Ohio. We did not actually have to march all the way to Columbus from Warren—some 100 miles. In many counties the authorities were so anxious to be rid of us that they met us with trucks at the county line and transported us in style to the next line. But it was not like this all the way, so we did considerable walking and met many people to whom we gave our message.

We had our own softball team and would choose up games with youthful onlookers. Sometimes we stayed overnight at a county fairground and held big meetings with dramatic and musical entertainment. Progress toward the state capital was not too difficult. We had many arguments with the police but no fights. In Zanesville, a policeman became so jittery that his revolver went off by accident, but fortunately no one was hurt. It was only after we had reached Columbus, presented our petitions to the Governor in orderly fashion, and were preparing to leave, that we ran into trouble.

We were lining up our columns when the state police suddenly ordered us to move forthwith. We protested that we were not quite ready but would be in a few minutes, and we began to sing: "Amter is our leader, we shall not be moved." At this point the police moved in on us, swinging their clubs freely, hitting women and young people as well as men. It was a vindictive act, designed to disrupt the march which had been spendidly organized and highly disciplined. We maintained order as well as we could despite the panic caused by the police, reformed our ranks outside Columbus and reached our homes without further trouble.

A rival organization of the Unemployed Council, the Unemployed League, was holding its national convention in Columbus while we were there. Led by the Rev. A. J. Muste, a lean and lanky veteran of the labor struggles of the Twenties and a Christian socialist, the League was more of a native American movement than the Council which was based largely on the foreign-born. The unemployed organization in Warren, of which I was the head, was affiliated with the League and I was elected a delegate to its national convention. While in Columbus as a hunger marcher, I also attended sessions of the League convention, got the floor, and in line with our policy, appealed for unity between the two national organizations of the unemployed. Nothing happened at the time, but some years later the League and the Council merged into what was called the Workers Alliance.

Upon my return to Warren, I was promoted to the leadership of the Young Communist League of the area, whose headquarters were located in Youngstown. To this center of the fabulous Mahoning Valley steel region, I now moved. The Youngstown section of the Communist Party cut a swathe across three states and took in the Ohio towns of Warren, Niles, Steubenville, East Liverpool and Salem; the Pennsylvania towns of Farrell and Newcastle, and Weirton and Wheeling in West Virginia. In this enormous area the Communist Party never had more than 600 members at its peak, but at times it enjoyed considerable influence.

The steel industry was the life-blood of the region, but now it was running at only 15 to 25% of capacity. For the people of the area this was a grim disaster. The steel workers were unorganized, except for the tiny and impotent Amalgamated Association of Iron, Steel and Tin Workers (AFL). This organization consisted of a fraction of the most highly skilled workers, and cared nothing about the mass of workers who in turn looked upon it as practically a company union. The mills themselves were military fortresses, with small private armies of uniformed, armed company police to intimidate the workers and block organization. City and town government, controlled by the steel corporations, ruthlessly suppressed all union activity. For all practical purposes, trade unions were illegal and subversive; organizers were arrested, beaten up and driven out of town; workers suspected of union activity were summarily fired and blacklisted throughout the industry. To ferret out militant workers, the companies employed large numbers of spies. The threat of deportation was continually held over the foreign-born workers who made up the bulk of the working force in the Valley. Over the steel towns hung a heavy pall of fear, repression and poverty.

Could these vast mills, controlled by the most powerful and brutal corporations in the world, ever be organized? A mere handful of us were trying and the odds seemed overwhelmingly against us. I used to stand on a bridge overlooking the Republic plant in downtown Youngstown and watch the Bessemer converter shoot a giant tongue of fire into the night. It scorched the heavens and was a wondrous and fearsome sight. I felt puny. Could mere man ever win out over such enormous aggregations of capital?

One thought, however, gave me confidence. Had there not been a time when these mighty mills were, in fact, toppled, stilled and silenced, with hundreds of thousands of steel workers marching out to the cry of "Strike, strike!" That was in 1919; the great walk-out had been organized by William Z. Foster who had become one of the outstanding leaders of the Communist Party. Although in the end the strike had been broken, the miracle had actually happened. That it would happen again one day, I was certain. And happen again it did, only four years later and under circumstances which none of us in 1933 could foresee.

The Communists had opposed Roosevelt in 1932 and they did so for the next two years. We still saw no difference of any importance between the GOP and the Democratic Party. We did not understand (and few others did either) that the shift from the Republicans to the Democrats that had started in 1928 was the beginning of a profound upheaval in our land that would be climaxed by the New Deal Era. Two world-shaking events had been mainly responsible for this new era—these were the Great Depression here at home and the coming to power of Adolf Hitler in Germany. But in 1933 we were deeply suspicious of Roosevelt; we did not see that the earlier Al Smith and Roosevelt Administrations in New York State had been portents of a new liberalism. We looked upon the first promise of the New Deal, the National Recovery Act (NRA) with its codes and Blue Eagle insignia, and the bold moves of the first 100 days of the new administration as signs of an incipient, neo-fascism reminiscent of Mussolini. We could not have been more mistaken.

Hitler's triumph in Germany was a catastrophe, the full gravity of which was not immediately apparent. The German Social-Democrats blamed the Communists for the advent of the bloody Fuehrer, and the Communists blamed the Social-Democrats. Both combined had a majority of the German nation. Whoever was more to blame, it was obvious that both groups, along with most of humanity, were equal victims of the tragedy. There was no doubt in our minds that the German Socialists had refused to unite with the Communists against the common menace, but we were beginning to see now that mistaken Communist policies had also contributed to the failure of anti-Hitler unity, had, in fact, made it impossible.

Between them, the Communists and Socialists had more votes than Hitler who was financed by the steel magnates. But because they could not unite, Hitler won and proceeded to wipe out both working class organizations. The Socialists had been opposed to unity with the Communists on principle and this had led to their undoing. The Communists appealed to the Socialists for unity but insisted it be on Communist terms. They opposed unity to defend German bourgeois-democracy against Hitler and argued that Socialist-Communist unity must be conditioned on accept-ance of the dictatorship of the proletariat.

The Communists operated under the theory that the Social-Democrats were "social-fascists," a harmful concept and an in-surmountable barrier to unity. This theory held that the Socialists were paving the way for fascism and consequently could be con-sidered its allies. Serious errors of both movements contributed to Hitler's victory, but neither could be called his allies. They were his enemies and the members and leaders of both groups ended up in Nazi concentration camps, in Nazi torture and execution chambers.

This terrible object lesson was not lost on the world, and cer-tainly not on Communists, Socialists and trade unionists. Hitler's regime of murder and of war preparations now confronted man-kind with the greatest danger in all history. In the wake of Hit-lerism and the almost world-wide depression, fascist movements arose in many countries. Here at home, fascist demagogues like Father Coughlin, Gerald L. K. Smith and Huey Long flourished. Something else began to flourish here and abroad: popular anti-fascist movements, determined to combat fascism everywhere.

One of the first acts of President Roosevelt had been to recog-nize the Soviet Union and to exchange ambassadors, ending a 16-year pretense that the Soviet government did not exist (an idiocy now being repeated with respect to China and with the same howling lack of success). It began to be clearer to us that the Roosevelt Administration, even though it moved in several directions at once in the early days, was not neo-fascist but anti-fascist, not anti-labor but pro-labor, not reactionary but progressive.

The labor movement recognized in the NRA a charter for organizing the unorganized: the more forward-looking of the labor leaders like John L. Lewis and Sidney Hillman understood that the great unorganized mass-production industries could be organized only along industrial union lines, although this ran counter to the craft union ideology of the AFL's top officialdom. Lewis, Hillman and others formed a committee inside the AFL to promote industrial unionism. This brought them into open conflict with the top bureaucracy and led to their expulsion and the formation of the Committee of Industrial Organizations, the CIO. For years the Communists had been plugging doggedly and almost alone with their small industrial unions. Now they found their ideas and slogans taken up by powerful forces. With years of experience behind them, with their skeleton union organizations in many industries, and with their widespread contacts, the Communists got in on the ground floor of the burgeoning movement.

From caustic opponents of the New Deal, the Communists now became its ardent supporters. We began to participate seriously in politics. We formed alliances with the advanced trends within the Democratic Party, while looking forward to an independent mass farmer-labor party. We sought to join with all who opposed fascism, regardless of whether they were for or against capitalism. When some misguided admirers here of the Hitler youth movement initiated a congress of young people, it was taken away from them by the combined efforts of the most important youth organizations and the participation of the Young Communist League. These now formed the American Youth Congress in which the Young Women's Christian Association, other Christian and Jewish youth organizations, various student movements and the Socialist and Communist youth organizations collaborated.

Meanwhile in France, Italy and Spain, nation-wide united fronts were being formed by Socialists, Communists and liberals. This was the atmosphere in which the Communist International opened its 7th World Congress in Moscow in the late summer of 1935. The Congress officially ended the unrealistic, sectarian and ultra-revolutionary policies which had isolated the Communists everywhere from a majority of the people and in Germany had contributed to Hitler's victory. The Congress approved the new policy of subordinating the ultimate goals of the Communist movement to the drive against fascism. Important new changes were made in Communist theory: Communists could now support their own capitalist-democratic governments, even participate in them; socialists were their brothers and comrades; unity was essential not only within the labor movement but also with the middle classes and even with capitalists who opposed fascism. This was the People's Front. Its aim: the election of Popular Front governments and the forging of a collective security pact of the western capitalist democracies and of the Soviet Union against fascism and war.

New impetus was given to the efforts of the American Communist Party to become a serious political trend in American life, an indigenous socialist organization. A variety of new anti-fascist movements came into being here, in which Communists took part: the American League Against War and Fascism, the National Negro Congress, the Southern Conference for Human Welfare, the Southern Negro Youth Congress, the Commonwealth Federation of the State of Washington, the New York American Labor Party initiated by the International Ladies Garment Workers Union, the Amalgamated Clothing Workers, and others.

American Communists began to study American history with its democratic, labor and socialist traditions. Earl Browder, the party's general secretary at that time, coined the slogan "Communism is 20th Century Americanism" and our influence grew not only in the labor and Negro people's movements, but in intellectual circles as well. These years of 1934 to 1939 were the heyday of Communist prestige in the United States.

With thousands of others, I was part of that tempestuous history before I was old enough to vote. Those years were an education which, despite all the minuses, I would not exchange for anything.

The new change in the Communist movement was symbolized by what happened to William Z. Foster's *Toward Soviet America*. Written in 1932, this was an atrocious book even for those sectarian and super-leftist days, outlining a blueprint for the U.S.A. along the exact same lines as the Russian revolution. Now it was officially discarded by the party, including Foster himself. It was forgotten and ignored by everybody, except J. Edgar Hoover and assorted prosecutors and investigating committees who considered it such a handy weapon that they have not let go of it to this day. The concept of the People's Front against war and fascism was a sound one and enormously effective. It should have become a permanent feature of Communist theory and practice. Instead it proved to be a temporary expedient and tactic and this was its Achilles heel.

When I moved from Warren to Youngstown, I lived with various families who shared their scanty larder with me. After a year of living this way, I managed to get on relief which amounted to $1.75 a week for single men and was later raised to $2.25 and to $2.75. Then as various works projects got under way, I obtained a job at $7 a week on a National Youth Administration project, at $25 under the Works Progress Administration, and at $35 on Public Works Administration construction. Many public works were built which still stand in Youngstown today—bridges, roads, grade crossings, buildings—all of them monuments to the government programs of those days. Even had we never built anything of permanence, this program would have been more than worthwhile; it was an investment in human beings. Nothing is more demoralizing than to be out of work with no prospect of getting a job. The projects restored the confidence of millions of Americans in themselves and in their country, gave them back their self-respect, brought them hope again.

One day in May, 1935, I was arrested in the open-shop steel town of Newcastle, Pa. I had been distributing leaflets in the course of a strike in a small factory there, when I was picked up. The town mayor acted as judge in the case. I was not even given a chance to plead, let alone explain my case. The mayor proceeded to read me a lecture and denounced me as a foreigner in Pennsylvania since I had come in from Ohio. Without permitting a word to be said, he pronounced me guilty and sentenced me to spend thirty days in jail, or drink a glass of castor oil. No loving relatives had ever succeeded in forcing castor oil down my throat when I was a child, and no two-bit would-be Mussolini would either. I served the thirty days.

Sunday evenings an evangelist group came in to preach to us; we had no choice but to listen. They irritated me no end for they assumed we were all sinners and all guilty, and appealed to us to repent. I might even have stood this, but when the group leader denounced Russia, I rebelled and began to contradict him. "Were you ever in Russia?" he finally asked. "No," I admitted, adding, "Were *you?*" He agreed that he had not been there either, so that ended the matter. After the group left, the sheriff came in and wanted to know what had happened. I told him that I had no objection to the preaching of religion, but politics was something else again. He agreed. There was no more politics after that.

I am told I have a fairly good reading voice (at the Smith Act trial in 1949 Judge Medina was to designate me the "best reader," before shipping me off to prison) and for this reason the National Youth Administration chose me to represent "the typical unemployed youth" of Youngstown on a vocational-guidance radio program. The program was sponsored by the local YMCA and I was interviewed for ten straight weeks on the types of work that might interest young people—but got no job.

We organized a WPA youth club among the many young fellows of my own age who worked on the project. The YMCA gave us a reduced rate and we established our club on the premises. Later we started a rifle club at the "Y," using their basement for a range, and practicing regularly with .22 rifles. This was the first time I had ever used a gun; I had no idea that I would soon be putting this new skill to more serious use in Spain.

The fascist dictatorship in Spain was ousted at the end of 1935; free elections were set for February of the following year. A peoples' coalition was formed by all parties opposed to fascism, from the Republican Party on the right to the Communist Party on the left. They put up a People's Front ticket, won an overwhelming victory at the polls and proceeded to form a cabinet. No Communists were included in this new cabinet, although they had won a number of seats in the Spanish parliament, the Cortes, and supported the government. This is how the new democratic Spanish Republic was born, and it was quickly recognized by most governments, including our own. But powerful fascist forces controlled the Spanish Army, and these now plotted the overthrow of the Republic. The Communists urged the new government to take strong measures against the conspirators but, tragically, the plea went unheeded. On July 18, 1936, General Franco, then commanding the Spanish forces in Morocco, launched an armed revolt against the Republic after he had been assured of active assistance from Hitler and Mussolini.

The sympathy of democratic-minded people everywhere was overwhelmingly on the side of the Republic, or Loyalists, as those loyal to the Republic came to be known. At the time of the rebellion there were no Communists in the government. The issue of communism was a false one, with the fascists using the lie to mask the nature of their rebellion.

The world was thrilled by the heroic, almost barehanded resistance of the Spanish people. Although almost the entire regular army went over to the fascists, the latter were repulsed in most of the large cities. It soon became clear that the Spanish people were fighting against great odds. They had to fight not only their own regular army, but also substantial military units from Nazi Germany and Fascist Italy.

Rumors appeared in the newspapers that an international brigade of volunteers was being formed to aid the beleaguered Republic. The news that the first contingent of such a brigade had actually gone into action on November 7th in Madrid, created great excitement and enthusiasm. This first contingent consisted of French anti-fascists, along with Germans and Italians who had been living in France as refugees from fascism.

One day a leader of the Young Communist League arrived in Youngstown and told us something about the International Brigade. When he said that Americans were volunteering too, I was overwhelmed with admiration and envy. Then the thought struck me: Why couldn't *I* go too? My voice trembled as I put the question to my friend. "Why can't *I* go too?"

"Why not!" he replied—the two most wonderful words I had ever heard.

From then on I was a man transformed. The first volunteer from the state of Ohio, I lived for nothing but to get to Spain.

IV

SPAIN

A SHOWDOWN WAS APPROACHING AT LAST IN THE STEEL MILLS. AFTER a slow and painful start because of the intimidation, the drive of the CIO Steel Workers Organizing Committee took on momentum and men streamed into the union offices to sign up. The hopes of hundreds of thousands of workers were finally to be realized.

Ironically, just at this moment my main interest lay elsewhere. I applied for a passport. Since our government had declared American passports invalid for travel in Spain, I wrote on my application that I was going to Germany—my plan was to travel on the S.S. *Deutschland*. For profession I put down chemist; if I had written WPA worker, the question might have arisen of how I could afford a European trip. Years afterwards at the Smith Act trial, the prosecutor made much of this, charging that I had lied and was not a credible witness.

It is true that I concealed my real purpose—not, however, to defraud or injure anyone but to fight against fascism. If there was any real lie in the matter, it lay in our State Department's policy of "neutrality" toward the war in Spain—a policy which FDR later conceded was his biggest mistake in the field of foreign policy. If there was ever a moment of truth in my life, it was in volunteering to fight in Spain. I was determined to get there, come hell or high water.

42

One day, the passport arrived. I had spent the preceding month cautiously raising money through friends for my steamship ticket. Since then I have met hundreds of people who have said they had wanted to volunteer at the time but had no idea how to go about it. A few others from the Youngstown area volunteered and we arranged to go together. At the beginning of February—this was 1937—friends gave us all an affectionate farewell party and we took the train for New York. It was goodbye to Youngstown, to thousands of good friends, and four wonderful years.

In New York the Passport Division stamped our documents "Not Valid for Travel in Spain"; this was meaningless since the Spanish government did not require passports of us. We got in touch with a committee that was assisting the volunteers; they gave us all the necessary information, chiefly their Paris address. To my family, I said I was off for Europe, not saying where or why; my destination had to be kept confidential and I did not want to worry them. It would be a year before they learned where I had gone.

Since the S.S. *Paris* was leaving sooner, we decided to travel on it instead of the *Deutschland*. By Feb. 6, we were on our way; we discovered that on board there were several hundred other young men about our own age, most of them with identical black suitcases. The government could hardly have failed to know where we were going. The voyage itself was uneventful, our chief problem being to quiet down the more exuberant spirits among us and keep them from talking too much. Six days later we disembarked at Le Havre, where the French customs inspectors took one look at our suitcases and our fleece-lined sheepskin coats and congratulated us.

In Paris the headquarters of the committee was rocking with activity; volunteers were being processed now from all over the world. Only three days in which to see Paris! Whatever little money we had, we spent. We knew we would have no use for any in Spain. I fell into a great piece of luck—I found 10,000 francs in a taxicab. Every last franc was soon gone; nothing could be easier.

Beautiful as Paris was, we were all impatient with the three days' delay. A train carried us to Perpignan on the Mediterranean at the Spanish border. There we simply boarded a bus for Figueres, and in a few minutes we were in Spain and that was all there was to it.

Entering the country did not remain easy for long.

A few days later, the French closed the border. The democratic governments of France, Britain and the United States had embarked on their fatal policy of "non-intervention," placing an embargo on the shipment of arms to their sister republic of Spain, and in the name of neutrality standing by while the Axis powers blotted out democracy. From then on, volunteers found entering Spain heart-breakingly difficult. They had to climb the Pyrenees at night on foot, and sometimes were arrested by the French. Others came in by boat and some of these men were torpedoed and lost their lives before ever setting foot in Spain. We had been lucky enough to ride across the border in brilliant sunlight and in style.

At Figueres we were brought together with other volunteers in a massive medieval fortress. The place had all the filth and stink of feudalism, but who cared about that? We met people from scores of countries, eagerly exchanged experiences and discussed the war. Forming squads, we marched up and down the huge yard of the fortress in close-order drill. Confusion and bedlam reigned since there were as many different languages and march routines as there were countries represented. It was all in good humor.

We left our dank dungeon in a troop train bound for Albacete, base of the International Brigade. Our route took us through Barcelona and Valencia and we stopped at all the small towns. At each station, crowds of Spaniards met us and presented us with huge baskets of oranges, the men cheering, the women throwing kisses, the children chortling with delight. Our few possessions were soon handed out as souvenirs.

At Barcelona we disembarked for an overnight stay and paraded through the city to our barracks in a sort of triumphal procession. Barcelona was impressive, clean and modern, with its own type of rococo architecture. Propaganda posters had been developed to a fine art in Spain and they were plastered everywhere, displaying power and vividness. In addition to the posters, huge slogans had been painted in red on every wall, shouting "Muerte al Fascismo" (Death to Fascism), "Viva Espana Popular" (Long Live People's Spain), "Viva Rusia" (Long Live Russia).

Today it is difficult to appreciate the enormous prestige which the Soviet Union enjoyed in Spain. The Soviet Union, with Mexico, was almost alone in coming to the assistance of the Republic. The only government willing to sell arms to Spain, the Soviet Union from the very beginning sent in massive shipments, especially while the French border was still open. Most of the volunteers were Communists and credit for the International Brigade went to the Soviet Union too, although no large number of Russians ever came to Spain. The words, "the cause of republican Spain is the cause of all advanced progressive humanity," had been spoken by Joseph Stalin, an idea that was to plant itself deep in the conscience of mankind.

When we arrived in Albacete, we really got down to business. Outfitted with uniforms (French) and with rifles (Russian) still packed in cosmoline, we were assigned to units. My outfit was an experiment, an international battalion composed of four companies, an English-speaking one, a French-Belgian, a Slav and a German-Austrian. The battalion commander was Italian and the commissar French. This was an independent battalion not assigned to any of the International Brigades.

The International Brigades were five in number, each with its dominant language: French, German, Italian, Slav and English, although numerous nationalities were scattered among them. The International Brigades had their own base but for training purposes only. Actually, the brigades were part of the Spanish Republican Army, subordinate to its command and discipline.

I discovered to my surprise that as regular members of the Spanish Army we were to receive pay. I knew nothing about armies and the thought of money had been farthest from my mind. We were given the same rate of pay as the Spaniard: for a private 10 pesetas a day, equivalent to the American dollar-a-day army pay of that time. To American volunteers, the money never meant much since we had little opportunity to spend it. To the Spanish soldiers who had families to support, it meant a great deal.

In his book *Masters of Deceit*, J. Edgar Hoover writes: "American communists used glittering promises, underhanded tricks, and downright fraud to coax young men to go to Spain. An enlistee might be promised a lucrative position in Spain, cash rewards, or travel accommodations. A young girl would entice unsuspecting men; in return for her favors they would promise to enlist."

If this were not so malicious and did not come from so powerful a source, it would not be worth a reply. No one had to be coaxed to go to Spain. There were no promises other than the possibility that we might lose our lives. The idea of "lucrative cash rewards" is so laughable to anyone who fought in Spain that it hurts. A few American aviators, professional soldiers and adventurers were hired directly by the Spanish army in the beginning because there were no Spanish aviators; these mercenaries never belonged to the International Brigade; the army's experience with them was so bad that they were soon dismissed.

As for enticements by young girls, the truth is that the American volunteers left wives, children, sweethearts and families behind them, and scores of American young women volunteered as nurses and ambulance drivers. The selfless idealism of the Americans who fought in Spain has been confirmed by Vincent Sheean, Claude G. Bowers, Ernest Hemingway, Herbert Matthews.

We began to whip our new battalion into shape in the small town of Madrigueras, near Albacete. The greatest difficulty was the Babel of languages. Along with our military training, we took time to establish good relations with the people of the town, a matter which especially interested me. An international show for the children, we decided, would be the best way to start. The local movie house was rented, and the school teachers marched in their children. Inside we passed out candy and toys and staged a number of skits representative of our many nationalities. The biggest hit was a red-headed Scotsman who wore kilts and played the bagpipes (the Basques, by the way, play a sort of bagpipe, too). But the climax came when we led a burro down the aisles of the theater and up onto the stage. This dramatic device happened to be my own idea and the result was remarkable: sheer pandemonium. From then on the town was ours.

I was a private then and for my effectiveness with burros and public relations, my company elected me company commissar ("comisario" in Spanish, meaning commissioner). The office of commissar was by now an institution in the Spanish army. It had been established because of the nature of the war and the problems faced by the army. Since the old army had gone over to the enemy, this was a completely new army, created from scratch. When the fascist revolt broke out, the people spontaneously formed a militia, which took political form as the various political parties and union federations organized their own units.

This worked for the early days of the war but it soon became apparent that a regular army with a unified command was needed, that political subdivisions were impossible. This was a delicate matter since the new setup brought opposing political trends into direct contact and often conflict with one another. The government therefore created the office of commissar—officers entrusted with unifying all political factions with the aim of saving the Republic. Fighting against great military odds, the army would have to make up for this with its unity and with the average soldier's understanding of the profound issues of the war.

The commissar was entrusted with this job of education. In rank he equalled the officer in command of the particular unit and they signed all orders jointly as a symbol of the unity of army and government. While a military officer in combat, the commissar was a combination morale officer, chaplain, information and education officer in the rear. His province included relations between soldiers and civilians, and with illiteracy widespread in Spain, he organized classes in reading and writing.

It is not true that the commissars were representatives of the Communist party. They were subordinate to the government and charged with the duty of subordinating the political differences among the soldiers to the common goal of victory. The institution originated in the army of Cromwell and in the French Revolution, and in modern times in the Soviet Red Army. In the latter, however, where only one political party existed, the function of the commissar was different than in Spain.

Apart from marching, our military training consisted of taking apart and putting together our rifles and machine guns. Each of us was allotted a total of three rounds of rifle ammunition for target practice. Then came the great day.

We were assigned to combat with a Spanish brigade on the southern Cordoba front. When we reached this area, we were put on a second train with orders to make contact with the enemy. A decoy train preceded us. We rode in silence, each one immersed in his thoughts. Suddenly we heard a whistle, a whine, then the burst of a shell. It had landed beyond us, the smoke rising.

I felt a sinking sensation in my stomach and an overpowering urge to hit the earth. The train seemed too confining. We stopped, reversed our direction and then were ordered to disembark. We did so, and ran right into an artillery barrage. Before we could take up safe positions, three of our men were killed and several wounded. Exactly three weeks after we had landed in Spain and after each of us had fired only three rounds of ammunition in training, we were in combat.

War has its own form of existence. It calls for different qualities than are considered important under normal circumstances. Strong men weaken, weak ones become strong. At some times courage becomes more important than brains; at times it is the other way round.

Joe Dallet of Youngstown wrote to his wife when he arrived in Spain: "This is a funny place. Some of the most prominent people back home . . . turn out badly here, while some insignificant people like Johnny Gates rise to the top."

The reality of war turns out to be entirely different than the expectation. All in all, it is a dirty, filthy murderous business and great will be the day the world learns to dispense with it.

One day I received a letter with a clipping from the *Youngstown Vindicator* containing my picture and a story that I had been killed in action in Spain. I immediately wrote the *Vindicator* that I had read about my death but could not confirm it. Like

Mark Twain, it was pleasant for me to be able to write so objectively about my demise.

Another letter, from Gus Hall, who now headed the new union in Warren, told of the steel workers' organizing drive, which was a big success. (Hall was convicted along with the other Communist leaders at the first Smith Act trial.) He wrote that a strike had broken out in Little Steel—actually huge steel companies that are "little" only alongside US Steel. The walkout was solid, but several workers had been killed on a certain day on the picket line in Youngstown. That day had been a particularly quiet one in Spain: it was evidently more dangerous to be a striking steel worker back home than a soldier in the Spanish war.

The Cordoba front was long and broad and sparsely populated, the military lines thinly held on both sides. Big breakthroughs and big retreats took place, but they were neither decisive nor permanent. Although the lines shifted spectacularly, in the end they went back where they started. Not a key front, nevertheless good men died there.

Almost worse than the action were the long spells of quiet. Periods of inactivity were physically safer but they also spelled boredom, demoralization. These were the times when the red tape and idiocy of military life reigned supreme. A private in my company developed a badly abscessed tooth and was in great pain. Since no dental facilities were available in our brigade, I asked permission to evacuate him to division headquarters in a large town some distance away. This was denied on the grounds that no soldier could be spared. Actually our front had been inactive for weeks, there was no sign of enemy action, and the soldier was in such utter misery that if combat broke out he would be worse than useless.

I protested the decision, storming with my superiors, but to no avail. When the face of the stricken soldier almost drove me crazy, I took things into my own hands. Commandeering the battalion ambulance, I had him taken to town where his tooth was treated. When my superior officers found out, they were furious and rightly so.

Had a battle taken place, the battalion would have been without its ambulance, many men could have lost their lives because I was taking care of one man's toothache. I was let off with a reprimand but I deserved severe punishment for my individualistic action. The question of simple humanity involved here could have been taken care of without having to hijack an ambulance. Later, when I was to assume greater authority in Spain, I also used my power at times in a way that flouted humane considerations.

We were an isolated group of Americans on the southern front, and the main body of Americans in the Lincoln Brigade, then fighting near Madrid, asked that we be transferred there. This was a good idea. We were a small group to begin with and were becoming smaller all the time, which increased demoralization. Our brigade command agreed to the transfer, but I remained behind. I got along well with the Spaniards, perhaps because of my knowledge of the language. While I envied my buddies who would be rejoining their fellow Americans, I felt it my duty to stay with my original outfit. I was now promoted to brigade commissar with the rank of lieutenant colonel, the lone American in an overwhelmingly Spanish brigade.

But my fellow Americans still felt I was in the wrong place and they did not let matters rest. Several months later I was called to Albacete; I was given the choice of joining the main body of Americans, or of going back to the States to help with the campaign for aid to Spain. Actually this was no choice. I had come to Spain to fight for the duration. Reluctantly I agreed to leave my outfit on the Cordoba front to take charge of the American base in Albacete.

Joe Dallet had come to Spain a few months before, but I had not seen him since Youngstown. Dallet had become part of a newly-formed Canadian battalion, the Mackenzie-Papineau, commanded by Robert Thompson, a young American from Oregon. But the day I arrived in Albacete to take up my new duties, Joe was killed in action.

It happened at Fuentes de Ebro and up there I heard the story. Joe was battalion commissar and it seems that during the training period he had been a strict disciplinarian, rubbing many of the men the wrong way. On the eve of the battalion's first action, the

Brigade staff met to discuss whether Joe should not be removed from his post because of his unpopularity. He was not removed. But he had been very hurt over the criticism and determined to prove himself to the men the next day. Anyone knowing Joe well could have guessed what would happen. At the signal for attack, he was the first to jump out of the trenches. He was killed a good distance in front of the rest of his men.

At Fuentes de Ebro a new tactic was tried out which, though unsuccessful on that occasion, became the dominant pattern of World War II. This was the armored column breakthrough. The idea was to use a large number of tanks to break through the enemy front lines and then, instead of stopping, keep right on. A battalion of infantry was to ride on top of the tanks, while the main body of infantry would follow on the ground and take over the enemy front positions. Meanwhile, a column of trucks carrying still more infantry would be poised to ride through the breach and dash for Zaragoza, a large city 50 miles distant.

It was a brilliant plan but it failed. We had 100 tanks, the most we succeeded in massing during the entire war. These were light tanks (the Spanish conflict proved them entirely inadequate for modern war) and they were manned by Slavs. The troops on top of the tanks were Spanish, while the infantry that was to follow through and mop up was British, Canadian, and American. The tanks broke through successfully and kept right on with the men on top. But they advanced so swiftly that the follow-up infantry was left far behind.

The enemy lines had been crossed but the enemy troops in the lines had not been wiped out and after the tanks moved on, the fascists had enough time to recover and to open fire against our oncoming infantry. Our infantry attack was stopped in its tracks with many casualties. The tanks up ahead were cut off and finally destroyed or captured. The column of trucks was never even able to start rolling. Failure of the operation was laid to a breakdown of communications resulting from so many different languages among our troops. Everything depended on split-second timing and coordination of the various arms. In World War II, the concept was perfected and proved extremely effective.

Many other military techniques were first tested in Spain. Anti-tank defense was developed. The ability of small groups of men to halt tanks with gasoline bombs and grenades was demonstrated. Anti-tank guns were tested, the 37 mm. guns proving effective against light tanks but not against heavier ones. The Nazis tried out their heavy bombers and their saturation bombing technique. As part of their experiments, they destroyed the town of Guernica, a religious shrine and of no military importance whatsoever. We discovered that mass bombings in themselves were not decisive; they had a terror value especially against civilians but they were relatively ineffective against soldiers in the field. In fact, the very rubble created by the bombings could be transformed into defensive positions against an enemy advance.

We found, however, that airpower was extremely effective when combined and coordinated with all the other military arms. Antiaircraft artillery was also tested, the Nazis using electrically-coordinated multiple batteries for the first time. Trench mortars were used widely; cheap to manufacture, simple to operate. They were deadly and dreaded weapons. Guerrilla tactics were developed by our side and were found to be most useful in conjunction with the activities of our regular units.

But Spain was not only a military rehearsal for World War II. It was a political harbinger, too. It showed that fascism was not invincible, that it could be defeated in battle by a people united in a democratic cause and even against superior odds. Not domestic but international developments defeated the Republic—the shameful desertion by the countries that should have been her allies, in face of the ever-mounting assistance given Franco by Hitler and Mussolini. The Franco-Hitler-Mussolini coalition and the International Brigade of Spain were in embryo the Fascist Axis and the Grand Alliance of World War II.

In the Spring of 1937 an organization called the POUM instigated an armed insurrection in Barcelona against the government of the Republic. Consisting of Spanish Trotskyists and Anarchists, the POUM claimed the revolt was an effort at proletarian revolution and the immediate abolition of capitalism in Spain. The government, whose premier was a Socialist, looked upon the uprising as a stab in the back, as treason in the midst of a war against fascism, and proceeded to crush it. We in the International Brigade did not participate in Spain's internal politics and the POUM putsch did not directly affect our units then fighting at the front, but we considered the counter-measures of the government entirely reasonable.

There is a vogue today, set by the late George Orwell, to say the POUM should have been supported and that the government was wrong to crush it. This would mean that the Spanish government should have let itself be overthrown. A comparable situation—perhaps easier for Americans to understand—would be if a group of radicals had organized an armed uprising in Chicago against the Roosevelt government in 1944 when our troops were landing in Normandy. It is hard not to feel that the present-day champions of the POUM seem to want to out-Bolshevik the Bolsheviks.

The POUM claimed that the issue in Spain was proletarian revolution. But this was what the supporters of Franco also claimed, although from the opposite direction. On the other hand, the government and the Communists declared the only issue was democracy versus fascism, and they acted accordingly. Those who think the POUM could have saved Spain should ponder whether the western powers which refused aid to the democratic capitalist government would have helped a revolutionary anti-capitalist POUM regime.

I find it strange, too, that some persons who condemn the Czech Communists for having taken over full power in their country in 1948, can condone the attempt of the POUM to take over in Spain in the midst of a life-and-death struggle with fascism.

Another tale going the rounds now that memories have dimmed, is that the Soviet Union decreased its sale of arms to Spain in the latter stages of the war because of political differences with the government, in order to help the Communists win greater concessions. Soviet shipments did decline as the war went on. But it is reasonable to consider this was inevitable once the French closed the border and the Germans and Italians were permitted to maintain a naval blockade of all Spanish ports in Loyalist hands. The simple facts are that Spain was strangled by the fascist blockade on the one hand, and on the other by the western policy of neutrality and embargoes.

There is also a story to the effect that Soviet arms were channeled mainly to Communist units of the army. The so-called Communist outfits, which must certainly include the International Brigades, were pitifully short of arms even in the best days. We had virtually no artillery (the most decisive weapon) and only a handful of tanks and planes. We had enough rifles, grenades and machine guns to fight a long time, but not nearly enough to stave off final defeat at the hands of a foe plentifully supplied with everything we lacked. The arms we did have, we used exclusively for one purpose: to kill fascists. I think it is fair to say that Spain lost because Spain could not get arms, not because Communists received more than others.

Contrary to the general impression, there were hardly any Russians in Spain. At the beginning a few Russian aviators and tank specialists came over with the first shipments of arms to show the new army how to use them. But they left as soon as the Spaniards became proficient. Among the 3,000 men who composed the 15th International Brigade, there were only two or three Russians and they, we soon learned, were neither supermen nor gods, but human beings with the same frailties as the rest of us.

Stalin, however, did seem like a god to us. As the leader of the one big power which was helping democracy in Spain, we did not believe him capable of any wrong. As far as we were concerned, the Soviet Union was tops, while the prestige of the western democracies was at its lowest ebb. When the Moscow purge trials took place in 1937, we accepted them at face value. Franco had announced that he was marching on Madrid with four columns and that he would be aided there by a Fifth Column operating within Loyalist ranks, and this was confirmed in our minds by the POUM uprising. It seemed entirely logical to us that there had also been a Fifth Column operating in the Soviet Union.

I found no reason to question the public confessions of top Bolshevik leaders like Bukharin and Radek. They had been known as dissidents for years. Their personal ambitions, I thought, had led them to the fatal step of counter-revolution. It seemed incredible to me that men of their stature could confess to these grave crimes unless they had committed them; I could not conceive of myself ever confessing to crimes of which I was not guilty. The possibility of Stalin coercing them into false confessions we refused even to consider. Could such vileness be perpetrated by the man who was doing more than anyone else in the whole world to help democracy in Spain?

As American base commissar in Albacete, my job was to assist the 3,000 Americans who were scattered all over Spain in various infantry, artillery, tank, transport, medical, quartermaster and training units. All of their complaints, and there were many, came to me. Most of the requests had to be turned down, an unpleasant task which was made slightly easier by the fact that I had as long a front-line record as any American and could not be called a rearguard commando.

My biggest problem was with an announcement, made earlier, that American volunteers could be sent back home after six months' service. This was now to be rescinded and the task of telling men who expected to return home that it was all off fell upon me. I pointed out that we had enlisted for the duration, that fighting fascism was no part-time job. A policy of rotation might have made sense if there had been an inexhaustible supply of replacements from America, but this was not the case. A six-month enlistment meant that after two months of training and three months in combat, a volunteer would naturally begin to think of going home. This would impair military efficiency; a soldier would tend to avoid unnecessary chances on the eve of being taken out of the lines. Meanwhile, a policy of part-time foreign volunteers would have a negative effect on the Spaniards. All this was listened to quietly and the men accepted it. They did not blame me for changing the policy, but they did criticize the men who had originally made the well-intentioned but utterly unwise promise.

On visits to the units containing Americans, I saw much of the country—a beautiful one with vast variety of terrain and climate; snow-capped mountain ranges and arid, desolate plains; great rivers and drought-ridden areas; a tropical Mediterranean coast and a rock-ribbed Atlantic coast; a land of oranges, grapes, figs, olives, peaches, pomegranates and flowers, and with plenty of coal, iron, tin and mercury; a land of enormous wealth plagued by the widest extremes of rich and poor. A splendid spirited people in a country then being devastated and plundered by fascism.

The most exciting visit was to the 15th International Brigade—the Americans liked to call it the Lincoln Brigade although this did not set well, of course, with the many other nationalities in it. The Brigade was made up of four battalions, an American whose real name was the Lincoln Battalion, and a British, a Canadian and a Spanish battalion. Attached to the Brigade staff were an anti-tank battery, a special machine-gun company and an observation company. Commander of the Brigade was Col. Copic, a Yugoslav who had been a member of the Yugoslav parliament. Chief of staff was Major Robert Merriman, who had taught economics at the University of California. Dave Doran, Young Communist League leader from Pittsburgh, was commissar.

At full strength, the Brigade numbered some 3,000 men, about half of them American. The Brigade had been through many battles and suffered many casualties, fighting at Jarama and Brunete near Madrid, and at Quinto and Belchite in the Aragon. The name of Abraham Lincoln had been taken by the American battalion because of the parallel between the Spanish war, started by a pro-fascist revolt, and our own Civil War, instigated by a pro-slavery insurrection. The battalion banner bore the inscription "So that Liberty Shall Not Perish from the Earth," and its members bestowed nothing but honor on these words.

I had known Dave Doran well in the States. He was a brilliant and audacious young man in both politics and battle. At Belchite, the brigade had surrounded a fascist unit but its destruction would have been a long and costly process. Doran got his hands on a loudspeaker and had a young fascist, just captured, broadcast an appeal to surrender—which the enemy unit did.

Another exploit of Doran's came during the visit to Spain by Major Clement Attlee, the leader of the British Labor Party. Since

that party had not yet made up its mind about Prime Minister
Neville Chamberlain's non-intervention policy, Doran thought it
would help matters if Attlee visited the British Battalion. This
the Labor Party leader had no intention of doing but this did not
faze Doran who proceeded to set things into motion. Attlee, too
busy to come to the Brigade, was touring all sorts of installations
in Madrid. One day as he emerged from a government building,
he found a delegation waiting for him. He was quickly escorted
to an automobile, and before Attlee knew what was happening
and believing this was still part of the official tour, he was
brought before the British Battalion already waiting for him and
lined up in full dress parade.

The band played "God Save the King," the British commander
saluted Attlee in the snappiest manner, presented him with the
battalion colors of Spanish and British flags and ceremoniously
announced that the machine company, best in the battalion,
would henceforth be the Attlee Company. What could poor Attlee
do but respond in kind? Overwhelmed, he accepted the honor and
promised to do all in his power to aid the cause of democratic
Spain.

And indeed, after Attlee went back to London, the Labor Party
did launch a campaign against the appeasement policy of Chamberlain. Of such small and unheralded incidents important history is sometimes made. Never was there a more benevolent kid-
napping with such good consequences as the one master-minded
by Dave Doran. The Attlee Company never cast any discredit on
its illustrious namesake, later to be Britain's Prime Minister. On
many occasions he was to talk with pride of the company that
bore his name.

In March 1938, the war took a sudden turn for the worse. The
fascists launched a well-prepared general offensive to separate
Catalonia in the north from the central and southern regions. The
plan was to drive along the Ebro River to the Mediterranean and
cut Spain in two. The 15th Brigade was located near the Ebro.
It was decided now that I should join them there, and I took up
new duties as assistant to Doran.

The fascists had massed an imposing array of artillery, tanks, planes, and fresh divisions. Soon the entire Loyalist army was in full retreat and we were forced back from one position to another. Whenever we tried to hold our ground, we found our flanks giving way and we had to retreat once again. Our biggest problem was to prevent panic and keep the retreat from turning into a rout, but here we did not succeed. What was left of our Brigade was completely surrounded and to escape we had to fight our way through the fascist lines.

To facilitate escape, the Brigade divided into two parts, with Copic taking command of one column and Doran the other. I went with Doran. Later we heard that Copic's group ran into a tank concentration and was forced to scatter and make its way out individually. Our group held together until one evening when we decided to move across country at night in single file. Doran headed the column and I took up the rear. It was a dark night and each man had to keep contact with the soldiers directly behind and in front of him. The men were so exhausted that it is no wonder that somewhere a link in the chain was broken. Word came to me in the middle of the night that contact with Doran had been lost. I immediately took command of what was left of the column and placed George Watt, who had been active in the student movement back home, in charge of the rear. The next day Doran's group ran into the fascists and Doran and Merriman were among the killed.

Our own column had been moving along cautiously in the dark. About two hours before dawn we reached the enemy lines and managed to filter through between two hills on which the fascists were emplaced. They heard us and called out, but, of course, we did not answer. Dawn was coming up and they saw us and opened machinegun fire, but we were already out of range. Artillery uses up expensive ammunition and normally is not expended against individual human targets, but that day it was. The fascists had more than enough to spare. And as we dispersed and scattered they played with us, sniping at us with their artillery, directed from planes overhead. Although we had now got through the main fascist lines, we were not out of the woods; there were still fascist patrols to contend with.

I was now with a group of three. We ran into a fascist foot patrol but got away successfully into the brush. Deciding now that it was unsafe to move by daylight, we hid and went to sleep, and moved only under cover of the dark. That night we reached the river near the town of Mora del Ebro. We could find no boats, no materials with which to build a raft. Coming upon a small house, we decided to go in. I was leading the way, grenade in hand, when from inside came a call: "Who's there?" My impulse was to throw the grenade and run, but I was suddenly struck by the realization that the words had been spoken in English and the voice sounded like George Watt, who had been in the rear of our column the previous night. I answered "It's me." Sure enough out came George and several other of our men. They had bedded down for the night—very foolishly, I thought, in view of how close they had come to being killed by their own men. Watt told me later that his group had come just as close to opening fire on us. It made a good story to tell afterwards, and a never-settled debate on which of us had been more unwise.

The river was very wide at this point and the current swift. Some of the men were not sure they could make it, so fatigued were we all, but we decided to join forces and swim across at dawn. We stripped naked, threw away all our belongings, and made for the opposite bank. Three of us got across safely just as the day was beginning to break. The bodies of two other men were washed up on the shore several days later. Besides myself, those who made it were Watt and Joseph Hecht, who was later killed in World War II. In the excitement I had kept my hat on.

Between the river and the road stretched a field of cockleburrs which we now crossed on our bare, bruised feet. This was the last straw: naked (except for my hat), hungry and exhausted, I felt I could not take another step. I had sworn never to surrender to the fascists but I told Watt that if they came along just then, I would give up (actually, we would not have had much choice, having no arms).

We lay down on the side of the road, with no idea of who might come along, too beat to care much. Suddenly a car drove up, stopped and out stepped two men. Nobody ever looked better to me in all my life—they were Ernest Hemingway and *New York Times* correspondent Herbert Matthews. We hugged one another, and shook hands. They told us everything they knew— Hemingway, tall and husky, speaking in explosions; Matthews, just as tall but thin, and talking in his reserved way. The main body of the Loyalist army, it seems, had crossed the Ebro, and was now regrouping to make a stand on this side of the river. The writers gave us the good news of the many friends who were safe, and we told them the bad news of some who were not. Facing the other side of the river, Hemingway shook his burly fist. "You fascist bastards haven't won yet," he shouted. "We'll show you!"

We rejoined the 15th Brigade, or rather the pitiful remnants of it. Many were definitely known to be dead, others missing. Men kept trickling across the Ebro, straggling in for weeks afterwards, but scores had been captured by the fascists. During the first few days, I took charge of what was left of the Lincoln Battalion; we were dazed and still tense from our experience. Meanwhile, the enemy conducted air raids daily against our new positions, but we were well scattered and the raids caused more fear than damage.

On one of those days, we were visited by Vincent Sheean, a handsome fellow who was then a correspondent for the *N.Y. Herald-Tribune*. He sat down with us in one of the holes we had dug for shelter beneath the trees. While we chatted, an air raid took place; there was little danger but the men were quite nervous. Sheean said nothing but it was his first such experience and later he wrote about it in *Not Peace But a Sword*, surely one of the finest books about Spain:

"Cover was not available, except that by getting as close as possible to the bits of mountain scrub around the ravine we might hope to be invisible from the air. We each grabbed a bush and hung on to it. We were scattered enough so that all would not have been killed even if a bomb had landed in the ditch. The bombs were raining down now, somewhere near, in a close series of reverberating explosions. In a minute or two the planes came directly over us, flying very high—a large number of Savoia-Marchetti bombers, their distinctive white-and-silver bodies flashing beautifully in the sun. We tried to count them and came to no agreement. On their left a swarm of black devils that looked like Junkers were sweeping along to keep them company. They passed over, the thunder of their bombs still sounding, and we breathed a little more freely. "They're coming back," somebody reported, having crawled to the edge of the ditch to have a look. We got back to our bits of mountain scrub again and made ourselves as unnoticeable as we could. The planes swept over us again . . . . This time I was fairly sure of my count, and it was more than fifty. . . . I saw no Republican airplanes. . . . The bombs continued for another two or three minutes, dying away down along the riverbank to the south. We gathered again in the middle of the ravine and proceeded to eat our chestnuts, washed down by the remains of the champagne cider. . . . The episode (once it was over) meant nothing to the men in the ravine. It was another bombing from the air. They had been through hundreds of them . . . [but] . . . This was the first time that I had been beneath so many bombers, and very nearly (or so it felt) the first time I had been in an air raid. It was curious, the feeling of relief when the planes could be heard no more. Even more curious was the way in which the men in the ravine took it all as a matter of course. 'When I start to make laws,' Al said, 'I'm going to make a law abolishing all airplanes. Anybody who makes an airplane or sells one or flies one will be put in jail.' "

Spain was the conscience of the world and also its crossroads. It appeared as if almost everybody who was anybody came to see us, political figures like Nehru, and the outstanding authors of the period. Among the latter, Hemingway, Sheean and Matthews were our favorites. They spent much time with us and wrote fairly, objectively, with feeling.

Our Brigade was sorely in need of replacements and these began to arrive, mostly youthful Spaniards, raw recruits but willing and quick. The flow of American volunteers had slowed down to a trickle. This required putting the Brigade on a new basis, with emphasis on the training of Spaniards. Major Valledor, a Spaniard from Asturias, replaced Copic as brigade commander; I was named brigade commissar to replace Dave Doran; Malcolm

Dunbar, former British commander of the anti-tank battery, became chief of staff. Major Milton Wolf was named commander of the Lincoln Battalion. He had fought in every major battle of the battalion and, along with Steve Nelson, the first commissar of the Brigade, at this time back in the States, was the most loved and respected of all the Americans.

Spanish now became the main language of communication in the Brigade and we began to train Spanish officers for our posts. A great new offensive, our biggest undertaking of the war, was now in preparation. The objective: to cross the Ebro and recapture the territory we had lost. This would require a high degree of tactical skill, as well as special engineering equipment for crossing so large a river. In hidden *barrancos* miles from the Ebro, we practiced mock crossings over and over again until we were sure we could do it in our sleep. Other units were training, too, and a vast Army of the Ebro was being assembled.

This was a tense period. The nerves of many of the men became edgy, including my own. In my impatience, I used my new authority to denounce and even jail men who dared to dispute my word, convinced that this was necessary for military discipline. Following one such incident, a friend said to me: "You know, you are a Brigade commissar and if a private says something you don't like, you can do anything you want, even jail him. But if you say or do something a private doesn't like, there is absolutely nothing the private can do to *you*."

This hit me between the eyes. Power can corrupt, it can be abused; there must always be a consciousness of the danger, and checks and restraints. I learned a lesson that day, but it was the kind that needs to be learned over and over again. It was a lesson that I lost sight of many times over the years as I rose higher in the Communist movement.

The success of the new offensive depended on taking the enemy by surprise. We had strict orders to conceal our plans even from our friends. A few days before the offensive, Herbert Matthews came to me to ask whether anything was likely to happen soon; if not, he would visit the southern zone of Loyalist Spain, from which we were cut off—what would I advise him?

It was a fine dilemma: if I told him not to go, it would be the same as telling our secret; if I let him go, our grand project would not be covered by the most able and influential correspondent of the war. Reluctantly I told him there was no reason he should stay around. This is why Matthews was in the southern zone when our offensive began; fortunately he managed to get back in time to cover most of it. (I hope he forgives me now—the incident illustrates how well our secret was kept when even the most knowledgeable journalist in Spain remained in the dark.)

There is even more important evidence of how well we guarded our plans: our offensive succeeded in taking the fascists completely by surprise. One evening in July 1938, as soon as it turned dark, our units began to stream toward the Ebro along a stretch from the Mediterranean and far inland. All roads were choked, but the movement was well-timed and coordinated; the long training had paid off. Lights were strictly forbidden, even cigarettes. When we reached the Ebro, we took boats out of their camouflaged hiding places and began to row across the river. Some men were in such exuberant spirits that they swam across —a far different kind of swim than the one several months earlier in the opposite direction. Once on the other side, we found the fascist positions thinly held, as our intelligence reports had led us to expect, and we quickly overwhelmed them.

Our orders were not to consolidate our gains but to keep pushing ahead as far as possible. We marched rapidly against little opposition and by daylight were many miles inside enemy territory. The advance continued steadily, notwithstanding that large fascist units were now far in our rear. Had they decided to fight, they could have played havoc with our communications, but they were panic-stricken and terrified—as we had been a few months earlier. Whole units would come across a lone Loyalist soldier and surrender. One of our men brought several hundred fully-armed fascists right into our Brigade headquarters. They could easily have wiped out our entire staff, but they meekly laid down their arms and were marched to the rear under a small guard.

We captured vast stores of ammunition and supplies, took thousands of prisoners. In the first few days there were few casualties. It was the biggest victory of the war, but we suffered from lack of transportation and striking power. The bridges across the Ebro had been destroyed the previous spring; the newly-laid pontoon bridges were knocked out by enemy planes almost as quickly as they were built. Since we had no airforce, the fascist planes enjoyed total air supremacy and we had to build our bridges at night. This left only a brief time for our trucks and supplies to cross the river, for at daybreak the enemy planes would appear again to smash the bridges.

The result was that we had few trucks, apart from some that we had captured, and our advance had to be on foot. This gave the fascists time to recover, bring up reserves and establish strong defensive positions. After three days, we began to encounter strong resistance. Even then we could have smashed through if we only had artillery, tanks and planes. In fact, artillery alone would have done the trick. We spent ourselves storming the fascist positions again and again with only our small arms. Finally our offensive ground to a halt. We had achieved enormous successes, but we had failed in our objective of reuniting the two zones of Loyalist Spain. We had struck serious blows against the fascists, but we had not destroyed the bulk of their forces. They had inexhaustible reserves in the support that Hitler and Mussolini were pouring in. We had no such reserves. The front became stabilized, but we knew it was only a matter of time before the enemy would take the offensive. We consolidated our large bridgehead and prepared various defensive positions to fall back on if necessary. We were determined that the fascists would have to fight for every inch of ground and that there would be no repetition of our panicky retreat of the spring before. Our victory elated us; it was wonderful to know that we had turned the tables on the enemy and given them a taste of their own medicine. Most important, we had proved that fascist armies were not unbeatable.

The enemy offensive began in September. It was not a surprise attack but it built up steadily and massively. Artillery, planes and tanks were concentrated to a degree that we had never experienced. Slowly we were pushed back, but this time it was step by step and when we retreated it was to prepared positions. We resisted stolidly, but the cost was terrific. No further reinforcements were available, and our ranks were being decimated.

We did, however, get one more volunteer. James Lardner, youngest son of the famous Ring Lardner, had come to Spain as a newspaper correspondent. A quiet, serious young man, he had been deeply stirred by the war. One day, he asked me what I thought about his volunteering for the Lincoln Battalion. I told him that the war was in its final stages, that things looked bad. The stream of volunteers from the States had stopped. Lardner volunteered. The morale of the men in the Brigade was strongly affected at the news. In the last days of action by the Lincoln Battalion, young Lardner was killed. Later Vincent Sheean wrote, in *Not Peace But a Sword*, the chapter entitled "The Last Volunteer."

The going became rough as September wore on, but nothing could have been as bad as the news we received at the front in September, 1938. Britain's Prime Minister Neville Chamberlain and the French premier Edouard Daladier traveled to Munich to sign a pact with Hitler and Mussolini. Czechoslovakia was to be handed over to Hitler without a shot. As it turned out, the pact sealed the fate of Spain too. Instead of guaranteeing peace in our time, as Chamberlain had promised, the pact made World War II inevitable.

At the front the gravity of the situation was realized full well; the entire world was approaching catastrophe. Although in the midst of intensive combat, we took time out to send a cable to President Roosevelt, expressing our alarm, and warning that if the democracies did not come to our immediate assistance, "the bombs that were falling on Madrid and Barcelona would surely fall on London, Paris and New York."

The die had been cast at Munich; our appeal fell on deaf ears. Later the bombs did fall on London, Paris and Pearl Harbor; the whole world was engulfed in war around the same issue being fought out in Spain—democracy against fascism. It was to take six long years, rivers of tears and oceans of blood before fascism would be defeated.

At this grave juncture, the Spanish government, headed by Dr.

Juan Negrin, made a dramatic effort to change the picture. The decision was reached to withdraw the International Brigades from combat and to send us home. This was a last desperate move by the government to dramatize before the League of Nations that the Spanish Republic was not dependent on foreign aid. It was made in the hope that the League might at last force Hitler and Mussolini out of Spain. The hope was a vain one. The League did nothing except take an official census of the International Volunteers as we left Spain. The farce of non-intervention was carried through to the very end, which finally included the end of the League of Nations itself. The refusal of the League to act only made the fascist dictators impatient for the kill. They stepped up their aid to Franco.

We were in fierce combat at the front, having one of our worst days, when the newspapers arrived on Sept. 23 at Brigade headquarters with the news that this was to be our last day of fighting. Tomorrow we would be withdrawn. We tried desperately to keep the news from reaching the men, knowing they would lose whatever will to fight they still had. The incessant pounding of the past days had put our men in a state of numbness and shock. The news leaked out and spread like wildfire. Our last day was a nightmare. That night we were relieved by crack Spanish troops, and just in time too, for under the circumstances we were no longer fit for combat.

It took two more months to leave Spain. Transportation had to be arranged for the long voyage back; we had to be outfitted with civilian clothes; the League of Nations had to count us; it was almost more difficult to leave Spain than it had been to get in. Meanwhile, the Spanish people wanted to give us a proper farewell. Fetes and banquets were held everywhere as people showed their gratitude to the 25,000 men from all over the world who had come to help Spain in her hour of need.

The main farewell took place in Barcelona on Oct. 29. For the last time in full uniform, the International Brigades marched through the streets of Barcelona. Despite the danger of air raids, the entire city turned out. Whatever airforce belonged to the Loyalists, was used to protect Barcelona that day. Happily, the fascists did not show up. It was our day. We paraded ankle-deep in flowers. Women rushed into our lines to kiss us. Men shook our hands and embraced us. Children rode on our shoulders. The people of the city poured out their hearts. Our blood had been shed with theirs. Our dead slept with their dead. We had proved again that all men are brothers. Matthews wrote about this final day, remarking that we did not march with much precision. "They learned to fight before they had time to learn to march."

Finally, on a day in December 1938, we boarded a train near the French frontier and left Spanish soil. The French government sealed our train and we were not permitted to get off until we reached Le Havre and the ship that was waiting to take us home. The Italian and German members of the Brigades were interned in French concentration camps; there they led a miserable existence until World War II freed them and they were able to use the experience of their Spanish days in the various Allied armies which they joined.

Three months after we crossed the Spanish border, and two years and eight months after Franco had begun his revolt, the Republic of Spain fell to the fascists. It was a bleak day for mankind.

V

THE MARCH TO
WORLD WAR

I HAD STARTED OUT IN SPAIN A PRIVATE AND HAD RISEN TO THE highest rank of any American there. I had come to Spain as an obscure Communist, but in my absence the Young Communist League elected me to its National Council in 1937. It was my original plan to return to Youngstown, but the YCL decided I should assume a national post in New York. After an absence from my family for six years, I now lived with them once again. Before taking on my duties in New York, however, I paid a visit to Youngstown, to see the relatives of men who had been killed in Spain, meet old friends, and speak at several large meetings.

My new post in New York was executive Secretary of the Friends of the Abraham Lincoln Brigade, headed by David Mc-Kelvey White, a Spain veteran and son of a former Ohio governor. The war was still going on and many problems remained: some Americans were still in Spanish hospitals where we had been forced to leave them; some were prisoners in Franco's dungeons. Men who had returned needed help finding work; the wounded and disabled required medical assistance and job re-training. We held many affairs to raise money and win support for Spain. In March, the war ended. By April, all Americans had returned from

Spain, including prisoners of Franco. Since the work of the Friends of the Lincoln Brigade was largely finished, the organization dissolved, its rehabilitation duties now being taken over by the Veterans of the Lincoln Brigade, composed of all who had fought in the war.

I was now able to devote all my time to my first enthusiasm—the Young Communist League. A vital, throbbing organization of close to 20,000 at this time, the YCL was headed by Gil Green and the Negro youth leader, Henry Winston. Many League members had fought in Spain and this had been a major factor in its growth. Joe Starobin, whom I had not seen since college days, edited the League's lively magazine, the *Young Communist Review*. Many other schoolmates, veterans of the unemployed days, organizers of the labor movement, were now in leading positions of the YCL and the CP. A convention of 1,000 delegates was held in May 1939, and attracted 20,000 people to a public meeting in Madison Square Garden.

"Character Building and Education in the Spirit of Socialism" was the new slogan of the convention, suggested in a speech by Earl Browder. This slogan had, in fact, been inspired by Gil Green, an unusually able man with a keen understanding of American youth. The YCL was working closely with church and many other youth organizations in the American Youth Congress. Their influence upon us stimulated our new emphasis upon education and character.

We presented a revue called "Socialism in Swing," with lyrics and music that could have graced a Broadway musical. Madison Square Garden rocked with a jitterbugging show that must have made Karl Marx do some spinning of his own. As it was, many live communists were shocked—jitterbugging was definitely not anticipated by the Marxist classics. But our young members loved it. We felt we were definitely moving forward. The prestige of the communist movement had soared chiefly as a result of its struggle against fascism, and was on the way to being accepted as part of the democratic current. Earl Browder was invited to speak at universities; he was listened to seriously as representing a trend of increasing importance.

Browder was a native of Kansas, son of a family that went back generations to early America. An old-time Socialist, he had been one of the founders of the Communist Party in 1919. Shy, diffident, no flaming orator, he was nevertheless far more successful in rooting the Communist Party in American life than any previous leader. Within the party itself, his prestige was enormous and he overshadowed Foster, whom a severe heart attack in late 1932 had incapacitated for four years, and whose policies, moreover, were considered old-fashioned and sectarian.

As a student of American history, Browder made serious efforts to link the communist movement to the democratic, revolutionary, labor and liberal traditions of the country. The party won substantial influence in labor unions numbering more than a million members. Its reputation was high in Negro life, among farmers, youth and in the arts, sciences and other professions. When Browder ran for president on the communist ticket in 1936, it was actually a token campaign as far as votes were concerned; the main slogan of the campaign was "Defeat Landon [the GOP candidate] At All Costs." This could only mean that the party was urging people to vote for Roosevelt, not for Browder. But the campaign gave the party an opportunity to speak over the radio, appear before large audiences and participate in the popular movement around Roosevelt.

Not that communists, and those who associated with them, were immune from attack. The official presence of communists in the American Youth Congress, for example, made that influential organization the target of widespread criticism, although the fact that Mrs. Eleanor Roosevelt was one of the chief patrons of the Congress, tended to soften the blows. But the time came when the Congress felt compelled to clarify its relationship to communism.

In 1939, the Congress adopted a resolution which declared its opposition to all forms of totalitarianism—nazism, fascism and communism. To most of the organizations affiliated with the Youth Congress, this resolution offered no problem, but it did for the Young Communist League. We were, of course, opposed to the reference to communism and would have voted against the resolution except for a complicating factor. The YCL was only one of a large number of national youth organizations in the Congress, the overwhelming majority of which were strongly anti-communist; but the YCL had an altogether disproportionate number of rank-and-file delegates at the Congress. This happened because many YCL members belonged to other youth organizations as well, from which they were often elected as delegates to the Congress because of their good work. This gave the communist organization a mechanical majority at Congress gatherings if it chose to wield it. It is not unusual in our country for members of political organizations to belong also to other organizations; but in our case our members felt bound to carry out our own policies in other organizations even where this resulted in conflict.

Besides, communists in these organizations usually concealed their political affiliation, not only for fear of losing their livelihood if their employers got wind of it, but also for fear of not being accepted by the particular organization. This gave rise to suspicions that communists "bored from within," and were subject to a higher discipline than the non-communist organization to which they belonged. At this particular Youth Congress, the problem was this: if the national leadership of the YCL, officially present as delegates, voted against the anti-totalitarian resolution, the majority of delegates might follow suit. This would defeat the resolution. But the victory would be a superficial one. It would misrepresent the true sentiment of the Youth Congress and characterize it publicly as pro-communist, which it very definitely was not.

The official YCL delegates decided therefore to vote for the resolution with an explanation of our reservations. Our spokesman said that communism should not be lumped with fascism, that it was indeed its very opposite, that communism had much in common with democracy, was actually, as we believed, the highest form of democracy. The resolution passed overwhelmingly.

As national educational director of the YCL, to which I had been elected at the 1939 convention, and because of my personal activities as an anti-fascist in Spain, I was assigned to write an article for the *Young Communist Review* which would explain our vote at the American Youth Congress. The article was a mess of contradictions. The logic of my argument was that we should have opposed the resolution; I could not explain the real reason that we voted in favor; I could not write that we were afraid the resolution would be defeated if we voted nay—this would have been evidence that a majority of delegates at the Youth Congress were under Communist influence.

But the policy then pursued by the YCL in the American Youth Congress was the exception in communist practice rather than the rule. In many organizations we used our mechanical majorities to adopt policies in line not with the will of those organizations, but with our own; and this would lead at times either to the destruction of those organizations or to the isolation of the communists and the decline of their influence. The communist movement in this country was never able to work out a sound and sustained relationship with other organizations.

In 1939 the education department of the YCL also found itself with a difficult problem of theory. In the early part of the year, the official *History of the Communist Party of the Soviet Union* had been published and translated amid much fanfare. Stalin was reputed to have played a major part in writing the book and it became the most authoritative textbook for the world communist movement. How the book applied to the American scene was not an easy question to answer, however, for our American program seemed to contradict some of the major conclusions of the book. The book contained a number of theoretical postulates which it declared were universally valid, one of them the "law of violent proletarian revolution" expressed by the following passage:

"Marx and Engels taught that it was impossible to get rid of the power of capital and to convert capitalist property into public property by peaceful means, and that the working class could achieve this only by revolutionary violence against the bourgeoisie, by a *proletarian revolution,* by establishing its own political rule—the dictatorship of the proletariat—which must crush the resistance of the exploiters and create a new, classless, Communist society."—*History of the Communist Party of the Soviet Union,* p. 9.

This seemed to be at complete variance with our own repeated denials that we advocated the forcible overthrow of the government of the United States. A self-study guide issued by the League's education department, posed the question: How can you reconcile the law of inevitable violent proletarian revolution with our opposition to violent overthrow of our government? Our reply to our own question was that no contradiction existed. The tendency of every ruling class when confronted with a majority will to replace it, we said, was to resort to violence. This violence was instigated by the ruling class, not by the people, and was inevitable. Moreover, once the public came to power, they would have to defend themselves against the violent attempts of the former rulers to regain their positions. As proof, we pointed to the American Civil War and the recent Spanish conflict, where democratically elected governments faced armed revolts by the former ruling classes. Our explanation left many questions unanswered. But this was the way we understood the matter at the time.

Following the fall of Spain and of Czechoslovakia, the Communist Party emphasized anew the danger of general war and the need for a collective security agreement between the West and the Soviet Union to "quarantine the aggressor," as FDR had put it in 1936. The British and French finally appointed representatives to meet with the Russians, but they named unknown third-stringers, hardly a sign of sincere intentions. For their part, the Russians had offered to guarantee the defense of Czechoslovakia if the West agreed to do so too, but this was rejected by the British and French. When the Russians proposed to join the West in defending Poland in the event of aggression and on condition that the Red Army be permitted to fight against the enemy on Polish soil, this too was turned down.

The newspapers reported that behind the scenes the British and French were negotiating with the Axis powers. Reports also appeared of a possible agreement between the Nazis and the Russians, at which we Communists scoffed as slanderous and utterly impossible. True, Stalin had warned, in March 1939, that the Soviet Union would not pick the western powers' "chestnuts out of the fire" for them, but we did not interpret this as a hint of dealings with the Nazis. When Vincent Sheean wrote of this possibility in the *Red Book* magazine, I dismissed it as silly speculation. (Sheean had also made a speech at a meeting sponsored by the Friends of Lincoln Brigade, in which he quoted Lord Acton's famous assertion that "Power corrupts and absolute power corrupts absolutely." This was the first time I heard the quotation; I was totally incapable of understanding it then and I shook my head: Poor Sheean, I said to myself, is weakening under imperialist pressure and succumbing to the anti-Sovieteers. . . .)

The announcement on August 23, 1939, that the Soviet Union and Germany had signed a non-aggression pact came like a thunderclap, not least of all to the communist movement. Leaders and rank-and-file members were thrown into utter confusion. The impossible had happened. We looked hopefully for an escape clause in the treaty, but the official text provided none. For several days there was no clarification from Moscow and we American Communists were left painfully on our own. It would have been better if we had remained on our own.

A national conference of the Communist Party had previously been scheduled for that weekend and it took place amid pathetic consternation. Eugene Dennis, then the party's legislative secretary and a member of the Political Bureau, the highest party committee, seemed to make the most sense, calling for a fight on two fronts: against the fascist enemy and against the appeasing democratic governments which could not be relied on to fight fascism. This attitude, a reasonable continuity with our former position, did not last long. Statements now began to come from Moscow— both from the Soviet press and the Communist International— which made clear a big change in policy was under way. When the Nazis now invaded Poland and Britain and France declared war against Germany, the Soviet position was that British and French imperialists were responsible for the war, that this was an imperialist war and that neither side should be supported.

The world communist movement followed in the wake of these statements. Until that moment the communist parties had been demanding that their governments fight against fascism; now that the West had at last declared war on the Axis, we denounced them and opposed all measures to prosecute the war. We demanded that the war be ended; how this could be done without the military defeat of Hitler was left unclear. Some communist leaders in the west, like Harry Pollitt, then general secretary of the Communist Party of Great Britain, projected a policy of working to establish governments that would energetically fight the fascists, but these leaders were removed. Now in disgrace, Pollitt went back to work as a boilermaker. Dennis did not persist in his original position, which had been similar to Pollitt's.

Actually, a good case could be made for the Soviet Union's non-aggression pact with Germany. For years Moscow had tried to reach an agreement with the West against fascism. Instead, the West had come to an agreement with fascism at Munich and behind the back of the Soviet Union. After Munich, the Soviet Union had every reason to believe that the West was not negotiating in good faith but was maneuvering to push Hitler into an attack upon the USSR. Convinced that Hitler was bent on war, unable to conclude a defensive alliance with the West, the Soviet Union decided to protect itself through a non-aggression pact. The West had only itself to blame for what happened. Churchill had warned the British government against such an eventuality. The Soviet Union undoubtedly gained temporary safety and additional time to prepare for the inevitable onslaught.

But it also paid a heavy price. What it gained materially, it lost in moral prestige. It is questionable whether the one balanced the other. The Khrushchev revelations 17 years later indicate that the Soviet Union did not use the time gained to maximum advantage in preparing defenses against Hitler—which raises the question of whether Stalin did not have illusions about Hitler and whether the Soviet Union may not have been genuinely surprised when the attack finally came.

Whatever justification there may have been for Soviet policy, was there any at all for the new course now adopted by the Communist Party of the United States? For years we had been saying that when it came to a choice between bourgeois democracy and fascism, we would unite with everybody against the latter. Now we discarded this sensible policy. We insisted now that there was no significant difference between the bourgeois-democratic countries and the fascist ones, and we began to act as if the western democracies were virtually fascist themselves.

We attacked the Roosevelt administration once again as we had done back in 1933, calling it dictatorial and pro-fascist. Although we said we supported neither side, in effect our main attack was against the West. We did not support fascism, but our sharpest criticism was reserved for the western democracies. We could have defended the action of the Soviet Union as an unavoidable defensive move, as a lesser evil forced upon it by wrong western policy, and we could have continued our own policy of unity against fascism. But to have done so would have been to court condemnation by the Soviet Union and the Communist International for differing with the Soviet Communists and hence betraying proletarian internationalism; any leaders pressing for a reasonable course would have been deposed, as was Pollitt. No such heresy arose in the American Communist Party.

The complete turnabout cost us heavily. It lent credence to the charge that the policy of the anti-fascist people's front was a Trojan Horse maneuver, a tactic toward the end of securing complete power for ourselves, that our anti-fascism was not sincere. Not only reactionaries but the entire democratic current denounced us. New epithets were coined at our expense: "red fascists" and "Communazis." There was a certain poetic justice in this since we had once called the Socialists "social-fascists." The truth was that regardless of Socialist or Communist mistakes, neither of them were ever any kind of fascist.

The unity we had helped to create, the alliances we had established with important forces in American life, were shattered overnight. Philip Murray, James Carey and other leaders of the labor movement refused to have anything to do with us. A. Philip Randolph, head of the National Negro Congress, left because of our presence; Joseph P. Lash, a Socialist and head of the American Student Union, broke with us. Prominent intellectuals like Granville Hicks left the party. Even though our loss of members was far less severe, our loss of influence was important.

We turned on everyone who refused to go along with our new policy and who still considered Hitler the main foe. People whom we had revered only the day before, like Mrs. Roosevelt, we now reviled. This was one of the characteristics of Communists which people always found most difficult to swallow—that we could call them heroes one day and villains the next. Yet in all of this lay our one consistency; we supported Soviet policies whatever they might be; and this in turn explained so many of our inconsistencies. Immediately following the upheaval over the Soviet-German non-aggression pact came the Finnish war, which compounded all our difficulties since, here also, our position was uncritically in support of the Soviet action. The American Youth Congress, in which the Young Communists had stepped so carefully, now underwent great strains as we tried to bend it toward our policy without regard for consequences.

At a Youth Congress gathering on the White House lawn, at which FDR spoke, the President was booed. The Youth Congress could not survive a turn like this. It passed out of existence, and to our shame we were not sorry to see it go. Our slogan was now "The Yanks Are Not Coming," and we gleefully sang songs ridiculing President and Mrs. Roosevelt.

Yet we were not totally isolated. Other forces opposed the war too. Among these was John L. Lewis, who had broken with FDR for his own personal reasons, not shared by most of the miners. A strong isolationist current existed in America, as well as the traditional pacifist trend, and now we sought allies here. We often found ourselves in strange company, with some of the most reactionary, anti-labor and pro-fascist elements who were part of the isolationist America First Committee. But while we located some new friends, we had become estranged from the mainstream of American democratic and progressive life. Many people had looked upon us with trust. This we now lost, and were never able to win it back fully even when circumstances changed again.

All this seems so simple and obvious now. But it did not appear so to most of us at the time. The fatal appeasement policy had caused us to distrust the West, and with good reason. Meanwhile our admiration of the Soviet Union had grown, especially with its long years of struggle for collective security against fascism and its virtually lone stand in assisting Republican Spain. Immediately after the outbreak of the second world war, there took place for several months what became known as the "phoney war," when the British and French conducted no operations against the Nazis and seemed more interested in fighting the Soviet Union via the Finland route. This only confirmed our suspicions that the western powers did not want to fight the Axis but sought to transform the war into one against the USSR.

As a matter of fact, whatever doubts many of us had about the non-aggression pact were dissolved during this period. Suppose that Russia had not signed a pact with Germany, we reasoned, would the western powers come to the aid of Russia if it were attacked, when they had refused to help Czechoslovakia and Spain? But we were content to expose the aims of the western powers as phoney; we had no interest in trying to change the phoney war into a real one that would destroy the Axis.

Of course, it was more than simply our admiration for the Soviet Union, and our hostility to the appeasers, that explained our support of it, through every twist and turn of events. It was the deeply-ingrained conviction that the Soviet Union was the bulwark of a world movement, a base from which socialism would advance on a world-scale. While we were not "puppets" or "agents" of anything specifically in the Soviet interest as distinguished from the national interests of other peoples, we did imagine ourselves members of a common front, participants on our sector of a common battle. If we had to take it on the chin because the particular battlefront was unfavorable to us, this was nonetheless necessary in the interests of the overall struggle. It is true that we were never consulted on the world strategy of which we assumed ourselves a part and by which we were governed. We accepted it though it was a strategy worked out by others. And we saw it as the only possible strategy since those who had worked it out were assumed to be the wisest of all communists.

Roosevelt seemed to us to be moving in a reactionary, anti-labor direction. Repressive legislation, such as the Smith Act, was passed. The Voorhis Law was enacted to compel us to register as foreign agents, as a result of which the American Communist Party decided to disaffiliate from the Communist International, making clear, however, that we did this only to protect ourselves from the new and unjust law. Earl Browder was sent to prison on a technical charge of passport fraud. With a long period of repression now seemingly ahead, the party went on a semi-legal basis. The actions taken against us seemed to us a certain sign of impending fascism; it did not occur to us that these measures were prompted not only by the usual pressure from reactionary forces, but also by a desire on the part of others to retaliate against us for our mistakes. Nor were we able to envisage sharp turns that might alter the situation completely.

The phoney war came to an abrupt end when in June 1940, the Nazis sliced through the Low Countries and invaded France. The highly touted Maginot Line dissolved like so many blocks of butter. France fell, the British suffered their disastrous Dunkirk, and the bombing of Britain began. The war was serious now. Churchill had come to power in Britain and he obviously was no appeaser, while most of Europe was by this time a Nazi fortress. But our policy remained unchanged.

When FDR began his lend-lease policy and proposed the first peacetime draft in our history, we denounced these moves as steps to war and insisted our country continue as a neutral. Meanwhile, for every gain which brought the Nazis closer to Soviet borders, the Soviet Union made a countermove. When the Nazis invaded Poland, the Soviets occupied eastern Poland; when they conquered France, the Russians took over the small Baltic countries and Bessarabia in Rumania.

Hitler's air blitz of Britain failed and instead of undertaking his much advertised invasion of the British Isles, he began to move eastward. Evidently Hitler was afraid to tackle Britain so long as the Soviet Union remained powerful on his eastern flank. When Churchill and others warned the Soviet Union that she was next on Hitler's list, the warning was rejected as propaganda designed to disrupt the peaceful relations between Russia and Germany. The day before the invasion actually began, the *Daily Worker* derided rumors of the impending attack as wishful thinking on the part of imperialists.

By now I myself did not share this view and I was not the only one. Saturday evening, June 21, I had dinner with friends and argued not only that an attack was possible but it had been ever since Hitler moved into Yugoslavia in April, 1941. As a matter of fact, there had been much discussion in the YCL's inner circles about the Yugoslav uprising, and the potentially anti-Soviet orientation of Hitler; we even felt that the "unjust character of the war" was changing, and hence some felt our own policies ought to be changing. But it was characteristic of the Communist movement that while much discussion went on in private, and even in the formal organizational committees, little of it was allowed to come before the membership or be given public expression. It was part of our concept of discipline, and of our loyalty to a world front, that this kind of self-censorship prevailed. This dilemma of the conflict between opinions debated behind closed doors and public pronouncements was never resolved.

It was a sultry night, that Saturday night, and when I returned home I opened all the windows wide. It must have been past midnight when I became conscious of radios blaring all over the neighborhood. I listened casually, then began to catch phrases —the Nazis had crossed the Soviet borders, Russia was being bombed. This was it. The land of socialism was under attack. The news stirred me to action, which the fall of France had never succeeded in doing. I dressed quickly and went to the home of Max Weiss, who had no phone and who had succeeded Gil Green as head of the Young Communist League. The family was asleep and it was some time before Weiss came to the door. There was no more sleep that night; we pondered the meaning of the grim news and what we would have to do. We woke up other YCL leaders and arranged a meeting for early morning. There we decided that we must appeal to America and Britain to join with the USSR and give it full assistance in the common fight against Hitler. But before we were able to put these views into print, assurances were already coming to the Soviet Union from the various governments. They had not waited for our opinion on the matter.

The Young Communist League of New York State, which I now headed and which numbered 10,000 members, swung into motion. Our former slogans were junked. No longer did we chant "The Yanks Are Not Coming"; no longer did we oppose aid to Britain, lend-lease and the draft as steps toward war—we warned now of what would happen if we did *not* go to war. We were squarely for national unity behind Roosevelt, fully supporting his policy of aid to the allies now that the allies included the Soviet Union.

This is not to suggest that our lightning-change was made without pangs of conscience. Many of us were ashamed now of the policy we had followed since August 1939 and were determined to make up for it. We were justified in emphasizing the new danger to America from Hitler's attack on Russia; but had not the invasion of France and the bombings of Britain endangered us too? We who had fought in Spain had been called premature anti-fascists (which had always made us feel proud); when Russia was invaded we had become anti-fascists come-lately, of which we could not be proud. Even from the narrow point of view of supporting the Soviet Union, our policy of 1939–41 had been stupid. Had it prevailed, our country's ability to assist Russia in the moment of crisis, let alone defend ourselves, would have been considerably weakened. In fact, had our stand against aiding the allies won out, the United States might never have aided the Soviet Union at all.

A majority of Americans had awakened to the fascist danger later than we Communists did, but when they did awake they displayed a consistency which we Communists could not claim. One can speculate, of course, whether Roosevelt and Churchill would have promised help to Russia so promptly if the West had not suffered such terrible defeats at Hitler's hands the preceding two years. Nor should it be forgotten that people like Harry Truman, then an influential member of the Senate, proposed that in the Soviet-German war we should help whichever side was losing at a particular moment so that in the long run they might bleed one another to death. Surely this attitude was no less harmful to America's interests than our own since 1939. Proof of this was to come at Pearl Harbor.

Between June and December of 1941, we Communists did our utmost to repair the damage we had done to ourselves and others in the preceding two years. It was rough going. Distrust of us could not evaporate overnight. But now we were going with the stream, not against it.

Sunday, Dec. 7, 1941. The Communist Party was holding a national conference, the main address being delivered by Robert Minor, a Texan, famous cartoonist for the *St. Louis Post-Dispatch* in an earlier day, and now acting secretary of the party during Browder's term in prison. Minor's theme was the imminence of war between the United States and Japan and the need for the country to step up its defenses. While he was talking, someone ran into the hall with the news—the Japanese had bombed Pearl Harbor! There was stunned silence. The meeting was recessed so that fresh proposals could be prepared in view of the grave new situation.

Many of us knew what we had to do, as we had known once before when Americans were volunteering to fight in Spain. The next week I spent in helping the organization ready itself to give full support to the war, and in preparing for someone to take my place. On Dec. 16, 1941, I went to the main army recruiting office and volunteered. I was sworn in on Dec. 17, Private John Gates, army serial number 12037342. We were allowed three days to terminate our personal affairs before reporting for induction.

All over the country, young Communists, and older ones too, were volunteering. In fact, some 15,000 American Communists were to become members of the armed forces, a very large proportion of the organization's membership at that time. In many places, ceremonial meetings of the party took place, as send-offs. It so happened that the New York Communists were holding a meeting of leading people, some 2,000 in all, the day I was sworn in. Tremendous applause greeted the announcement that I had just joined the U.S. Army, on leave from the Communist Party. The audience stood as I saluted the flag and repeated the pledge: "I pledge allegiance to the flag of the United States of America, and to the Republic for which it stands; one nation indivisible, with liberty and justice for all."

Two days later the Young Communist League tendered me a farewell banquet. George Watt and I exchanged stories about the Ebro, and we said the cause of democracy for which we had fought in Spain had been taken up now by the whole world. Our spirits had never been higher. Many gifts were presented, mostly sets of military brushes than which nothing is more useless for soldiers in war. I said goodbye to my friends and later to my family. Early next morning I took the train to Camp Upton.

VI

FROM THE ALEUTIANS
TO GERMANY

THREE WEEKS AFTER I HAD ARRIVED IN SPAIN AND WITH NO MILITARY training to speak of, I was in combat. Upon enlisting in World War II, I trained and trained, and before I saw any combat, three whole years had passed. I may have been the most trained soldier in all World War II.

The first few days in the army were taken up with interviews, all the necessary information: my full-time employment in communist activity, my change of name, and so on. Since being a communist organizer was not a normal trade or profession, there was some trouble about classification. My title in the New York YCL had been executive secretary but the list of army skills contained no such heading. The closest thing was "secretary," which meant a typist or clerk. But I had not enlisted to do office work. I was put down finally as experienced in organizing and educating. My previous military experience in Spain caused a puzzled reaction.

"How old did you say you are?" the interviewer asked.

"I'm 28," I replied.

"Heck, you couldn't have fought in the Spanish-American war!" was his comeback.

It was amazing how many men had never heard of the Civil War in Spain, only three years after.

I wanted to serve in the Armored Force branch of the army; having walked so much in the infantry in Spain, I wanted to ride for a change. Besides, the Spanish experience convinced me that of all military arms, tank units were the most decisive. Scoring fairly high in the Army General Classification Test, I was placed in the first category and assigned to basic training in field artillery.

Just before leaving Camp Upton, Intelligence called me in, questioned me sharply about my communist background and warned me against engaging in subversive activities. I remonstrated that my intentions were quite the opposite, that I wanted only to get into combat as quickly as possible and to put my military experience to use against the fascists. The officer had no understanding of what I was saying; it made absolutely no impression on him. Later I learned that he placed the letters "S.D." on my service record. This meant "suspected of disloyalty." It was to dog me all my days in the army.

Christmas of 1941 found me at Fort Sill, Oklahoma, the army's famous Field Artillery Training Center, where basic training in army fundamentals began with the use of the 75 mm. howitzer, a standard weapon in World War I but already obsolete in World War II. I had no difficulty with training and came out first in my company. Local newspapers got wind of my presence and printed interviews about my record in Spain. After 10 weeks of basic, I was assigned as a cadre to help activate the newly formed 6th Armored Division at Camp Chaffee, Fort Smith, Arkansas. "Cadre" was a military term used to describe key personnel making up the basic skeleton of a military unit.

Chaffee was a new camp, not yet fully completed. Only a few men had arrived and we were put to work moving equipment and cleaning things up. Soon the new recruits appeared and we began to work in earnest. I was assigned to the 59th Armored Field Artillery Battalion, where our basic weapon was the 105 mm. self-propelled howitzer. I kept thinking how differently matters might have turned out if we had only had such a weapon in Spain. Two weeks after joining my new outfit, I was promoted to private first class, another two weeks later to gunner corporal, still two weeks later to machine-gun sergeant, and several months later to battalion operations sergeant, technical sergeant second grade.

I got along well with officers and men; soldiers with actual combat experience were few and far between. My buddies generally came to know me as a person before learning that I was a Communist. They did not hold my politics against me. I was a "good guy" in spite of it, they figured. When my officers recommended me for Officers Training School and Washington constantly rejected the idea for obvious reasons, the men in my outfit were always puzzled. Their reasoning was simple. I was a good soldier with considerable experience as a leader. There was no doubt I hated fascism—why not use me to the maximum?

My own outfit made use of my experience in many ways. I gave a daily 15-minute newscast, lectured on the military developments of the war, basing myself on the outlines prepared by the army orientation department, and taught a class in fire direction. The army had a good educational program but it often failed to get across for lack of trained personnel. Lectures were usually dull; I attempted to make the subject interesting by drawing on dramatic examples from my own experience. There was nothing unique in this. In one outfit after another, American Communists were being called upon to help educate the men.

I was proud that my outfit was being whipped into shape and certain the day was drawing close when we would be ordered overseas. The order alerting our division came down in late 1942; but a few days later another order arrived from the War Department. I was to be left behind when the division went overseas, and transferred forthwith to the service unit permanently stationed at the camp. Appalled by the stupidity and senseless bureaucracy of the order, I could hardly keep from crying. The officers and men were stunned, too. I was by now a key part of the outfit and the order to leave me behind was incomprehensible to them. My commanding officers assured me they would do everything to get the order reversed; in the meantime, to comply with the order, they placed me on special duty to prepare my battalion for overseas movement. Ironically, of course, the men thought me lucky to stay behind. If the order made no sense to them, neither did my unhappy frame of mind. They considered me somewhat touched in the head.

I decided to appeal to President Roosevelt. Under army regulations, any soldier can write directly to the President without having to go through channels. It was a long letter, containing the salient facts of my life, including my communist background and experience in Spain. Everyone makes some mistakes, I went on, and while we communists had been wrong in opposing the draft from 1939 to 1941, he, the President, had admitted he had been wrong about Spain. I was asking no special favors, only the chance to go overseas and fight with the outfit I had helped to train.

Subsequently I learned that the President gave my appeal consideration and sent a copy of my letter to the battalion commander, asking for his comments. Five of the battalion's officers, including the commanding colonel (a West Point graduate), two majors and two captains, forwarded their personal affidavits to the President testifying to my ability and integrity, expressing confidence in me and recommending favorable action on my appeal. All of this was strictly confidential; I found out about it only because enlisted men in the battalion office were friendly to me.

About this time I was granted a regular furlough. I determined to use it to drum up support for this case, which was no longer a personal matter. It involved a principle and affected thousands of soldiers. In New York I went to see Earl Browder who had recently been released from prison as a gesture of national unity on the part of the Administration. Browder held that the action in my case was actually a hangover from the preceding period. In his view, everything was changing (witness his own release) and things would surely change for me too. Upon his advice I consulted several Congressmen. A number of them made inquiries at the War Department about me—Vito Marcantonio, Joseph Clark Baldwin, Clare Booth Luce. A query also went to the Department from Henry Cabot Lodge on the initiative of a captain in my battalion, who had been an aide of Lodge's in the North African campaign.

Upon my return from furlough, my officers were confident that I would be transferred back into the battalion. In fact, an order to this effect arrived soon afterwards from Armored Force Headquarters. I thought victory was finally at hand, when everything was upset again. Newspaper columnist Drew Pearson published an account of my case just as I have described it here. Syndicated coast-to-coast, the column meant well but it contained all kinds of unauthorized, secret military information—the name of my battalion, the fact that it had been alerted for overseas, my letter to the President and his reply, and the officers' affidavits. As a result of this violation of military secrecy, the date for the outfit going overseas was postponed, the order restoring me to my battalion was countermanded and I was out of it for good. It seems that some of my friends, a bit overzealous in my cause, had given Pearson all this information, thinking the publicity would do me good.

I was compelled to settle down now as an acting first sergeant with the station complement at Camp Chaffee. But my case bore fruit, although not for me. Fifteen thousand American Communists had joined the armed forces and there were many cases like mine; now the growing protests and publicity finally caused a change in policy, as Browder had predicted, and Communists were permitted to go overseas. Many distinguished themselves, winning decorations and becoming officers, among them Robert Thompson who won the Distinguished Service Cross in the Pacific, Herman Bottcher in the same theatre who was awarded the medal twice before being killed, Joseph Clark who won the Silver Star in Europe, and many others.

The turn of fate that kept me in the States for so long, had important personal consequences for me. Shortly before I went into the army, Lillian Ross of Texas had come onto the state staff of the New York Young Communist League as state education director. Now she and her husband, Carl, decided to separate. Lillian was visiting her family in Texas and we met while I was stationed at the replacement training center at Camp Wolters near Dallas. For twelve years I had been too busy organizing and fighting to fall seriously in love with anyone; now it happened at last (on government time!). We were deeply in love. Lillian was beautiful and able and nothing so wonderful had ever happened to me. But before we could be married, I was shipped to the Aleutian Islands. Ours was a true wartime romance and but for the War Department's policy of not shipping communists overseas, it might never have happened.

The Aleutians were really a form of exile. Someone figured out a way of sending me overseas and yet not into combat. This time I was not so anxious to go. It was an unimportant theatre and I had found an absorbing new interest at home. But in October of 1943 I went, and after a long, rough, miserable voyage of two weeks on a tramp steamer, disembarked on the island of Amchitka, more than a thousand miles off the coast of Alaska in the Northern Pacific.

Here I joined the 209th Field Artillery, a national guard outfit from Kansas which had been in the Alaska area and the Aleutians for almost two years. There had been little combat in the Aleutians (only the islands of Kiska and Attu had seen some fighting) and now everything was quiet. Ninety percent of our activity consisted of "housekeeping," as it was called. The area was barren, desolate, isolated, largely tundra; the climate was forbidding and cold with much snow. Gales of 60 miles were almost normal and the wind constantly changed direction—it was a common joke that making water was dangerous because you might be doing it against yourself. We had to spend most of our time providing adequate housing, warmth and food. The only real military activity came from the air force which sent patrol bombers on reconnaissance flights. These took place ostensibly over Japanese areas, but it was an open secret that much of the observation was over Russian territory. The men felt terribly small and unprotected, stuck way out in the Pacific on a frigid two-by-four flyspeck (actually only two miles by ten), and so close to Japan. One comfort was that we were even closer to an ally, Russia.

Boredom was the big problem and we devised sports, entertainment and educational programs. For athletics we built a gymnasium for basketball and pingpong, boxing and wrestling shows. There was a radio station on the island and we broadcast amateur entertainment and quiz shows. We conducted archaeological expeditions and dug up human skeletons which we deduced were Russians (the Aleutians had been purchased from Russia along with Alaska) and Aleuts, the native Indian tribe who had peopled the islands and were now almost extinct. The area was very healthful. We concluded that few germs could survive the Aleutian climate. The only form of life that could stand it was human.

There was plenty of time for reading. I took full advantage of the paper-covered classics provided by the army, one of the best contributions the military made to a more literate America. I also took refresher courses in mathematics through the Army's arrangement with the International Correspondence School. This was necessary for a knowledge of artillery, but I also had ideas of becoming an engineer when the war ended. I felt keenly the fact that I had become a communist organizer at an early age and never had the opportunity to learn a normal skill or profession.

All these feelings and frustrations were poured into my letters to Lillian. I wrote long love-letters and filled page after page with ideas on every subject under the sun, expressing emotions that I had never suspected lay within me. As with so many young people in those lonely war years, these letters meant everything to us. Often there would be long lapses in communication because planes were grounded by climatic conditions and boats traveled slowly. Then tensions and frustrations arose which caused us to accuse each other of neglect. Reconciliation was sweet when letters started arriving again. My stay in the Aleutians was a serious mental strain and would have been more so had it not been for Lillian.

Along with her personal feelings, Lillian's letters were filled with news of exciting developments back home. Through its contribution to the war effort, the Communist Party was recapturing some of its lost prestige. Once again it was becoming a respected part of American life. The Young Communist League came to the conclusion that it had been a mistake to follow so closely the pattern of the Communist Party, which in turn was virtually patterned on the lines of the Soviet party.

The League now dissolved to make way for an anti-fascist

youth organization with a much broader appeal to young Americans. This was the American Youth For Democracy (Lillian became head of its New York division). Among other achievements, the new AYD organized the SOS movement (Sweethearts of Servicemen) and conducted a petition campaign to end Jim-Crow in baseball. I was proud of the newspaper photographs showing Branch Rickey of the Brooklyn Dodgers being presented with a batch of petitions by a delegation including Brooklyn's Communist Councilman Peter V. Cacchione, and Lillian—soon afterwards the Dodgers broke the ice by signing Jackie Robinson. The AYD also sponsored a memorial concert at Carnegie Hall on the occasion of the death of the Negro musician, "Fats" Waller.

In 1943 the Communist International, the world association of all Communist parties (from which the American party had disaffiliated in 1940) was officially dissolved. The International had outlived its usefulness, it was said. No single set of answers could satisfy the now matured Communist Parties in many different lands. Moreover, dissolution would be a contribution to the wartime alliance between the western Allies and the Soviet Union. Meanwhile, the Teheran agreements among Roosevelt, Stalin and Churchill held out the promise that Big Three wartime collaboration would continue into the postwar. In a letter to Lillian, I exulted over what Teheran meant for the future of the world; Lillian showed my letter to Earl Browder and he quoted it in an article in March 1944 as an example of how isolated American Communists scattered throughout the world were arriving at the same conclusions as the party back home.

"The change in world history brought about by the Moscow, Cairo and Teheran Conferences," I wrote, "poses a whole number of new practical and theoretical questions. The kind of world there will be after this war (already in its early stages) is so completely different from that of 1918! It will be a world in which the most decayed and reactionary elements of capitalism will have been decisively defeated, and in which the most democratic sections were able to survive only with the help of the socialist nations, and through the advancement of formerly-oppressed colonial peoples towards greater independence and consolidation as free nations. It will be a world in which governments of a new type, neither capitalist nor socialist in the old sense, will come into being. All this means that every old theory has to be re-studied again and that many new ones are presented for solution. Plenty of room for creative thought and action! There will be no lack of things for us soldiers to do once we get through fighting and come home. Never a dull moment!"

Browder had developed several bold ideas which were stimu-lated by the unprecedented situation, and now he proceeded to put them into effect. At a national convention in 1944, the Com-munist Party of the United States dissolved and reformed itself into the Communist Political Association. This was in recognition of a central fact of American politics, namely, that the people operated within the framework of the two-party system, that Labor exerted its political influence chiefly through one of these two parties, and that any socialist political movement claiming to represent the interests of the labor movement had to take Labor's existing attitudes and practices into account.

This action was the most serious effort to date by the Com-munist movement to become an integral and accepted part of American life, especially of the trade union movement. The change was also based on the expectation that the wartime Grand Alliance and American national unity against fascism would con-tinue into the postwar world. Word of the new developments in the Communist movement filled me with elation. True, I found that my fellow GIs did not share my rosy optimism about the postwar world; but I was sure we were right and that life would soon prove it. In any case, I was certain that this was the kind of world we must work for.

This new enthusiasm of ours for national unity, based on the fact of the American-Soviet military alliance, sometimes led us to ridiculous extremes. We supported Labor's no-strike policy, but to an unwarranted degree. The employers sought to take advantage of the patriotic policy of the American trade unions and com-pelled Labor at times to resort to the strike weapon to protect its rights and standards.

When the coal miners were forced into strike action, the communists opposed the strike. Again, many of my army buddies did not share my opposition to the miners' action. They felt the workers had been provoked and were justified in walking out of the pits. Subsequently Earl Browder received the chief blame for our policy toward the miners' strike; but it is also worth recalling that William Z. Foster, who had opposed Browder's major proposition, the Political Association, went far beyond anyone else in his articles denouncing John L. Lewis, even to accusing the Mine Workers' leader of treason. Such mistakes as these lessened the prestige of the communists in Labor's ranks.

The question of the second front by the Allies in Western Europe also confronted the communists with a complicated problem. The demand for a second front was militarily justifiable and was supported by many strategists in the American political and military commands, as against the British concept; but coming from the communists, the proposal was viewed with suspicion because of our past record.

Many thought we favored a second front primarily because it was in Russia's interest. Actually, it was very much in America's interest. Those who today lament that the Red Army was permitted to occupy so much of Europe as it did when in pursuit of the fascist armies, should consider that this was the inevitable result of the long delays in opening the second front.

My outfit had been in the Aleutians now for more than two years and was scheduled to return home on rotation. I was almost frightened to death at the prospect of being left behind on my desolate little island, since I had been there for only six months. This time luck was with me. I returned with the others and we staged a wild celebration in Seattle. Our furlough was for three weeks and everyone was soon reunited with his family, and I with Lillian.

When we got back from furlough, we found we had been assigned to Fort Sill as a demonstration battalion. I disliked the spit and polish that we had to exhibit and was still determined to get into combat. I could see only one way: to volunteer for the paratroops. I reported to the Army Parachute School at Fort Benning, Georgia.

In my class were 1,600 men, but only five of us were over the age of 30. The rest of the men were under 23. Parachute jumping is definitely a young man's game and I was soon called Pop. The younger men found the physical training under the supervision of All-American athletes fairly easy; for me it was most difficult. On the other hand, while the younger men found the psychological hazard of jumping from an airplane extremely difficult, this was somewhat easier for me because I had joined to get into combat. Even with this incentive, however, every jump was frightening; the paratroopers said nobody ever jumped, they were pushed. But finally I passed all the tests. The paratroops were an elite corps and I was not at all modest about my special wings insignia and characteristic jump boots.

In school we had made four daytime and one nighttime jump in order to qualify. Now we were assigned to parachute artillery where we learned to pack the 75 mm. mule pack howitzer into seven boxes and jump with them. Upon landing, we rounded up the boxes, assembled the components of the gun and put reins on ourselves to pull the gun into position. In the old mule-pack artillery, mules pulled the guns; in modern parachute artillery we were the mules. (Today even bigger guns are dropped already assembled and with a truck to pull them.)

Instead of being sent overseas, I was shipped to a parachute artillery battalion at Camp Mackall, North Carolina, where the old training cycle began again. Here Lillian joined me and on Feb. 5, 1945 we were married at Bennettsville, South Carolina, and spent our honeymoon at Southern Pines, not far from camp. The question of my getting into combat kept recurring because I would not let the matter rest. My battalion commander, a West Point major, promised that he would see what could be done, and one day he asked if I would be willing to go overseas as an individual replacement. I replied that I most certainly would, and several days later the order came down.

I was soon on my way to France, arriving there in late March 1945, and in early April I joined my new outfit, the 17th Airborne Division, in Germany. The Division had jumped a few days earlier on the east side of the Rhine. This was the last combat jump in the

European war and I had missed it. My battalion had the misfortune to jump into a concentration of German 88s and suffered extremely heavy casualties. The battalion commander turned out to be Col. Booth, my first company commander back in Camp Chaffee days. He was surprised to find me here at this late date; in fact, he was surprised to see me at all, and wanted to know of my misadventures of the past three years.

The Germans had little fight left in them by now, at least on the collapsing Western front. They were in full flight and we could hardly keep up with them. All these years I had worked to get into the fighting and now that I had succeeded, it was all over. Of course, I was not unhappy that the war in Europe was coming to a victorious end. We were stationed in the Ruhr, a steel center much like Youngstown, and I gazed at the mass of twisted girders and miles of wreckage, wondering whether Germany would ever emerge again as a power. History has taught the old lesson over again. Devastated as it was, Germany was obviously a powerful and modern country, very much like the United States.

Late one night in April we were on duty in the battalion fire direction center (my assignment was operations sergeant). Most of us were dozing; there was no military activity on our front. Suddenly the captain began to shake us awake. He had been listening to the radio, half-asleep himself. "Roosevelt just died," he said, almost in disbelief. But it was true enough and it sobered us all. Franklin Roosevelt had dominated our age. Many of the young men in the armed forces had never known any other President. What would happen now? It was hard to imagine Harry Truman taking his place, or anyone else for that matter—we had become so used to FDR.

V-E Day came on May 8 and was no surprise. Germany was obviously defeated and we were overjoyed when the Russians, British and Americans joined hands in Berlin. Now we took on new duties as an army of occupation. The Germans whom I met disgusted me; they were thoroughly beaten, docile, servile. Hitler had trained them to obey the conqueror, so now they obeyed *us*. None of them ever owned up to having supported Der Fuehrer.

With the war over in Europe, it was news from the Pacific, where the war against Japan continued, that now interested us.

When word came of the first atom bomb being dropped on Hiroshima, our men were not elated. These men knew the horror of war; such a terrible weapon, they felt, could be used one day against *us*. Many said there was something morally wrong about a weapon that could wipe out whole civilian populations. (Professor P. M. S. Blackett, the British physicist, wrote later in *Fear, Bomb and the War* that the bombing of Hiroshima and Nagasaki was unnecessary, the real purpose being to launch the cold war against Russia. General Willoughby, aide to Gen. MacArthur, also stated that Japan was on the verge of defeat when the bombs were dropped.) '

From Germany we went on to Austria and were stationed near Berchtesgaden in the Bavarian Alps. Here I was promoted to first sergeant, a post which I had declined for years because the duties were mainly administrative, but to which I had no objection now, especially since I was married and could use the extra money.

One day I read a small item in the army daily newspaper *Stars and Stripes*. It reported that a New York newspaper had published a translation of an article in which Jacques Duclos, a top leader of the French Communist Party, severely criticized policies of the American Communists. The article, originally appearing in the French Communist theoretical magazine, ridiculed Browder's concept of the postwar world as utopian, condemned the dissolution of the Communist Party, and described Browder's ideas as a "notorious revisionism" of Marxism, than which there is no more serious criticism in the Communist dictionary.

These accusations infuriated me I immediately sent off a letter to Lillian in which I reaffirmed my belief in the Browder policies and protested the French article as being completely ignorant of American problems and as constituting rank interference in our affairs. I hoped, I wrote, that we would give their criticism the sound rebuff it deserved.

It was not hard to imagine the consternation in communist ranks at home and, I was impatient for news. This soon began to come in letters from Lillian; she also sent me clippings of articles from the Communist press. The Duclos article had caused an upheaval in the American Communist movement. Excoriating Browder in the most extravagant terms, Duclos had praised the views of William Z. Foster, quoting from speeches and communications by Foster, of which the American Communists, except for the top leaders, had been entirely unaware.

Naturally, this created a sensation; the membership demanded to know why Foster's views had been kept secret from them. How Duclos found out about Foster's opinions I do not know, but clearly someone sent them to him. Foster's opposition to the Browder policies did not impress me. I wrote to Lillian that for years Foster had been the most sectarian and dogmatic of American Communist leaders; on the other hand, our most impressive gains had been made under the aegis of Browder.

Browder conceded that the Duclos article did not express the point of view of an individual French Communist, but was the considered opinion of the world's "most authoritative Marxists," meaning, of course, the Soviet Communists. The leaders of the American Communists, who, except for Foster and one other, had unanimously supported Browder, now switched overnight, and, except for one or two with reservations, threw their support to Foster. An emergency convention in July, 1945, repudiated Browder's ideas, removed him from leadership and re-constituted the Communist Party in an atmosphere of hysteria and humiliating breast-beating unprecedented in communist history.

Browder's view of the postwar world was undoubtedly over-optimistic. He underestimated the clash that would develop among the allies once the war was over. But he was not the only leader to make such a mistake; it was made by the leaders of every other political trend as well.

Browder did have a vision—that World War II would usher in a new kind of world where war would be unthinkable and where the communist and capitalist worlds would have to compete and collaborate. Perhaps he did not foresee the difficulties that would lie in the path and the hard struggles that would be needed to bring this about, but his prescience was sound in many major respects. Probably his greatest contribution was his effort to adapt the Communist Party to the American scene. Toward that end he demonstrated more creativity and greater imagination, independence and originality of thought than anyone before or since.

Only a few years later I was to learn from someone who spoke with Duclos in 1946 that the world communist movement did not consider Browder's most serious error his myopic view of the postwar era (they had all made similar estimates), but rather his dissolution of the Communist Party. Here was the unforgivable heresy. Browder had violated the one thing so sacred that no one could dare tamper with it: the concept of the Communist Party as it had been laid down by Lenin in 1902.

In 1946 Browder was expelled from the American Communist Party for refusing to accept the new policy and for publishing a bulletin not authorized by the party (and because Foster was determined to be rid of him). For several years Browder protested that his ideas were closer to the Soviet view than were the American party's.

But despite illusions about Stalin at the time, Browder's policy of dissolving the party and replacing it with the Communist Political Association was a forerunner of the great heresies that have rocked the communist world since World War II. American Communists did Browder a grave injustice when we expelled him (although he is probably thankful now that we did), but far greater was the damage we did to ourselves. We returned to old ways of thinking which in the end were to prove fatal. In the party itself, Browder's name became a dirty word. Anyone could be discredited by accusing him of holding "Browderite" views.

For several months following the publication of the Duclos article, I would not concede that Browder and the rest of us had been wrong. Although I continued to write bitter letters to Lillian, gradually I became convinced. The party did not hold this hesitation against me; it was considered only natural that being so isolated in far-off Europe, it would take me longer to see the light. I was elected *in absentia* to the National Committee of the reconstituted Communist Party in July. (I had also been elected the year before to the national committee of the Political Associa-

tion.) When I returned to America and to party activity, I became
as anti-Browder as anybody. At our 1950 convention, I delivered
a speech on Browder which was published under the title of
"Fight Against Browderism, Titoism and Trotskyism." The article
was acclaimed at the time, but surely it is the most stupid piece
I have ever written. The present party leaders today write the
same sort of thing about me.

Life in the army had become impossibly boring and no one
thought of anything but getting home. It was difficult to maintain
any kind of discipline or morale, which made the work of a first
sergeant especially petty and irritating. Although men were being shipped back on a mass scale, it still wasn't fast enough. The
army sought ways of keeping the men interested until shipping
space could be obtained for them; one project was to send men
to European universities if they desired.

I enrolled at the University of Manchester in England, spending three delightful months there, little of it at the university but
a great deal with my British friends from Spain. I used the time
to observe the British Labor and Communist movements; I took
in several performances of Shakespeare at the Old Vic and of
Gilbert and Sullivan operettas performed by the D'Oyly Carte
company.

Christmas Day 1945 I boarded a ship at Cardiff, Wales, and
was on my way home. It was a Liberty ship and the voyage
seemed interminable, almost three weeks. After docking at Camp
Kilmer, we were taken to the Separation Center at Fort Dix, New
Jersey. But separation was not happening fast enough for our
tastes—the weekend was starting and nothing could be done for
us until Monday. Nothing, that is, until we learned from the
grapevine of a hole in the fence through which, it was said, men
in our predicament sometimes "exfiltrated." In the early hours
of the morning, I stood before the door of our apartment in
Queens, rang the bell and a sleepy Lillian opened the door. For
the first time in my career in two armies I had gone AWOL.

Monday morning I was back at Fort Dix in time for reveille; no
notice had been taken of my absence. Then came all the last red
tape, payment of back pay, and in a simple ceremony much like

the one when we were sworn in on January 17, 1946, I was honorably discharged as a first sergeant in the 101st Airborne Division, and joined the Enlisted Men's Reserve Corps. But the big story of the moment for me was quite different: after more than four years I was a civilian again.

VII

POSTWAR AND POST-
BROWDER

I HAPPENED TO BE AWAY ON A TRIP ON JULY 20, 1948, THE DAY A
Federal grand jury indicted us under the Smith Act and I did not
know what had happened until the next morning's newspaper
told the story. When the United Press ticker in the *Daily Worker*
office had carried the first news of the indictment that morning,
the party leaders were informed and those present in the headquarters awaited the arrival of the FBI. Several hours later the
FBI men showed up, made the arrests and jailed the Communists
overnight pending arraignment. The FBI had had ample time to
make the arrests earlier in the day; bail could then have been
arranged at once, and the defendants would not have had to go
to jail that evening. But this would have interfered with the impression which the Department of Justice evidently wanted to
create. The arrested men were fingerprinted and mugged, and
their photographs and arrest numbers splashed across the front
page of all major newspapers in the country. We were "criminals"
long before the trial took place.

The account in the newspaper which I was reading the morning following the indictment carried the information that the defendants would be arraigned that day at the Federal Court-house in Foley Square. I returned to the city, reached the court-house shortly after noon and entered the designated room. No-body was present except the clerk. When he asked my business, I told him that I was one of the Smith Act defendants and had come to present myself for arraignment.

"Everybody's gone; it's too late," he replied.

Perhaps I should have taken him at his word, but I insisted that he go and summon the judge. When the judge appeared, I pleaded innocent, and a few hours later I was released on $5,000 bail. Why I insisted on being arrested then and there, I have never been able to figure out. Perhaps it was because I had become so accustomed to standing upon my rights before public officials that I even insisted on my right to be arrested and without any waste of time. I am inclined to think, however, that there was a certain private satisfaction in adding another touch of unreality to a situation which already seemed entirely unreal. Was it pos-sible, after spending six years of my life in the uniforms of the Spanish and United States armies fighting for democracy, that I was now to spend several years in the uniform of a federal con-vict? Was it possible that only three years after many Communists had been on good terms with a considerable part of official Washington, Communist leaders were to be imprisoned, charged with crimes against the government?

Unfortunately, it was entirely possible. This became even clearer in the next few days when few people in the country either dared or cared to speak up in our behalf. In three brief years since the end of the war, the country had changed. With the onset of the cold war and the rise of McCarthyism—which pre-dated McCarthy himself—the political situation at home had become more and more dismal. At the same time, the Communist Party, with the ouster of Browder and the reversal of party poli-cies, had become increasingly incapable of grappling with the new developments.

During these three years, my own life had changed greatly: from bachelor to married life, from one of many active Communist organizers to a member of the small inner circle of top leaders.

When I was mustered out of the army in 1945, Lillian and I took a two-week vacation in Florida and Cuba and then settled down in our Queens apartment in New York City. As with so many wartime marriages, this was our first opportunity to know each other well. With her blue eyes, classic features and handsome figure, Lillian was a charming and vivacious woman; she liked to sing and dance and was the center of attraction at parties where her specialty was the St. Louis Blues. At home Lillian played the piano just well enough to communicate with snatches of Chopin, Beethoven, and popular songs. Her parents were Czech Catholics and Lillian inherited the artistry and taste of the Czechs, along with the zany, independent spirit of her native Texas.

She imparted her remarkable sense of color to the decorations of our apartment and to the way she dressed. A practice of pressing her clothes each time she wore them made her invariably neat as a pin. I think the feature of her appearance which first had attracted me years earlier was the flower that she never failed to wear in her hair or pinned to a dress or coat. Regardless of the season, Lillian and her flower always brought a breath of Spring to the drab offices of the party on Twelfth Street in New York. She was natural and human, considerate of people, and did not affect the jargon typical of the Communist movement. She came from a working-class family, her father a cabinet maker. Lillian herself had always worked for a living, as an office worker and legal secretary, until becoming a full-time Communist worker in 1941.

Nothing came of my desire to study engineering. Although the GI Bill of Rights would have made this possible and I was still young enough to undertake it, the party had other ideas. Right now such an ambition was frowned upon as a weakening of revolutionary fiber, an example of the evil influence of Browderism—and I agreed. This was no time to lead a normal life, the party needed people for responsible posts; besides my conscience still bothered me for having been a "Browderite." I became national

Veterans Director of the party, responsible for helping to readjust the thousands of returning Communist veterans to civilian and party life, orient them on the big changes in the party since Browder's ouster, and project a program on behalf of American veterans in general. I attended, as an observer, conventions of the American Legion, Veterans of Foreign War, and the American Veterans Committee, and wrote articles for the *Daily Worker* and *Political Affairs*. A pamphlet on veterans problems was titled "Who Ruptured Our Duck?" the "ruptured duck" being the name given by the GIs to their honorable discharge insignia.

Inevitably I became deeply involved in the inner politics of the party's highest committee. Browder had been expelled and his ideas defeated; Foster had emerged the party's outstanding leader, the only one in fact unblemished by the Browder heresy. But within the leadership itself the struggle went on as two groupings developed, one around Foster, the party chairman, and the other around Eugene Dennis, who became in 1946 general secretary.

Supporting Foster were only Robert Thompson and Benjamin J. Davis, Jr., the former being the youngest member of the leadership, three years younger than myself. A hero of World War II, winner of the Distinguished Service Cross, a battalion commander in Spain where he had been wounded in action, Thompson was courageous and able in military matters. In politics he was a novice who seemed unable to grasp the fact that the military approach is wholly inadequate in politics and human relations.

In the upheaval accompanying Browder's ouster, Thompson became the head of the important New York organization, comprising half the total national membership of the party. Here he replaced Gil Green, probably the most able of all the party leaders at the time, who relinquished his post because he felt personally guilty for past party policy as one of the most prominent Browderites. Green now went back to Chicago, where he had been born and where he hoped to redeem himself. When Thompson was given the New York leadership, he was politically an unknown quantity, promoted on the basis of his wartime reputation. Benjamin J. Davis, Jr. was the son of a Republican national committeeman from Atlanta, Georgia, and a graduate of Amherst and Harvard Law School. He came into prominence as an attorney in the Angelo Herndon case during the course of which he joined the Communist Party. Coming to New York, he joined the staff of the *Daily Worker*, and along with Brooklyn Communist Peter V. Cacchione, was elected to the City Council of New York when the system of proportional representation was in effect. A big, powerful man with a passion for oratory, he has been the most prominent Negro Communist since James W. Ford.

Foster, Thompson and Davis constituted a minority of the leadership and were ranged against a majority centering around Dennis. Ineffectual in many ways, almost painfully shy, a poor speaker, Dennis nevertheless was an astute politician. He was experienced in American politics and adept at getting things done behind the scenes, a skilled wire-puller and manipulator. His impressive exterior belied his introverted personality, for he was tall, ruddy, robust, with a mop of grey hair; a handsome and striking-looking Irishman. Despite his inadequacies as a public leader, Dennis resisted Foster's policies at this time and was our best symbol.

The Foster group pressed for super-militant policies which in Communist terminology we called "left-sectarian" because they isolated us from the people. Our group stood for broader, more flexible policies which our opponents, again in Communist parlance, called "right opportunism," which meant sacrificing principle for the sake of mass popularity.

Actually, this was a continuation of the struggle of ideas that had led to the victory of Browder's policies in 1944 and to their defeat a year later. The fight now between the majority and the Foster minority in the leadership became extremely sharp. But both groups joined in keeping the struggle behind closed doors, one side for fear of challenging Foster openly since his prestige was so great; the minority because their constant pressure was successful in extracting important concessions from their opponents. It is also likely that Thompson and Davis, who looked upon most of us as weak, unreliable, and as concealed Browderites, had their eyes on the top posts but were not ready to make this known.

Even though I was part of the group opposing the Foster policy in those days—actually little more than a rearguard action —I did not always put up the kind of fight of which I can be proud. In 1946, a conference was called to review our "Negro work," as we called our activity in behalf of civil rights. The purpose of the conference was to review—and inevitably reverse— the policies of Browder in this field, and to revive the old theory that a Negro nation existed in the South which had the right to separate from the United States if it wished.

On the initiative of the Communist International in the 1928– 30 period, American Communists had developed the theory which asserted that the Negro people in the plantation areas of the South constituted a distinct and oppressed nation; we demanded "self-determination" for this Negro nation in the Black Belt, in- cluding the right of separation from the United States if the local population so desired.

This was an arbitrary and mechanical transplanting of Stalin's teachings on the national question to the American scene, aris- ing not from the aims of the Negro people in the South but from abstract theories in Moscow. While the inventors of the theory made ample use of the historical studies of Dr. W. E. B. DuBois, this noted Negro scholar himself rejected the idea of a distinct Negro nation in the South. The theory played into the hands of the white segregationists, as well as into the hands of Negro na- tionalists like Marcus Garvey who advocated a back-to-Africa movement. But no important Negro organization or individual outside Communist circles ever expressed anything but horror at the concept.

American Negroes favored equal citizenship and the aboli- tion of all forms of separation, and bitterly opposed the "separate but equal" doctrine of the Supreme Court of 1896 in its Plessy vs. Ferguson decision. Over the years the Communist Party had built up considerable influence among the Negro people, not how- ever through the theory of a separate nation in the South, but through the great emphasis which it placed on full economic, political and social equality, and on the need for Negro-white unity to achieve it. If the Negro nation theory served any purpose at all, it was to dramatize the special character of Negro oppression as rooted in the plantation system with its remnants of slavery, and the fact that the Negro people in this country constituted an oppressed national minority. But this did not justify use of a far-fetched theory which ran counter to the real aspirations of the Negro people and consequently hampered the efforts of the Communists in behalf of equal rights.

The first prominent Communist to challenge this separate Negro nation theory had been Browder when he declared in 1944 that the Negro people had chosen the path of integration, not separatism. At that time, this became the new party policy. However, Browder also implied that the fight for integration had already been largely won, and would be finally achieved rather effortlessly and painlessly in the postwar period. This underestimation of the difficulties that lay ahead on the road to integration, was used later to justify a return to the original hare-brained theory.

At the 1946 conference on this subject it was conceded that the Negro people desired to be part of America, not separated from it; but there was a band-wagon rush to reinstate the theory of the right of self-determination of a supposed Negro nation in the Black Belt. Only two persons at the conference had the understanding and courage to stand up and disagree. One was Gil Green. He called the theory wrong and unrealistic, and said that even if it were adopted, it would eventually have to be shelved. Green was mercilessly castigated for his stand, even being accused of "white chauvinism," that is, a feeling of white superiority over Negroes. The other was Doxey Wilkerson, a leading Negro educator who had left his profession in order to become a full-time Communist functionary. His speech opposing it was not even deemed worthy of publication. Wilkerson's opposition was especially significant since he was the only top Negro Communist who dared to take such a stand. This required considerable courage because he was running the risk of being labeled by other Negro Communists an "Uncle Tom," a characterization of Negroes who compromised, or were alleged to do so, in the fight for Negro rights. I agreed with Green and Wilkerson and said so privately. But I lacked the political courage to get up and say what I thought and to vote against the proposition. I was still new to the top leadership of the party, just fresh out of the army, and I lacked the necessary self-confidence. Moreover I was still plagued by the fear that I might be reverting to Browderite weakness.

The rehabilitation of an old theoretical monstrosity sent the party off in a direction opposite to that of the influential Negro organizations. So isolated did we become from Negro life, in fact, that when the U.S. Supreme Court in May, 1954 handed down its historic decision on school desegregation, we were taken completely by surprise. This prime issue was not even a central point in the party's program at the time.

Gradually the party reverted to policies similar to those of 1939–41, the period of the Soviet-German pact. Subtle at first, the changes gathered momentum as the years went on and as the cold war became hotter. Contrary to the accusations by the Department of Justice in the Smith Act trials, the reversal of policy after Browder's removal had nothing to do with an alleged return to advocacy of the forcible overthrow of the United States government. The issues were entirely different.

The key to the change was the break-up of the wartime alliance between the western allies and the Soviet Union. As the war neared a close, each of the powers on the winning side began to maneuver for the most advantageous position in the postwar period. The Soviet Union sought friendly governments in Eastern Europe for its own future safety and to permit local Communists to exercise maximum influence. In the West the United States tried to bolster the weakened capitalist regimes and reduce the powerful influence of the Communist Parties, especially in Italy and France. In March 1946, Winston Churchill lent his prestige to what amounted to an official proclamation that the cold war was on. This was his famous speech at Fulton, Missouri, where the British Prime Minister was introduced by President Truman.

At this time the situation was still in flux. The new governments in eastern Europe were coalition governments in which

Communists shared power with other parties. The Communists called these states "peoples' democracies" to distinguish them from the Soviet-model "dictatorship of the proletariat" and many Communist parties actually changed their name. Today when much attention is focused on the question of independent paths to socialism, as advocated by Tito in Yugoslavia and Gomulka in Poland, it is often overlooked that such ideas were officially condoned by Moscow between 1944 and 1947.

One year after Churchill's speech at Fulton, however, the lines became sharply drawn. The Truman Doctrine was launched for Greece and Turkey and to "contain Communism" everywhere; the Communists were ousted from the national unity governments of France and Italy (which they did not strongly resist, evidently preferring to go into opposition). In reply, the Communist Parties of the Soviet Union and of eight countries in Eastern and Western Europe set up the Communist Information Bureau, popularly called the Cominform. Coalition governments in Eastern Europe were broken up and the Communists proceeded to take over full power and establish "dictatorships of the proletariat." Against this background, American Communist Party policy became still more narrow and self-defeating. In opposing the cold war, we placed the entire blame on the Truman policy and we would not concede that any share in responsibility for the tensions could be attributed to the policies of Moscow and the Cominform. It is my opinion—which I know many readers will not share—that powerful, reactionary forces here at home were mainly responsible for the cold war; they did not conceal their opposition to peaceful coexistence and their active hostility to socialism. What I could not bring myself to see in those days was the considerable responsibility on the part of Moscow as a result of wrong policies of Stalin (and if I ever saw it, I considered it my bounden duty not to say so).

As policy hardened in the international communist movement, the Foster group increased the pressure to make everyone toe the mark. The *Daily Worker* which reflected the coalition policies to which the Dennis group still tried to cling, was the target of attacks from Foster, Thompson and Davis.

The editor-in-chief at that point was Morris Childs, an old-time leader of the party and formerly head of the Illinois District, and he bore the brunt of the onslaught. In the hope of holding off the opposition, the grouping around Dennis decided to throw Childs to the wolves and replace him with myself. A meeting of the national committee in June 1947 recommended that I become editor-in-chief of the paper.

This was tantamount to election to the post; while the paper was technically independent and had ceased to be the official organ of the party since 1940 for legal reasons, its policy and main financial support came from the party. Childs was not even informed of the move to replace him until the proposal was put forward at the meeting. He was rightly indignant. It was an inhuman way to treat a person, but it was also a common practice in the party. Childs' feelings in the matter did not bother me too much at the time; I considered the move politically expedient and the manner in which it was carried through relatively unimportant. Nor did it occur to me that in sacrificing Childs, we were only encouraging the Foster group to press all the harder. To make a stand and carry the fight to the membership did not enter our minds. Such things didn't happen in the party where in the name of "party unity" the membership was usually kept in the dark on inner differences. (Another casualty was Jack Stachel, the party's trade union director. Over the years Stachel had been in opposition to Foster and was considered by him a congenital "right opportunist." When Walter Reuther won the presidency of the United Auto Workers in 1946, this was looked upon as a defeat for the party. Foster was quick to blame Stachel and had him removed from the important post of trade union director, and replaced by John Williamson.)

If Foster, Davis and Thompson thought that in me they were getting someone more pliant to their wishes, events proved them to be mistaken. I moved now into the *Daily Worker* offices. While it is the usual practice to learn the newspaper business from the bottom up, I learned it from the top down. The editor-in-chief of the *Daily Worker* was always a political designate, not a journalist, in order to insure party control. This at times irked the professional journalists on the paper who did the work while the chief editors came and went. The staff protested slightly in my case, but accepted me.

I was proud to join the staff of the *Daily Worker*. The men and women who worked for it had great talent and were held in high esteem by the devoted readers of the paper. It had always been extraordinarily difficult for a radical movement in the United States to sustain a daily newspaper because of high costs and lack of advertising. The *Daily Worker* was a deficit operation which had to be subsidized by the heroic efforts and sacrifices of all too few readers. For the last ten years of its existence the *Daily Worker* operated under an annual deficit of $200,000 which was raised chiefly by the herculean labors of the Communist Party. The existence of the *Daily Worker* as a daily newspaper for 34 years was a small miracle, admired by radicals in general and by many in the newspaper profession who knew what it meant to get out a daily paper on a shoestring and with our tiny staff. The history of the *Daily Worker* deserves a book by itself and cannot be done justice here. Newspapermen were critical of us for our obvious lack of independence when it came to the Soviet Union but envied our comparative freedom in many domestic matters, where we did not have to truckle down to Big Business and big advertisers.

The managing editor was Alan Max, a graduate of Columbia and Harvard, versatile, a writer of plays and short stories, and one of the best humorists and satirists in the country. Our foreign editors were Joseph Starobin and, later, Joseph Clark. We had men who were well respected in the profession for their special fields, Abner Berry in the Negro rights area, Milton Howard, chief editorial writer, George Morris in labor, and Lester Rodney in sports. We had many fine reporters including Harry Raymond, Rob Hall, Joseph North, Art Shields, Virginia Gardner, and many others.

I felt self-conscious at my lack of experience amidst these journalistic veterans but I looked upon it as a great challenge. On the whole, the staff was distrustful of party leaders, feeling they were too sectarian and orthodox and cramped the style of the paper.

I set out to prove this was not so, and before long staff members let me know that I had won their confidence.

The editorship of the paper provided a welcome break from the routine and encrusting life of a top party leader. In April of 1948, I flew to Italy to cover the elections there, although from a journalistic standpoint my trip was hardly a howling success. I did, of course, see something of the Italian Communist movement which impressed me with its great size and pervasive influence in all aspects of Italian life and made me envious because of our extreme weakness in the USA. On election night, I cabled the first fragmentary returns to the *Daily Worker*, including the customary safeguard that they were not conclusive. The editors back home were carried away by my election night enthusiasm—I was getting the returns at Communist headquarters—and wrote a headline that the Communists were winning. Although the Communists scored important gains, they did not win the elections and when I returned home I had a lot of explaining to do for that headline. At any rate, nobody recommended me for a Pulitzer prize on the basis of my first major assignment as a journalist. (In November of the same year I felt a little better when the *Chicago Tribune* printed a headline that Dewey had been elected president.)

I had considered going on from Rome to Yugoslavia in order to interview the people in the Cominform which was still stationed in Belgrade. Andre Marty, one of the French Communist leaders, later expelled and now dead, strongly advised me to make the trip (I have often wondered why). The Italians, on the other hand, discouraged me, saying the Cominform actually had no staff in Belgrade, and suggesting that Tito was a difficult man to get along with. This I attributed to the differences that had arisen between Italian and Yugoslav Communists over Trieste; I did not suspect that a bitter feud was going on between Tito and Stalin, which the Italian Communists, as members of the Cominform, must have known all about. Although I had actually obtained a Yugoslav visa, I decided not to go. On my first newspaper assignment I not only did not do well on the story I had come to cover, but I missed a tremendous scoop. I must admit that even had I gone to Belgrade and learned of the Tito-Stalin conflict, my sympathies would have been pre-ordained, and I could not have published a word of it anyway.

It is hard to come to terms with oneself for having been completely blind to the bad turn which events were taking in that period in Eastern Europe. There was plenty which I could not know, but even what I could, I would not. The scrapping of the coalition governments and the setting up of one-party systems inevitably narrowed the popular bases of these governments. This resulted in the Communists adopting ever more dictatorial and repressive measures to maintain power, leading a decade later to the mass upheavals in Poland and Hungary.

The Cominform described the world as divided into two sharply drawn camps, the camp of imperialism and war headed by the United States, and the camp of socialism and peace, headed by the Soviet Union; all trends of neutralism toward these two camps were roundly condemned. The concept of independent roads to socialism which had flourished briefly was now denounced; the similarity of the new Communist countries and the Soviet Union was emphasized now, and all Communist countries were called on to follow the Soviet pattern in every aspect of life with disastrous consequences to their economies and liberties.

Whoever resisted these new policies was now ruthlessly purged. The Yugoslav Communists, standing up against all pressures, were expelled from the Cominform in July 1948 and excommunicated from world communism, and Tito's government denounced as pro-capitalist, even fascist. This in turn set the stage for vast new purges. Since Tito was the worst of all possible enemies, anyone associated with him or with his ideas of an independent, national development of socialism was considered an imperialist spy deserving to be eliminated. In frame-up trials (which I did not then view as frame-ups and fully endorsed), Slansky, Rajk, Kostov and others were executed, while Gomulka, Kadar and many more were removed in disgrace and thrown into prison.

A spy psychosis and hysteria gripped all Communist countries, not unlike the McCarthyite lunacy which in our own country made a shambles of civil liberties, education, culture and science, and drove some people to suicide. The Soviet government clamped down on all liberalization tendencies; western influences on art, music, literature and science, resulting from contacts during the war, were now taboo. An exclusiveness and chauvinism developed to ridiculous extremes, such as claiming that practically everything good in the world had been invented by Russians (and under the Czars, no less!) and rejecting everything Western, including the science of genetics. A most sordid development occurred in 1948 when all Yiddish-language secular institutions were summarily dissolved and the most outstanding Jewish cultural figures disappeared from sight—put to death in 1952, it became known later, on false charges of belonging to an international Zionist conspiracy. But during this entire period, I would not believe that Soviet Communists were capable of repression and criminal acts; I scornfully rejected the charges against them as imperialist propaganda.

When I returned from Italy in the Spring of 1948, the presidential election campaign was getting under way, and we were reaching the low point in the party's relations with the labor movement. Shortly after the end of the war, the employers had launched an offensive against Labor with the Taft-Hartley Law as the goal. Craftily using the Communist issue as an opening wedge, they incorporated a provision in the bill requiring anti-Communist affidavits. If the Communist Party could be effectively pictured as a menace, it would be possible to pass the anti-union measure, and big business and government leaders now went to work on this, assisted by many labor leaders who did not realize that a trap was being set for them.

Now if ever the Communist Party needed policies which might keep it from being isolated from the labor movement. But our new policies were all headed in the opposite direction. Browder had not fully anticipated the postwar anti-labor offensive, and this fact was exploited by the Foster group to scrap all commonsense relations with the labor movement. Instead of emphasizing the economic questions which afforded the best possibilities for maintaining unity, the party insisted on forcing the issue around foreign policy matters like the Marshall Plan, and around political action questions like the Progressive Party.

Because of its exclusively military approach, the Truman Doctrine had not appealed to most of Labor; but the Administration recaptured the initiative when it put forward the Marshall Plan which seemingly emphasized economic aid. The Plan's authors invited the Communist powers to participate although terrified at the possibility that the invitation might be accepted. The gamble paid off when the Soviet Union rejected the bid, missing a golden opportunity to frustrate the plans of those who wished to isolate the Communist bloc. Czechoslovakia, in fact, at first agreed to enter the Plan but withdrew under Soviet pressure. It is possible that the world situation might have taken a somewhat different turn had the Soviet Union chosen to join rather than oppose the Marshall Plan. While the Marshall Plan aimed at bolstering capitalism in Europe, especially in West Germany, and at weakening Communism, events could not have unfolded exactly as they did, if the Communist countries had participated.

A strong progressive trend in the Democratic Party led by Henry Wallace opposed Truman's cold war policy and advocated peaceful coexistence between East and West. When Wallace was ousted from the cabinet, he chose finally to head a new party and be its candidate for President; this meant breaking with influential forces within the Democratic Party who agreed with Wallace's policies but not with his departure from Democratic ranks. At the same time, lacking the support of Labor, the new Progressive Party was doomed to failure.

The Communist Party knew this, had said so as late as June 1947. At that time (I was then also in charge of the party's legislative work) I presented a report to the national committee which strongly favored a third party but insisted that any such move was bound to fail unless backed by important segments of the labor movement. Specifically, support of the United Auto Workers, the Amalgamated Clothing Workers and others was mentioned as vital to the success of such a party. The meeting had unanimously approved this emphasis on labor participation as a precondition for a third party, but now only a few months later, we recklessly reversed ourselves. For one thing, we now considered the international situation as thoroughly desperate, which if correct, should only have made us seek still closer ties with labor, not risk a break. Moreover we were infatuated with the prospect of a great name like Henry Wallace at the head of a third ticket and we convinced ourselves that the rank-and-file of labor would revolt against its officialdom.

Up to this point, our electoral policy had been one of limited and critical endorsement of the Democratic Party, coupled with active support for its more progressive trends and candidates. We could have continued to be critical of Truman and supported those Democrats who opposed him, meanwhile directing our main attacks upon the GOP. Instead, we broke with a policy which had united us with some of the most influential forces in political life, and cut ourselves off from the mainstream.

The leadership of the CIO proceeded to use the Marshall Plan and the Progressive Party as issues with which to expel eleven Left-led unions, charging that they were under Communist domination and disloyal to CIO. Whatever mistakes were made by the Communists, a policy of expulsions of trade unions over political differences was fundamentally wrong; it is bound to weaken the labor movement itself. It has been argued by some on the Left that the CIO leaders were so determined on these expulsions that even if they had not had the Marshall Plan and the third party as ready-made issues, they would have found others. This may be true. But even if their aim was expulsion at all costs, then the Communists only made it easier for the expulsion policy to be carried through.

The Progressive Party had the curious effect of forcing President Truman to kidnap some of its program and adopt it as his own, thereby restoring his popularity and assuring his election. But as the basis for a new political movement, the Progressive Party was a disastrous failure, although it refused to admit this in 1948 and would not give up the ghost until many years later, during which time the Left sank into deeper and deeper isolation.

The Communists drew few conclusions at the time from their setbacks in the 1948 elections and in the trade union movement.

They could not see that the situation in the labor movement had changed and that Communists could maintain any influence in the unions only as part of broad coalitions generally under the leadership of non-Communists. Instead, the party persisted in trying to control every union in which it had influence at almost any cost, with the result that defeat followed upon defeat. The greatest losses took place in the New York area where, under the leadership of Thompson, the most unreasonable and inflexible policies were pursued. In the National Maritime Union, the Transport Workers, District 65 of the Distributive Workers, the Hotel and Restaurant Workers Council and many others, Communist influence was destroyed.

As the 1948 campaign moved along, the newspapers carried rumors that a federal grand jury was considering an indictment of the Communist leaders. Something like this had long been brewing. In 1947, Lewis K. Schwellenbach, then Secretary of Labor under Truman, had sent up a trial balloon in the form of a proposal to outlaw the Communist Party.

The party itself replied quickly with a Communist Veterans Encampment in Washington, where a group of us who had fought for our country placed a wreath on the Iwo Jima Memorial. And in the country at large, controversy raged over the proposal, climaxed by a debate between Thomas E. Dewey, opposing the outlawing of the party, and Harold Stassen favoring it. The debate put the finishing touches to Stassen's campaign and insured the nomination for Dewey.

As a result of the fiasco of the Schwellenbach proposal, the Administration took a new tack. Outlawing a political party was too crude, too offensive to people; therefore other means were sought, notably the Smith Act. As the '48 election approached, the Republicans were accusing the Democrats of being soft on Communism, and Truman wanted to cut the ground from under the charge. Besides, how could Washington keep insisting that our allies outlaw *their* Communist parties, if *our* Communists were allowed the run of the place? Still another consideration was said to be Truman's fear that the Progressive Party might take so many votes in New York from the Democrats that the GOP would carry the state (which, in fact, happened). Arresting the Communists before election day might keep the Progressive vote down. Week after week, the grand jury remained in session without being able to agree on an indictment. The jury's term was about to expire and we breathed easier; it was too late now for any move against us. But on the very last day of its term, the jury acted. We were arrested and faced one of the most crucial political trials in the country's history—and under the worst possible circumstances for the Communists.

VIII

TRIAL

PERHAPS ONLY AN ARCHITECT CAN DESCRIBE A COURTROOM OBJEC-
tively. To me, Room 110 in the Federal Court House in Foley
Square in New York City, with its high ceiling and paneled walls,
its rows of long benches seating about 300 spectators, and its
majestic judge's bench and jury box, was a funeral parlor, a
sepulchre; the quiet of the place was morbid, the lighting arrange-
ments depressing, the atmosphere suffocating. No doubt, the various officers of the court found the place a congenial, comfortable,
cheery place in which to earn one's living and make one's reputation.

The trial, which was our life for the next nine months, opened
on January 17, 1949, the same day, incidentally, that I received my
honorable discharge from the Enlisted Men's Reserve Corps of the
U.S. Army. There were eleven defendants, the twelfth, Foster,
having been severed from the case because of his serious, chronic
heart ailment. After two months of a jury challenge, a jury was
chosen and the government began its case. The first eight weeks
were taken up with the prosecution witnesses, a group of paid
informers, some of whom became so discredited in later years that
the Justice Department had to drop them.

The Party selected me as first witness for the defense and I was on the stand for three weeks. When under cross-examination the prosecution sought to draw from me the names of people who assisted me on the veterans' pamphlet "Who Ruptured Our Duck?" I refused to give any names; those who had worked with me included artists, lay-out men and others privately employed who surely faced the loss of their jobs if they had been publicly identified. Moreover, their identity had absolutely no connection with the charge against us. Judge Harold R. Medina ordered me to answer anyway; when I still refused, he sentenced me to thirty days in jail for contempt of court. Henry Winston and Gus Hall stood up at this point and protested the decision. They were ordered imprisoned for the duration of the trial. This set the pattern. Green, the next witness, was sent to jail for a chance remark in replying to a question; so was Carl Winter of Detroit when he refused to say whether his father was a Communist. These sentences could have been served after the trial was over, but Judge Medina insisted on immediate punishment, a vindictive procedure which also hampered our defense.

For the next four weeks I "commuted" daily, except for weekends, between the Federal House of Detention at West Street, overlooking the Hudson River, and the courthouse at Foley Square. The West Street jail was small, dingy and crowded. It had not been built originally as a prison but was converted from an old truck garage formerly owned by Al Smith. Each morning before going to court and on return, I had to strip naked while a guard searched every part of my body, including the private parts, for possible contraband, like narcotics, weapons or illicit messages. I was still on the witness stand and the restricted conditions of the jail made the proper preparations difficult. I was taken to and from the courtroom in handcuffs in a prison van. Medina called me a "truculent witness" and this experience was one of the reasons.

I was there together with Winston and Hall, and one day a demonstration took place in front of the jail protesting our imprisonment. The picket line chanted "Free Winston, Gates and Hall—They're fighting for us all." They made considerable noise and left a deep impression on the other inmates, some of whom became quite excited, thinking the demonstrators were going to smash down the prison gates and let all of us out. But West Street was not Jericho and the Communists were not Joshuas and the walls did not come tumbling down, to the great disappointment of some of the prisoners. But our prestige inside of the jail was enhanced because everyone knew we had friends.

Toward the end of my 30-day sentence, the *Daily Worker* asked its readers to greet me personally the morning of my scheduled release in front of the Federal House of Detention. The night before I was to come out, the prison authorities took me from my cell at midnight and informed me I was free then and there and goodbye. I knew they wanted to forestall the demonstration and I protested against this surreptitious and "premature" release.

Since the area was a lonely and deserted waterfront neighborhood, I insisted on the right to phone my wife to let her know I was coming out earlier. At first the authorities turned down this request, but they relented when I said that otherwise I would not leave. An escort of guards took me to a cab and in half an hour I was home with Lillian. The effort to prevent the demonstration did not succeed, however. My release had come too late at night to be reported in the morning papers and several hundred people gathered at 9 a.m. in front of the jail, waiting for me to come out. Great was their surprise when I suddenly alighted from a taxicab on the opposite side of the street. The *Daily News* carried an amusing story on how Gates had tried to prevent his release from prison.

Rarely has a case received as much publicity as ours; rarely has the public known so few of the actual facts about a major trial. The average person thought—and still thinks—that we were tried and found guilty of espionage, sabotage, treason and planning to overthrow the government by force. None of these crimes was even charged against us. We were actually accused of "conspiracy" to organize a political party which would teach and advocate the duty and necessity of the violent overthrow and destruction of the United States government. We were not accused of practicing force and violence, or of advocating it, or of forming a party which so advocated, but of "conspiracy to organize" a party—meaning getting together in a convention to form a party which would so advocate at some time in the future. The "conspiracy" charge is a highly technical one, having nothing to do with being conspirators in the cloak-and-dagger sense. In every anti-trust suit, corporations are accused of "conspiring" to violate the law—but they are not therefore pictured in the press, as we were, as conspirators.

The actual charge in our case was thrice removed from acts of violence and had nothing whatsoever to do with espionage, sabotage or treason. Moreover, the government did not even have to prove that the individual defendants themselves taught or advocated the forbidden doctrine (and the record shows the government did not prove this); the charge of conspiracy is so loose that it made any such proof entirely unnecessary.

The case hinged around the reconstitution of the party in 1945 which, according to the prosecution, meant the return to a policy of advocating force and violence. The reconstitution of the party meant a return to mistaken policies that finally destroyed the organization as an effective political instrument; but this had nothing to do with force and violence. We had not advocated it prior to 1944, so we could not "return" to it in 1945.

Three of the defendants, Henry Winston, Gus Hall and myself, were not even present at the convention which reorganized the party; at the time we were members of the armed forces of the United States. This fact alone should have resulted in our eventual acquittal if the present standards established by the Supreme Court had been applied in our case.* For that matter, under the present standards, *all* the original defendants would have been acquitted.

The idea that the small, weak, uninfluential Communist Party of 1948 represented a threat of violent overthrow of the most

* In its decision reversing the California Smith Act case, the Supreme Court ruled that "we should follow the familiar rule that criminal statutes are to be strictly construed and give to 'organize' its narrow meaning, that is, that the word refers only to acts entering into the creation of a new organization, and not to acts thereafter performed in carrying on its activities, even though such acts may loosely be termed organizational." (Yates v. U.S., June 18, 1957)

powerful government in the world, even if the party so desired, was ludicrous. As the main evidence of this charge, the government introduced the classic works of Marx, Engels, Lenin and Stalin, and pointed to the well-known fact that these were used as textbooks in Communist schools.

Years later, in 1957, the Supreme Court ruled that this type of evidence was insufficient to convict under the Smith Act; proof was needed that each defendant actually incited to violent action. No such evidence was presented against us in our trial. I challenge anyone to find one piece of testimony to this effect in the 20-volume record of the case.

The real reasons behind our indictment revolved around entirely different matters from force and violence. One of these was the cold war and the Truman Administration's determination to suppress all opposition to its international policies—what Dean Acheson at the time euphemistically called "total diplomacy" and which later, at least with respect to the government's loyalty program, he conceded was a major mistake.

The other purpose was simple enough: to demonstrate in an election year that the Democrats were not "tainted," that they could be as tough on Communists as the GOP claimed that only Republicans could be. As though being a victim of the cold war were not enough, the Communist Party also had the misfortune to be caught in the crossfire of big-time partisan politics.

The anti-Communist hysteria was so intense, and most Americans were so frightened by the Communist issue, that we were convicted before our trial even started. We would have been found guilty of any charge brought against us, I am sure, and it was a foregone conclusion that we would get the maximum sentence. When at the end of the trial Judge Medina said he wished he could give us more than the five years permitted by law, I had no doubt that if death had been permitted, death is what we would have received.

There have probably been few judges in American jurisprudence who have received more awards and citations than Judge Medina. Surely this could not have been in response to a display of impartial conduct on his part; after all, this is the simple duty of any judge and is seldom rewarded. The conclusion is inescapable that Medina has been showered with honors because, to put it bluntly, he "did a job" on the Communists. The judge has been enshrined in the public eye as a hero and martyr, for which there is little justification. I grant I am hardly an impartial judge in the matter, but then it is my contention that neither was Medina. One would think from the fuss raised by the judge that he was the victim and that he, rather than we, served five-year prison sentences. Medina has been pictured (chiefly by himself) as terribly harassed by the defense lawyers, but it was the lawyers who went to prison for contempt and, in some cases, suffered disbarment.

On his perennial tour of the lecture circuit, Judge Medina tells and re-tells the story of how he felt his life was threatened by the defendants and how he dreamed of suicide. If His Honor actually felt this way during the trial, he could hardly have been impartial, unbiased and unprejudiced toward us; it was his duty to bring his feelings of persecution out into the open and turn the case over to a judge who would not feel that the defendants before him were trying to murder him.

Judge Medina not only bore a marked resemblance to actor Adolphe Menjou; like Menjou, he was a consummate actor. From the outset he assumed the star role in the proceedings. Evidently believing that the prosecution could not produce any evidence to back up the charge on which we were indicted, he proceeded to prosecute us on a charge which he dreamed up himself: we and our lawyers were supposed to be conspiring to obstruct justice by dragging out the trial—a charge which the U.S. Supreme Court rejected.

Although our case was a hopeless one under the circumstances, the defendants made every mistake in the book. We permitted the trial to become a duel between judge and defense; it is difficult enough to get a federal jury to vote against the government prosecutor, it will never vote against the judge. Medina baited and provoked our lawyers and they fell into the trap. With the press solidly behind the judge and against us, no matter what we did was reported in a bad light, and our defense tactics often made a bad situation worse. A good picture of the proceedings and of Medina's conduct can be found in the opinions written by Justices Frankfurter and Douglas in the contempt case of one of our lawyers, Harry Sacher.

Justice Frankfurter wrote:

"The particular circumstances of this case compel me to conclude that the trial judge should not have combined in himself the functions of accuser and judge. For his accusations were not impersonal. They concerned matters in which he personally was deeply engaged . . . No judge should sit in a case in which he is personally involved . . . At frequent intervals in the course of the trial his comments plainly reveal personal feelings against the lawyers . . . Truth compels the observation, painful as it is to make it, that the fifteen volumes of oral testimony in the principal trial record numerous episodes involving the judge and defense counsel that are more suggestive of an undisciplined debating society than of the hush and solemnity of a court of justice. Too often *counsel were encouraged* (my emphasis-J.G.) to vie with the court in dialectic, in repartee and banter, in talk so copious as inevitably to arrest the momentum of the trial and to weaken the restraints of respect that a judge should engender in lawyers . . . Throughout the proceedings . . . he failed to exercise the moral authority of a court possessed of a great tradition."

To which Justice Douglas added: "I agree with Mr. Justice Frankfurter that one who reads the record will have difficulty in determining whether members of the bar conspired to drive a judge from the bench or whether the judge used the authority of the bench to whipsaw the lawyers, to taunt and tempt them, and to create for himself the role of the persecuted. I have reluctantly concluded that neither is blameless, that there is fault on each side, that we have here the spectacle of the bench and the bar using the courtroom for an unseemly discussion and of ill will and hot tempers."

While the Supreme Court upheld the contempt convictions of the defense lawyers, it threw out Medina's charge that the attorneys had engaged in a conspiracy to subvert the administration of justice and to undermine his health. Since the judge announced early in the trial that he believed that such a conspiracy existed, this also must have prejudiced his conduct. Despite the higher court's finding, the judge has continued in his innumerable speeches and voluminous writings to insist on the existence of this conspiracy.

Unless the reader has had occasion to be the defendant in a political trial, cooped up in a courtroom for nine months, it will be difficult for him to imagine our frustrations—especially when we had to sit and listen while witnesses swore to imaginary conversations which could not be disproved and which, under the Smith Act, could usher us straight into prison.

One of the prosecution witnesses alleged that a Communist leader, not on trial, had stated that the Red Army would march down on the United States via Alaska and Canada. Several of us could not refrain from smiling broadly. I had been in the Aleutians and knew the utter impossibility of such a march, except perhaps by sea-lions. Medina interrupted the proceedings to remark that he noticed the defendants were smiling and rebuked us.

I arose and inquired whether the judge was ordering us never to smile in the course of the trial. "It is bad enough that we are on trial for our right to think," I said, "without forbidding us now even the right to smile." This helped to break our tension and relieve our frustration. But it can hardly be said to have advanced our case or impressed the jurors, if any were in a frame of mind to be impressed by anything we might have done or left undone.

It must be said in justice to our lawyers that they not only performed miracles of courage and zeal in our behalf; they were not chiefly to blame for our ill-conceived tactics. Time and again they advised against doing certain things, but since we were the clients, they would defer to our wishes.

Something was even more seriously wrong, however, than our day-to-day tactics; this was our futile attempt to prove that the classics of the Marxist writers meant what we said they meant, instead of what they plainly did mean, if taken literally. It is clear now that instead of becoming involved in doctrinal disputes which nobody could understand, we should have concentrated on the civil liberties aspects of the case: the right to read, write, say and think any political thoughts we pleased—as set forth as a sacred right in the First Amendment to the United States Constitution—even the right to say and think things which we never dreamed of saying and of which we were accused by perjurous witnesses.

Our trial was the first to which the Communist Party was subjected under the Smith Act but this was not the first application of the law. Leaders of the Socialist Workers Party, who were Trotskyists, had been indicted and convicted in 1941. We hated and despised the Trotskyists, whom we considered to be anti-Soviet, and while we did not, as has often been alleged, support their prosecution and conviction, it is true that we did not come to their defense against the Smith Act. This failure returned to haunt us; it demonstrated that we were for civil liberties when it applied to our own rights but not in the case of our opponents.

As a result, many people who believed that the Smith Act was unconstitutional, nevertheless did not support us; they were convinced that if we ever came to power we would deprive everybody, except the Communists, of their democratic rights. We operated toward the Trotskyites on the Stalin dictum that they represented not a legitimate political trend but a counter-revolutionary conspiracy of spies and saboteurs, that they were enemies of the working class and entitled to no legal rights. This became the basis on which Stalin destroyed all political opposition and established his complete autocratic rule. Ironically, the attitude we took toward the Trotskyites was the same as that taken by the government toward us. We reaped the harvest of the seeds we ourselves had sown.

During the trial I was invited to speak by the Student Council of the University of North Carolina at Chapel Hill. While I was en route there by plane, the meeting was cancelled by the university authorities, a fact which I did not discover until I arrived. The cancellation had come so suddenly that the students were unaware of it too; and that evening about 1,000 of them gathered at the closed and darkened meeting hall. They milled around, angry at the decision. When I inquired whether they would want to listen to what I had to say off the campus grounds, they eagerly assented.

We marched off to a corner of town where I proceeded to make my talk on how according to American law and justice a man was presumed to be innocent until proved guilty, and should be tried for his acts and not his ideas or what someone said were his ideas, and that when anyone was deprived of his right to speak, the people were deprived of their right to listen and to seek the truth. There was considerable agreement with what I said; this was one of many incidents I was to encounter over the years which demonstrated that young students were often more mature and more zealous in the defense of democratic liberties than their supposedly more adult leaders.

During this period, I appeared on the radio program "Meet the Press," and I also debated with James Wechsler, editor of the *New York Post,* at Sarah Lawrence College. Dr. Harold Taylor, head of the college, acted as moderator. The subject of the debate was the Smith Act. I knew that Wechsler was an ardent civil libertarian and opposed the law, but while I devoted my talk to the Smith Act, Wechsler stated his position against the statute in a couple of minutes and spent most of his time on what was wrong with communism. I was indignant at these unfair debating tactics, as I felt them to be, but was nevertheless placed on the defensive.

One point which Wechsler made stuck in my craw. He said that one thing which he objected to most strenuously about communists was that we were so certain and cocksure about everything that we never entertained any doubts. I responded by saying that doubt was the hallmark of liberals and led to paralysis of action, while communists made up their mind and acted. Although I disagreed vigorously with Wechsler, his argument wounded me and I was never able to get it out of my mind. I thought about it again and again as the years passed, especially as events occurred which finally led me to understand what he was driving at.

As the day neared when the case would go to the jury, our position became more and more hopeless. Could a jury possibly find its way through seven months of reading aloud from abstruse books on economics, philosophy and revolutionary tactics against the Czar?

Moreover, even if they admitted to themselves that they had no idea what it was all about, would the jury give us the benefit of the doubt when newspapers and government officials were busy picturing us as saboteurs and espionage agents?

To this day the average American still has that picture of us, thanks to the reckless statements made over the years by people like J. Edgar Hoover. In this respect, it is worth noting some passages in Hoover's most recent book, *Masters of Deceit*. Hoover writes: "The Communist Party, U.S.A., has not reached the point where preparations for sabotage are vital to its future plans . . . So far the communists have carefully refrained from any show of terrorism . . . acts of sabotage are not now part of the Party's program . . ."

He maintains that nevertheless sabotage is an important element in the communist science of revolution, and while the party does not practice it now, it may do so in the future. Hoover is admitting here that in the almost 40 years of the existence of the American Communist Party, sabotage, terrorism and force have never been part of its program and have not been "vital to its future plans." Yet the average American has a totally different impression, which the FBI itself has helped to create.

On the matter of espionage, Hoover writes: "To be a Party member does not automatically mean being an espionage agent," adding, however, that it makes him "potential" spy material. He declares that "today, with some exceptions, the Soviets are attempting to operate their espionage networks independent of the Party, staying away, as much as possible, from Party assistance." Hoover maintains that this will change, however, "when the need arises." Again the party is proscribed not for what it does, but for what it might do in the imagination of its opponents!

There are many laws to combat acts of sabotage and espionage, laws which are just and necessary. But not one of them has ever been invoked against the Communist Party for the simple reason that no evidence linking the party with espionage ever existed. In the absence of any illegal actions, new roundabout laws were devised to make "dangerous thoughts" and "potentials" illegal, such as the Smith Act and the McCarran registration act.

And even here, the need for any evidence was circumvented by resorting to the legal theory of conspiracy of which the late Justice Robert Jackson wrote: "The modern crime of conspiracy is so vague that it almost defies definition . . . One might go on from the reports of this and lower courts and put together their decisions condoning absence of proof to demonstrate that the minimum of proof required to establish conspiracy is extremely low . . ." (Krulewitch v. U.S.)

In my 27 years in the party, I never came in contact with any kind of espionage; I never came across the slightest indication that the party was involved in espionage. I took it for granted that the Soviet Union conducted espionage activities, but from my general assumption that all nations did. Our own country has done so—and continually boasted of it—since the days of Nathan Hale. For the Soviet Union to have tried to make the American Communist Party a part of its espionage apparatus, would have been the height of stupidity, as J. Edgar Hoover concedes. It is true that spy networks recruit wherever they can, and it is possible that a Soviet network recruited some individual Communists along with individual Republicans and Democrats. If so, it was taking a risk of doing grave harm to the Communist Party, of discrediting and compromising the party, its members and leaders in the public eye.

Beyond this, espionage, regardless of who engages in it, is a dirty business. The technique, like that of war, is the same in every country; Soviet spy methods and American spy methods are probably quite similar. What is needed is the kind of atmosphere in the world that will make it possible to banish all of these evil arts.

As bad as espionage itself, if not worse, is the trumping-up of espionage cases for political purposes; this too is a fairly universal practice. As the years have passed and cold war passions abate, many political cases have been reviewed in our country and in the Soviet Union and the victims exonerated. But we have not yet taken a second and calmer judicial look at the Hiss, Remington, Rosenberg, Sobell and other espionage cases which were exploited so damagingly by McCarthyism.

Our own case under the Smith Act went to the jury the afternoon of October 13, 1949. Federal court juries are notorious for being handpicked on a highly select blue-ribbon basis. Acquittal by such juries was rare; where Communists were involved, an acquittal was highly improbable. At best, some of the defendants hoped a juror or two might hold out, resulting in a hung jury and a new trial. The nature of the jury can be seen from the presence on it of Russell Janney, author of the best-seller *Miracle of the Bells*. Janney, a well-known anti-Communist, had declared in a speech shortly before the trial that "we must fight communism to the death."

The jury deliberated a few hours, had a good night's sleep and came in with its verdict shortly after 11 A.M. next morning. The judge ordered us to stand up and the foreman pronounced the verdict—Guilty. Although I had expected this outcome, the words were a shock. The judge immediately remanded us to jail pending sentence a week later. Turning and waving to our wives and friends in the courtroom, we were hustled off to prison by the marshals. The following week we were sentenced to five years in prison and $10,000 fine each, the maximum sentence. Thompson received three years in view of his war record. Judge Medina denied our request to be freed on bail pending appeal, and we stayed in jail three weeks before the Court of Appeals reversed him on this point and granted bail, raising the amount from the original $5,000 to $20,000 each.

After the jury had brought in its verdict, Judge Medina had said: "Now for some unfinished business," and had proceeded to read the riot act to our attorneys. He charged and convicted them of wilful contempt, and sentenced them to prison terms ranging from one to six months. This was an evil time for the cause of lawyers who dare to defend unpopular and minority groups, and for civil liberties in general. With the convictions of the Communists and their lawyers, a giant step was being taken toward the hysteria that later was known as McCarthyism and which claimed victims far beyond Communist circles.

Any illusions that our appeals to the higher courts might be considered favorably were dispelled by the outbreak of the Korean war. Korea had been divided following the defeat of Japan, by agreement between our country and the Soviet Union, the Red Army occupying the northern and our army the southern zone. After several years both powers withdrew their armies but Korea remained divided. By 1950 the hostility between the two zones became extremely sharp, erupting into a major war in June 1950.

There is no doubt in my mind—I know this is a minority viewpoint—that the original provocation came from Syngman Rhee, the tyrannical dictator of South Korea. This should not be difficult to accept today—at least as a possibility—since the only two chiefs of state anywhere in the world who openly advocate and work for a new world war to realize their ambitions, are Rhee and Chiang Kai-shek. Rhee had launched military sallies many times across the 38th Parallel and each time was driven back. But in June 1950, the North Korean army did not stop with repulsing the latest provocation; it pursued the South Korean army and set out to conquer all of Korea. This decision brought the United States into the war under the aegis of the United Nations.

This was a major and fateful decision on the part of North Korea and it remains a mystery whether it did so on its own, or with the agreement of the Soviet Union and China. There is doubt whether the Soviet Union was in on the decision. Its representative was not present in the Security Council when the war broke out; and it would seem logical that if the Soviet Union had planned the war, it would have wanted to be in a position to veto any UN action. As for China, that country did not enter the war until General MacArthur, in turn not satisfied at repulsing the invasion of South Korea, crossed the 38th Parallel, sought to occupy all of North Korea and approached the Chinese border. It was the foolhardy effort to conquer each zone that brought the United States and China respectively into the war.

This was a terrible war; the use of napalm bombs by us was particularly reprehensible and has not been forgotten in Asia. The

Korean war brought world tensions to their most dangerous and explosive point since World War II, creating the grave possibility of the cold war becoming a general hot war. At home, the Korean war provided the background for the spread of McCarthyism which now reached its most vicious and most inhuman levels.

The estimate of how grave the international situation had become, that is, the extent of a danger of general war, predominated in the debates within the party's leadership at that time. In fact, the "war danger" was one of the celebrated controversies within the top leadership, having continued ever since 1946. It was one of the issues on which the same division between the Foster-Thompson-Davis group and the rest of the top leadership had shown itself, as I described earlier in discussing our attitude toward the party's line in the trade unions, among the Negro people, and with respect to political action. Closely linked with the "war danger" were our differences over the immediacy of fascism. Little of this debate ever came before the party membership, although allusions to it can be traced—if one knows what he is looking for—in the party's magazine, *Political Affairs,* and in the columns of the *Daily Worker.*

Those who took the view of the imminence of world war were naturally inclined toward a certain type of defense in the trial, and toward preparing the party for what they expected would be early illegality. To this group, "peaceful co-existence" became little more than a phrase. They claimed to be fighting for it, but they doubted it could be achieved. And since it was the party's view that the "decisive circles" of American capitalism were bent on war, any suggestion that any significant groups in the American ruling class or even among labor circles might oppose war, even for reasons of their own, was viewed as echoing "Browderism." The "war danger" was thus linked to a "go-it-alone" policy with respect to all other phases of party activity.

Late in 1950 I made a report on the Korean war to the National Board of the party and said that neither side could gain a decisive victory without the limited war in Korea becoming a worldwide conflict, which neither the United States nor the Soviet Union was prepared for or wanted.

This indicated, the report went on, a stalemate; the war would remain limited, and sooner or later it would have to be settled by concessions from both sides, roughly speaking around the 38th Parallel. I gave as my opinion that the Korean war was destined to be not the prelude to a third world war, as some thought, but one of the persisting aftermaths of World War II. Our main slogan had to be, therefore, to settle the war by re-establishing the 38th Parallel as the dividing line.

This estimate turned out to be pretty sound, although I did not yet realize that the stalemate existing in Korea was a general worldwide one between the two great power blocs, that neither side was able to dominate the world, whatever the intentions or desires, and that this constituted the basis for a general settlement of differences without resort to war.

This was the actual situation, but it was not yet apparent, so the war in Korea continued. When General MacArthur tried to spread the conflict regardless of the possible consequences, the underlying reality of a stalemate made it necessary to oust him. Meanwhile the war dragged on in its limited, inconclusive way until 1953, after the election of Eisenhower and the death of Stalin.

The opinions of Judge Learned Hand of the Circuit Court of Appeals and later of Chief Justice Vinson left no doubt that our convictions were upheld because of such events as the Berlin air-lift and the Korean war—actually named in the decisions—although these international developments took place after the conclusion of our trial, were quite beyond our control, and had no possible relation to the charge against us.

Six years after the Vinson decision, the Court, now under Chief Justice Earl Warren, in effect reversed the Vinson court; had we been fortunate enough to have our appeal heard under the principles set by the Warren decision, there is no doubt in my mind that our conviction would have been upset. The sharp difference between the two courts lay not primarily in the court's altered personnel, but rather in the changed political climate. If it is true, as Mr. Dooley said, that "the court follows the 'illiction' returns," it can be said with equal truth that the court has followed the ups and downs of McCarthyism and cold war.

On June 4, 1951, the Supreme Court handed down its 6-2 decision upholding our conviction, with Justices Black and Douglas dissenting. We had about a month of freedom before beginning our sentences. These last days we used to wind up personal affairs and to assist a new leadership to take our place while we would be in jail. A few days after the high court's decision, the Department of Justice indicted the "second-string" Communist leaders, as they were called in the press, headed by Elizabeth Gurley Flynn.

To many in the leadership, this meant that the United States was unquestionably on the threshold of fascism. Had not Hitler's first step been to outlaw the Communist Party? We saw an almost exact parallel. Undoubtedly this conclusion impelled four of the eleven convicted leaders to take what they considered a necessary step to save the party and fail to show up when we were ordered to appear on July 2 to begin our sentences.

Gil Green, Henry Winston, Gus Hall and Robert Thompson "jumped bail," as the saying goes, and this set the stage for a large part of the party going underground for the next few years. It was a difficult and reactionary period, but it was not fascism. Underestimating the democratic temper of the nation and the possibilities of a successful, open fight against McCarthyism, the party did considerable damage to itself.

For almost two years since our conviction in the Fall of 1949, we had staved off the day of reckoning, but now it was here. Once again we reported to the Foley Square Courthouse. We had said our goodbyes in the privacy of our homes, and we were ready. We held our heads high—the news photos showed my handcuffs high overhead—spirits unbroken. And in this way we mounted the steps of the waiting van and entered upon a life of five years behind bars.

IX

PRISON

Atlanta penitentiary was a famous place for me; Eugene Victor Debs had served there for his opposition to the first world war, as had Earl Browder in the early years of World War II. I was rather thrilled when I was placed in a cell three doors away from the one in which Debs had done his time. The Socialist leader had been pardoned by President Harding in 1921 and although none of the officers or inmates of that time were still around, the prison library contained books which told of Debs' experiences in that very place.

The prison had been built around 1900, a huge institution with some 2700 inmates and several hundred guards and other employees. It was a combination of the mediaeval and the modern. Most of the men were herded into small eight-men cells with a toilet in the center, and with one table and four chairs; the men slept in four double-decker bunks.

This overcrowding was the prison's worst feature. On the other hand, each man had earphones for listening in on the radio, and we received clean sheets once a week. While we had a prison hospital with a modern operating room and psycho-therapeutic treatment, we also had a "hole," as solitary confinement for extreme punishment was called. The cells were so crowded that the policy was to keep the men out of them as much as possible, either at work or at recreation.

The only "good" feature of the jail was its enormous recreational area with three baseball diamonds, two basketball courts, eight tennis and ten handball courts, shuffleboard, horseshoe pitching, volleyball and bocce courts, weight-lifting facilities, a quarter-mile track, a grandstand, and room for men who just wanted to talk and lounge around. We were allowed into the "yard" (the recreational field) every day if weather permitted. We saw a movie once a week. At Atlanta I personally experienced both the old and the new; learning to play tennis for the first time and, for the first time, spending a week in the "hole."

The food was ordinary and tasteless, but enough to keep a man from starving. Meat and desserts were strictly rationed, but bread, vegetables and potatoes were available in unlimited quantities, the only proviso being that once taken they had to be eaten on pain of punishment. Since we were in the South and most of the prisoners were from that region, the cooking was southern-style—everything was cooked in fatback, which I disliked intensely.

Unlike most state prisons, food could not be sent in from the outside nor could the men buy food of their own. This placed those with money at a disadvantage, but it was a fairer system for the majority. We were not allowed to have any money on our person. Instead, it was deposited to our account and we could spend it at the commissary at the rate of $10 (later to $12) a month for candy, crackers, smoking and toilet articles.

About half the men worked in prison factories for which they were paid up to $45 a month; although the scale was inadequate, this was one of the most progressive features of the federal prison system. The other half of the men, working on prison mainte-nance, received no pay, and thus suffered a form of discrimination. The prison industries in Atlanta included the manufacture of mat-tresses, canvas articles and clothing; trade schools were main-tained in the machine shop, carpenter shop, and in sheet metal and bricklaying; a print shop did government printing.

Upon entering the prison, the men were given intelligence and aptitude tests, classified just as in the army, and even asked what

they wanted to do. At my interview, I expressed my first prefer-
ence for the print shop, in line with my newspaper experience.
This was denied on the ground that the shop did confidential
work for the government from which I was disqualified. I then
asked for the machine shop in order to learn a trade, in the event
that I would not be permitted to return to the *Daily Worker* after
my prison term. I was told that I was much too educated for such
routine work. Whereupon I was given a mop and broom and assigned as an orderly to keep the cellhouse clean. My army experience all over again!

The seven of us who went to jail after the first Smith Act trial
were scattered through the various federal penitentiaries. Dennis
and I were the only ones to be sent to Atlanta. We were put in
different cells (though we saw each other every day in the year)
and Dennis was assigned to work in the greenhouse.

We got along well with the men. The fact that we were unpopular with the government made us popular with the prisoners.
Every prisoner in the place had been put there by the government
and this established a common bond among us all, despite the
great variety of reasons for our incarceration. Federal crimes were
those committed on federal property or against federal institutions
and those involving the crossing of state boundaries. The most
prevalent offense was car-stealing and transporting the stolen
property across state lines. The usual penalty was five years, sometimes as high as fifteen, and the offenders were young. The author
of the federal statute, former Rep. Dyer of Missouri, has stated
that he regretted sponsoring the law because he had not foreseen
such long sentences. The "aristocrats" of the prison were the bank
robbers. The nature of their crime required a high degree of intelligence, planning and daring and carried a minimum of 15
years. Besides, they stole from wealthy institutions, which con-
ferred upon them something of the mantle of Robin Hood and
Jesse James.

The men knew we were not ordinary criminals and they respected us. Although so much publicity had surrounded our case,
and we were looked upon as "big shots," we did not act as if we
were, did not seek special privileges and mixed with everybody.

Because we were educated and had acquired much legal knowledge from our long litigation, many of the men asked us for legal and personal advice.

It was assumed that leaders of a political party must have plenty of money and strong backing, and this led some inmates to approach us with angles of their own. They would ask us if we wanted anyone "bumped off" or otherwise taken care of. When we insisted that we were opposed to violence and had been falsely accused, they would smile knowingly and insist upon the matter. Only when we pointed out that in any case members helped the party out of love and not for money, did they lose interest.

In a few instances (this never happened to Dennis and myself) men hoped to curry favor with the authorities by physically attacking Communist prisoners. This occurred to Bob Thompson who was hit over the head from behind with a lead pipe by a fascist Yugoslav prisoner fearing deportation to Yugoslavia and figuring that this way he could get out of it. This was the exception and not the rule. Generally, the other prisoners regarded the Communists highly, recognizing, as not everyone outside did, that we were not criminals but that we had been imprisoned for standing up for our views and ideals.

If we got along unusually well with the men, this was not true of our relations with the authorities. Some officials were merely correct or neutral in their attitude to us; others went out of their way to make life difficult. These were petty politicians who in the current McCarthyite hysteria hoped to gain political advancement if they treated us harshly, or who feared demotion if they did not.

We were discriminated against in our job assignments and not permitted to work in prison industry, which meant depriving us of money as well as of the additional time off given for such work. We were also refused parole despite our good conduct. No Communist prisoner has ever been granted parole in recent years, the only category of prisoners so treated.

We ran into difficulty, too, with respect to correspondence and books. The inmates were permitted to write and receive letters only from close relatives and attorneys, and the nature of the correspondence was restricted to social matters. Letters written by

Dennis and me were returned to us on the grounds that they were not social. It seemed that the prison authorities had redefined the word "social" to mean only comments on the weather and kindred subjects, whereas we commented freely in our letters about current events. We insisted that we were within our rights, that "social" meant anything dealing with society, and that the word would inevitably be interpreted differently by prisoners who were non-political and by ourselves.

Prisoners were supposed to be allowed to order books from the outside providing they were not subversive or licentious; but we were denied the right altogether. After much unpleasantness for us and after the late Congressman Vito Marcantonio led a delegation in our behalf to James V. Bennett, federal director of prisons, we finally won the right to send letters commenting on matters contained in the newspapers which we read and to buy books from the outside if they were duly approved by the authorities. Even after this agreement had been reached, we continued to be harassed, the extent of the censorship occurring in almost direct proportion to the rise and fall of McCarthyism in the country at large.

In spite of our isolation, we managed to keep fairly well informed. Our wives wrote us informative, detailed letters and we followed events closely through newspapers and magazines. Prisoners were allowed one home-town newspaper each. Since the men came from all over the country, we would exchange reading matter and this way Dennis and I saw practically every major paper. Whenever the men noticed an item which they thought might interest us, they would call it to our attention. We read the *New York Times, New York Herald-Tribune* and *New York Post* regularly, subscribed to the *Nation, New Republic, The Reporter* and, through the other prisoners, read virtually every other magazine too.

Although we worked all day and went out into the yard after supper, we returned to our cells before dark and there was ample time to read during the long evenings. Four years of reading this way adds up. The library was fairly good as prison libraries go. There were also the books which we received from the outside.

Among those that I found most rewarding were the collected works of Mark Twain, Samuel Lubell's *Future of American Politics,* Arthur Schlesinger, Jr.'s, *Age of Jackson,* James Wechsler's *Age of Suspicion,* Matthew Josephson's biographies of Victor Hugo and Sidney Hillman, and biographies of Galileo, Debs, Darrow, and many others. I made a special study of the South, reading *The Mind of the South* by W. J. Cash; C. Vann Woodward's *Reunion and Reaction* and *Origins of the New South;* V. O. Key's *Southern Politics;* Heard's *Two Party South;* W. E. B. DuBois' *Soul of Black Folk* and his autobiography; the collected works of Frederick Douglass, and the novels of Ellen Glasgow. I doubt whether I would have read half as much had I been free. But I would still have chosen freedom any time.

This was also a period of intense re-examination of ideas. How had we gotten here? Was our imprisonment inevitable? The basic reason for our arrest, I was sure, was our opposition to the policies of the Truman administration, which we looked upon as pro-war and reactionary. On this I had no doubts or second thoughts, although I did begin to wonder whether Soviet policies in meeting the threat of war from the West had been right at all times. What weighed most heavily upon me was the almost complete absence of popular concern over our imprisonment. I was fascinated to read how Eugene Victor Debs ran for President as a prisoner in Atlanta and received a million votes, and of the great mass movement that finally won his release. The contrast with our case was painful. There was no mystery about the government's opposition to us; but how explain the lack of interest by the workers and the rest of the common people whose cause we had defended for so many years, and in whose interests we thought we had gone to jail?

I could rationalize this somewhat on the ground that people had been deceived about us or were intimidated by McCarthyism from coming to our support. Although I knew that both of these were true, still I felt that there must be more to the story. We must have committed some very serious mistakes of our own which also contributed to our isolation. Dennis and I discussed this again and again. We re-argued the trial and discussed mistakes by the defense, and reviewed all the policies of the party.

A few people, including Mrs. Roosevelt, Norman Thomas and A. J. Muste, did support amnesty for us. These particular personalities had been staunch defenders of civil liberties throughout the years. But even here something bothered me. If any people were justified in not coming to our defense, it was just these three whom I have named. Had we not heaped personal and political abuse upon them (alternating with periods of praise)? I asked myself how *we* would have responded had the situation been reversed, and my answer was not a comforting one. I came to feel that these individuals must have a moral superiority over us, that there must be something decidedly wrong with the attitude of communism toward democracy.

When we had been in jail a year, the government concluded its case in the hearings before the Subversive Activities Control Board, set up under the McCarran Internal Security Act to determine whether the party should register as a foreign agent. The defense now began its case after twelve months of testimony by government witnesses and the party asked me to be the lead-off man. I was willing and ready (among other things, it would give me an opportunity to leave Atlanta for a while), but I told Eugene Dennis that he ought to be the main witness. He was the general secretary of the party; his testimony would have much more weight and authority behind it.

As I had feared, he declined and I became extremely angry. How could he continue to be the leader of the party and shirk the responsibility to speak for it and defend it whenever the opportunity presented itself? Modesty and desire to stay out of the limelight were admirable qualities, but impossible for the head of an American political party. I had defended him against the attacks of Foster, Davis and Thompson and would continue to do so as long as I thought they were wrong, but his retiring nature made it increasingly difficult to support him in his post. I warned that his future as the leader of the party was at stake. Dennis remained unconvinced and adamant. I did not speak to him for days afterwards.

Our attorneys in the McCarran Act proceedings, former Con-

gressman Vito Marcantonio, John Abt and Joseph Forer, had to
work with me in preparation for my testimony. This would be
quite extensive since I would be answering a full year of government testimony. Their request that I be transferred tempo-
rarily to the prison at Danbury, Connecticut, where Marcantonio
had a summer home, was granted. In May I said goodbye to
Dennis and although we had sharp disagreements, it was a warm
and friendly leave-taking.

My trip to Danbury was by car and in chains. En route, one of
my stopovers was the West Street jail in New York, where I had
a chance to see Gus Hall. He was one of those who had jumped
bail and had been apprehended in Mexico City, for which three
years were added to his original five-year sentence. Also serving
time at West Street—for contempt—was one of our lawyers, Louis
McCabe of Philadelphia. It was a pleasure to talk with them
again, but it was only for a few hours; the next day I was on my
way to Connecticut.

Danbury was not a penitentiary but a correctional institution
for less incorrigible prisoners. The place was not as strict as Atlanta and was generally more pleasant. The food was better, and
I was put in a hospital room that was far more comfortable than
the 8-man madhouse to which I was accustomed. But it was still
a prison and I was kept in my room in solitary confinement.
Through the window I could see Jack Stachel, one of my co-
defendants who, after being convicted, had been sent to Danbury because of his heart condition, and also another one of our
lawyers sentenced for contempt (and later disbarred), Abraham
Isserman.

After many protests by my lawyers, I was finally permitted one
hour each day in the yard, where I could walk up and down a
10-yard stretch with a guard at each end to make sure I spoke to
nobody. Later I was permitted to confer for an hour with Stachel
about the proceedings at which I was to testify.

The institution was near New York City. Lillian (who had
visited me before in Atlanta) and my parents took advantage of
the short distance to come and see me. In Atlanta, visiting took
place on opposite sides of a massive table with an upright parti-

tion in the center to prevent bodily contact, although you were permitted an embrace at the beginning and the end of the visit. At Danbury you sat side by side with your wife on a settee and were even allowed to hold hands throughout the entire visit! This made for a far happier visit but heightened the pain of the parting.

I stayed at Danbury three weeks, conferring daily with my lawyers and getting my testimony ready. Among other things, this required reading and taking notes on back copies of the *Daily Worker*, which I was permitted to see for the first time. Finally the day of departure came; again I was put in chains and taken to Washington. I began my testimony in the SACB headquarters on June 9, 1952 and was on the stand six days, four of them on direct and two on cross-examination. Each day I was transported to and from the city jail, forced to submit to being stripped naked and to having all my bodily openings searched twice a day. I was handcuffed all the time except when I was actually in the hearing room and when I ate my lunch. This turned out to be a gala occasion, because I spent it with the lawyers, who were permitted to buy my food. They bought me the best.

The first few days were a considerable strain; I had grown unaccustomed to good food and went through the unusual torture of seeing duck, steaks, and roastbeef in front of me and being unable to eat them. Soon I got into stride, however, and I must have behaved like a starving man. Many friends came to the hearing room—they had made the trip from their home cities—and I was allowed to talk with the *Daily Worker* editors who were covering the event, Alan Max, the managing editor who had replaced me in my absence, and Rob Hall, our Washington correspondent. They were a sight for sore eyes.

I managed to say much more on the stand in these six days than I had in three weeks at Foley Square. Little time was taken up with legal wrangling between the attorneys and the SACB panel members. The government maintained that the American Communist Party had never differed with the policies enunciated by the Soviet Union and that this proved we were the agents of a foreign power and should be forced to register as such.

Registration would be tantamount to an admission of treason and the party had announced that under no circumstances would it register, regardless of what the SACB might decide, and regardless of the enormous punishment involved. Penalty for refusal to register was five years in prison *for each day* that an official or member of the party disobeyed the registration order. The McCarran Act was plainly the most unconstitutional and undemocratic law ever enacted by Congress and had been vetoed as such by President Truman, although his veto had been overridden. While I conceded that we had never differed with the Soviet Union, I denied that this meant that we took orders from abroad, or were agents acting for a foreign power.

I testified that the Soviet Communists and American Communists shared a common philosophy which we considered to be a science, that it was the nature of science to be universal, and it was not surprising that adherents of the same science came to the same general conclusions on relevant matters. We received no orders from abroad and took none, I maintained.

If we supported Soviet policies, this was because we believed them to be right and in the interests of world peace and all humanity, including the American people. Agreement with the Soviet Union could be wrong, but not criminal. Again and again the government asked me to give even a single example of where we had differed with the Soviet Union, and just as often I returned to my original answer.

In my own mind, however, the question continued to bother me long afterwards. I did not think then (and do not now) that mere agreement with the policies of a foreign Communist party makes anyone the agent of a foreign power and constitutes grounds for criminal action. But it was simply not human to have no differences or to think that Soviet policy had always been right and not mistaken even once. I could not help feeling finally that there must be something wrong in our relations with the Soviet Union.

One of the charges by the government had been that members of the party took an oath to defend the Soviet Union. In reply, I testified that the only oath I had ever taken in the party was when in 1941 I led a large meeting of Communist functionaries in the pledge of allegiance to the American flag upon my enlisting in the U.S. Army. I recalled in my testimony that I had first learned the pledge in elementary school in Manhattan while a child but that the Communist Party had taught me to understand it better than I did then. I told what the pledge meant to me now: that we were not yet one nation indivisible with liberty and justice for all, that we were divided into rich and poor, Negro and white, and that there was a different justice for capital and for labor, for Communists and non-Communists.

This testimony had an interesting aftermath. A congressional committee discussed it and concluded that something had to be done about the way the Communists were taking advantage of the pledge of allegiance. They decided to add the phrase "under God" to the pledge in order—they figured—to make it impossible for Communists to invoke it. That is how the pledge reads now, and I guess this testimony was indirectly responsible for the change. With or without the new phrase, the essence of the pledge remains the same with its promise of an indivisible nation and of liberty and justice for all still unfulfilled, still a glorious goal for the American people to achieve.

Under cross-examination the Assistant U.S. Attorney in charge of the government case, William Paisley, demanded that I tell him the whereabouts of my co-defendants who had jumped bail. I replied that I did not know as I had gone to jail the day they disappeared; but even if I did know I would refuse to tell him. When he persisted, I said that wherever Thompson was, I was sure that he was defending the United States in the same way that had won him the Distinguished Service Cross in World War II. Paisley still was not satisfied and I said that if he wanted me to become a stool pigeon and an informer, he was applying to the wrong address.

"If that is what you want, apply to J. Edgar Hoover, he is the keeper of the rats," I said. This statement was picked up by the press and broadcast over the radio. When I returned to Atlanta I found out that the men had heard it on the newscast, that it

had created a sensation and that I was now quite a hero in their
eyes.

This was the first time I had had a chance to know Vito Marcantonio. Short in stature, he was fiery, aggressive, volatile. He
had begun in politics as a protégé of Fiorello La Guardia whom
he resembled in many ways, later representing in Congress the
same East Harlem district which had first elected the "Little
Flower."

Marc, as he was known to tens of thousands, was a great vote-
getter, and was defeated only when the three other parties in
New York, the Democrats, Republicans and the Liberals, ganged
up against him and the American Labor Party which he led at
that point. He stood at the extreme Left in Congress and although
often identified with Communist causes, he was universally respected for his ability, courage and principled stand. I was
pleased that Marcantonio was impressed by my testimony. He
also seemed to like me, perhaps because I too was short and somewhat peppery. Unfortunately, I never saw him again; he died
before I was released from prison.

Usually even two minutes on the witness stand is two minutes
too many; but this time my six days passed all too quickly. Finally I had to give up my sumptuous luncheons and the dollar
cigar which a sympathizer in the courtroom donated daily (at
Atlanta we could buy only nickel smokes), and I set out for
"home." On the way back to Atlanta, I was escorted by two U.S.
marshals. We went by train, occupied a bedroom and I slept in
the bed, but with my wrists handcuffed and my ankles chained.
Even so, I derived considerable pleasure from the fact that my
guards had to sit up all night watching me while I slumbered.

Back in Atlanta, the old routine started again, the sweeping
and mopping, and, of course, regaling Dennis and other prision
friends with these high adventures. Now the authorities were
down on me more than ever because of the notoriety surrounding
my trip; perhaps they were incensed at my irreverent remarks
about J. Edgar Hoover. Soon an opportunity came along for them
to even the score. It came about this way. There was a master
lever for each one of the five tiers of cells which, when pulled,

locked every cell on the tier. In other prisons, such as Leavenworth, the inmates were not permitted to touch the levers. It was different at Atlanta. One day I was given the order to lock the men up. I refused. Hauled before the authorities, I explained that I was a convict and not a guard, that I would gladly release the men from their cells, but I would not lock them up. The response of the authorities to this was to throw me into the "hole" for seven days.

The "hole" meant solitary confinement and starvation rations. You were stripped naked and given coveralls and scuffs instead of shoes. After supper a mattress was thrown into the cell and removed the next morning before breakfast. The rest of the day the cell was bare and you walked or sat down on the cold concrete. Meals consisted of two slices of bread, a cup of black coffee without sugar, and a couple of vegetables—no meat or desserts.

For a week I had no one to talk to, nothing to read. Ironically, my cell in solitary was larger than the one in which eight of us normally lived; for a while I even relished the peace and solitude after the noise in my regular cell. Of course. the novelty soon palled. The "hole" is a barbaric system, a carry-over from the dungeons of the days of feudalism. I was not starved or beaten to death (although the men told stories of some who had been) but the purpose of the punishment was to humiliate, debase and degrade, to break down the human spirit.

This is what is wrong with the underlying philosophy of prisons. They do not serve to deter or reduce crime; in fact, they are often schools for crime. They rarely rehabilitate a human being and more often make him worse. If much of the money and personnel that go for prisons were put into efforts to improve the conditions of society and to perfect a system of parole and personal guidance, the results would be far better. The present system solves little. It aggravates the situation in many ways and costs more for society.

My experience in the "hole" only made me more bitter. I learned from many others who had gone through the barbaric treatment that they felt the same way. I was now transferred to a new job, a much more intelligent procedure than the punishment. This time I was assigned to heavy construction as a laborer, at which I at least had had more experience from the WPA days, than at sweeping and mopping. This was hard labor, harder than any other job in the prison, and undoubtedly the authorities assigned me there as further punishment. As it turned out, they could not have done me a greater favor. While the work was difficult, I was now out in the open and the fresh air did me good. Since the work was dirty, we took a bath every day, in contrast with the normal ration of twice a week. I came out of it healthier and cleaner.

We did maintenance work involving bricklaying, plastering, tile setting and carpentry, but our main project was constructing a tunnel ten feet wide and eight feet high. This was to carry electric lines and steam pipes from the old power house inside the prison to a new one just outside the walls. The fact that the tunnel was going through the prison wall to the outside world attracted a great deal of interest.

Rarely have I known so many men to be so deeply interested in so small a bit of architecture. At the same time the authorities made sure that nothing live would ever go through the tunnel except live steam and electricity. One day, they discovered a crude home-made acetylene torch inside the tunnel, which put an end to someone's dreams.

As we were digging close to the wall and fairly deep, I came across a battered old tablespoon. This became the occasion for the guard, with the prison many years, to tell the story of the last successful escapes from Atlanta, by Gerald Chapman and George Anderson. Chapman and Anderson were partners in the great million-dollar mail truck robbery back in 1921 for which they were serving 25 years. Chapman escaped first, on March 27, 1923, with another convict, bound and gagged a nurse in the prison hospital, filed the bars of a cell window, slid down the hospital wall on knotted sheets, short-circuited all the prison lights, threw a rope ladder over the 35-foot wall, and climbed to freedom. He was captured the next day 70 miles away and placed in the jail in Athens, Ga. Despite having been wounded in the kidney and arms, he escaped again a few hours later, this time for good. His buddy, Anderson, escaped from Atlanta with three others on Dec. 30 of the same year. There had been a tent colony for prisoners suffering from tuberculosis, and the escapees dug a tunnel from one of the tents 50 feet to the wall and under it. This had taken place near the spot where we were now digging. They used spoons and other tools to dig the tunnel, put the dirt into their pockets and emptied it in the greenhouse the following day. (I thought to myself that the spoon I had found could be the very spoon that was used, but it was hardly the kind of souvenir that I would be allowed to keep.) Although both men made good their escape, they were killed, years later, resisting arrest.

Soon after I found the spoon, the first escape in 30 years actually took place. Two men disappeared. The prison officials had no idea what had happened in spite of their well-organized system of informers. Work was cancelled and all men returned to their cells, while the guards methodically searched the prison grounds. When this failed to produce the missing men, it was concluded, of course, that they had escaped. How, the officials did not know.

For several days things were tight in the prison; then the officials decided on a clever stratagem. They pretended to go back to the normal routine, suspecting that some other prisoners knew of the escape route and would follow the first pair. Sure enough, a few days later two more men disappeared. But this time the guards in the towers were on the alert; they saw the men emerging from a clump of bushes several hundred yards past the wall. The alarm was given and the men were quickly seized. The "escape" route turned out to be an old abandoned sewer pipe, leading from a manhole on the handball courts, underneath the ball diamond and the prison wall, and coming out on the other side. The pipe was barely large enough for an average-sized man to scrape through. The authorities were supposed to have maps of all the sewer lines, but the map of this particular sewer was strangely missing—either it had been stolen or the men had come across it by accident.

I was put to work with others digging down to the pipe at the point where it passed under the wall and stopping it supposedly forever. The first two men who had used it were caught a week later in a wood about 30 miles away after being spotted by a lone hunter who reported them. I myself had no practical interest in prison escapes. But I derived keen satisfaction at the discomfiture of the officials and at the vulnerability of their high walls and their informer system.

Although the Atlanta penitentiary was a federal institution, segregation was enforced among the prisoners. This was so not only because the prison was in the South (even Lincoln's birthday was not celebrated in the prison), but segregation was the rule in all federal prisons in the North as well. In living quarters and the mess hall, whites and Negroes were kept strictly separated. While segregation could not be enforced with full strictness at work, Negroes generally were given the dirtiest and most menial jobs. There was some mixing in sports, but even here the organized teams were all-white or all-Negro. The main ball team of the prison would play outside army teams or college outfits; the visiting teams were often mixed while the prison team was all-white. Occasionally a big league club would visit the prison and play for us and, of course, had both Negro and white players.

Six of the tennis courts were reserved for whites, and two for Negroes. At one of the annual tournaments, I decided to pair up in the doubles with a Negro prisoner. There were some strange looks but nothing happened, and we reached the finals before we lost (we got this far because my partner was an excellent player).

I understand that later on Negro players were finally allowed on the institution teams together with whites, but all other forms of segregation remained in force. Dennis and I had to be careful in our associations with Negro and Puerto Rican prisoners (of whom there were many in Atlanta); we were under close surveillance at all times and this placed those with whom we associated under suspicion. In some cases, discrimination in jobs and parole was practiced against men merely because they were friendly to us.

Despite everything I could do to keep myself occupied, time still hung heavy and I had more opportunity to think than I had had for years. Events were developing in the outside world, confronting me with questions that I could no longer dismiss so easily. In March, 1953, Stalin died. I had enormous regard and admiration for him, and his death left a void in my scheme of things. But developments after his death forced me to question whether my absolute faith in Stalin had been justified. Immediately following his death, the Soviet government launched a peace offensive that resulted a few months later in the settlement of the Korean war. Soviet foreign policy had a new quality now, different from when Stalin had been alive. Had he been at all responsible for the Korean war? Had he been an obstacle to its settlement? The strange phrase, "cult of the individual," began to appear in the Soviet press. What did it mean? Who was the anonymous "individual"? To me it was obvious that the reference was to Stalin; I said so to Dennis, but he could not see it that way.

Just before Stalin died, a group of Jewish doctors had been imprisoned, charged with being part of an international "Zionist conspiracy" to poison the Soviet leaders. It was fantastic; still I accepted it as gospel truth, so firm was my faith. This had a sardonic counterpart at Atlanta when Dennis fell ill with gall bladder trouble and the prison doctors recommended an operation. His condition was becoming critical, but Dennis feared an operation by doctors who were probably not sympathetic with his politics. I advised him to go through with it and remarked sarcastically that in America surgeons were not influenced by politics in performing operations, but that if he were in the Soviet Union he might have good reason to fear, as I said, the doctors' plot demonstrated.

Dennis was shocked at my cynicism; but he went through with the operation, which turned out very successfully. As later events made clear to me, I had slandered the Jewish doctors and so had the Soviet leaders. After Stalin died the case was revealed to be a frame-up. When the doctors had first been arrested, Earl Browder had charged not only that they were being framed, but that the arrests had anti-Semitic connotations. This I had firmly refused to believe. Now I was forced to reverse myself. It was not easy.

Then Lavrenti Beria, the police chief and Stalin's right hand man, was arrested, tried in secret and executed. For once I could not swallow the stock charge that he had been an imperialist agent and spy and an enemy of socialism over the years. This, I said, I could not accept without proof. It seemed to me that political rivalries and a struggle for power were really behind Beria's execution. The fact that three successive police chiefs since 1934 had met their end this way, now filled me with dismay. Was there not something wrong with a system which, apart from the good, resulted in such horrors?

The Beria case came directly after the upheavals in East Berlin and in Czechoslovakia. While I did not doubt that anti-Soviet plotters were at work trying to undermine socialism—our Central Intelligence Agency was always boasting of its exploits—yet I could not accept this as the whole story.

Masses of workers had gone on strike and this meant the existence of deep dissatisfactions. When I coupled this with the undeniable fact of a continuous exodus of people from the Communist to the capitalist countries, often risking their lives to escape —and these were not chiefly former capitalists and landowners but ordinary people—I was forced to conclude that something was wrong in the Communist world.

Just what this was, I did not know for sure; I suspected that the Communist leaders had been pressing the people too hard in the face of the already terrible privations of the Second World War, and that they had not done enough to help ease world tensions and thus relieve the pressure upon their people.

The resignation of Georgi Malenkov as premier came as still another shock. Along with Beria's elimination, this disposed of two of the three men who had spoken over Stalin's bier. It lent credence to the reports of correspondents such as Harrison Salisbury of the *New York Times* that a fierce power struggle was raging behind the scenes in the top Soviet leadership.

I scoffed now at the reason given for Malenkov's demotion—that he lacked experience. It had also been obvious for some time that the charges by the Soviet leaders (which I dutifully echoed) that Tito was a fascist and was moving to restore capitalism, had not been borne out by the facts. Now there were several hints that the Soviet leaders were altering their former hostile attitude to Tito. All this did not make me question communism. But it shook my belief in Stalin's infallibility, in Soviet perfection. It made me eager to re-examine all policies, all ideas, everything. My mind was receptive to new ideas for the first time in many, many years.

It was in this context that I decided to read George Orwell's *1984*, which was in the prison library. There would seem to be nothing remarkable about deciding to read a book; but we had considered Orwell a Trotskyite, which meant his books were anathema, to be denounced but not read. For years I had been curious about *1984* because it had had such a profound effect on liberals and former Communists, but I could never bring myself to read it; even if I had, I would have rejected every word of it. When I first became a Communist, my mind was opened up to a vast new body of ideas, broadening my knowledge and outlook (for the works of Communist writers were largely proscribed in our capitalist America which has its own subtle forms of censorship).

But I also entered upon a closed system of thought which cut us off from large areas of human knowledge and eventually narrowed and stultified our minds. Reading Orwell did not open my eyes; rather it was the fact that events had opened my eyes and this caused me now to read Orwell. I did not like his book. I felt it to be negative and despairing of humanity. Nevertheless I had to admit that much of what he said was true; at least he was presenting an important aspect of truth, despite the faults and distortions of which I considered him guilty. I was certain that his savage picture of the danger of totalitarianism was true for capitalist society, as well as for communism. But then I had long known this about capitalism. What hurt now was the recognition that some of the evils which he depicted existed under communism.

All this self-probing was carrying me beyond a mere questioning of our former tactics and policies, and into an examination of fundamental propositions. My wife, in her visits and letters, had hinted that a sharp struggle was going on in the party leadership and that sectarianism and dogmatism were rampant. I found this hard to believe. It seemed to me that the ideas that were becoming obvious in Atlanta, must be having a similar effect on everybody but a few diehards. My constant disagreements with Dennis should have made me realize that this was not the case. While Dennis and I agreed that *we* had made many mistakes on policy, he would not admit the slightest doubt about *Soviet* policy. His absolute faith in the Soviet leaders was never shaken, whoever they happened to be at the particular moment.

These disputes were soon to be continued under happier circumstances. The day that had seemed impossibly far off when I first entered prison, came at last. On March 1, 1955, Dennis and I were released. Remaining behind us were Bob Thompson, who had been arrested in the California Sierras in 1954 and, for jumping bail, given four years in addition to his original three; Phil Frankfeld, who had been convicted in the Maryland Smith Act case; and Alexander Bittelman, convicted in the Foley Square trial of "second-string" Communist leaders.

We did not simply walk out of Atlanta, free men. Another indictment hung over us. We had already been convicted and had served time for being leaders of the party; but we had also been indicted, though not tried, for being members. This second indictment, under the membership clause of the Smith Act, still remained in force. Handcuffed, we had to spend several hours in the Atlanta federal building until bail was arranged for the second indictment. Finally the red tape was disposed of and we were free at last—to be besieged by press, radio and TV. Present to greet us were John Abt, our attorney, and Alan Max of the *Daily Worker*.

In the streets, the first thing I noticed were the little children. They seemed so tiny and delightful, like toys. I had no idea how much I had missed them, and I could not tear my eyes away. I also had a yen to see the sky at night, the moon and the stars. In the almost four years I had been in prison, we had always been sent back to our cells before dark. In a nearby restaurant, we toasted our freedom with drinks and ordered the biggest steaks available. Dennis could not get through his, so I ate his share as well—it made me sick later. When we arrived that evening by plane in New York, a large enthusiastic gathering was on hand to meet us at the airport, and there was great rejoicing. I was re-united with Lillian at last. We were driven home by friends, and Lillian had prepared a huge turkey for me which, alas, I was unable to eat.

Although we were now free, restrictions still remained upon us in addition to those of the second indictment. We had served three years and eight months of our five-year sentence; the rest of the time off was for good behavior as provided by the statutory regulations, but during this period we had to submit to parole supervision, reporting monthly to the parole office and accounting for our actions. Not permitted to return to the *Daily Worker* or to participate in other activities of the party, I went to work in a factory which printed and embossed plastic fabrics, and there I worked until Christmas 1955. The beginning of 1956 saw the end of our parole period and we now returned to our consuming interest—party activity, Dennis resuming his post as general secretary of the party, I my post as editor-in-chief of the *Daily Worker*. Just ahead lay the biggest political storm of our lives.

X

THE FIGHT THAT FAILED

THE CRISIS THAT SHOOK AND SHATTERED THE AMERICAN COMMUNIST Party did not begin with Khrushchev's secret speech on Stalin in February, 1956. This event greatly aggravated our crisis, but it had been building up for years, and would have come to a head much earlier had it not been for the Government's repression of the party. There had been serious, and increasingly irreconcilable differences, in our leadership for a long time. But a showdown had been postponed because of what we felt was the need to "close ranks" against the efforts to deprive the party of its democratic, constitutional rights.

Though I was not permitted to resume political activity for almost a year after my release from prison in March, 1956, hundreds of old friends came by the house, and it was not hard to get a fair briefing of what had happened to the party in our absence. Things were not good in the organization. In fact, they were bad. The situation in the country had changed greatly since June, 1951. The war danger was clearly receding. McCarthyism was being pushed back. The long-divided labor movement was now uniting. A new ferment gripped the South. Great, popular movements were afoot from which the American Communists were plainly quite divorced.

Our gloomy predictions of early war and inevitable fascism had been proved wrong. Obviously, we had been operating on mistaken premises for many years. As some of the party leaders returned from jail, and others from the "unavailable" status (this is what the practice of making oneself scarce to avoid persecution was called) the demand for drastic changes began to be heard on all sides. Past policies had to be re-examined, and those responsible for the miscalculations had to face the fact.

Confidence in the party's leadership had been seriously shaken. This was true, first, of our most important members and friends, those in the labor movement. Most party trade unionists had found it impossible to function as such. Those who had tried to follow party policy saw themselves defeated by workers who followed them in every other respect. The unionists were either being ousted from their positions, or else were in practice divorcing themselves from the party. They were not taking responsibility either for the making of party policy, or for carrying it out.

The California organization, second largest in the party, had long been at odds with the national leadership. This had been the only section of the party where the "unavailable" madness had not gone to such extraordinary lengths as elsewhere; the Californians had striven, and with success, to maintain the Party's legal status and to defend it ably. Their Smith Act trial had been conducted with skill. They had refused to accede to William Z. Foster's insistence that the trials must emphasize mainly the defense of Marxism-Leninism as a doctrine from A to Z; instead they had dramatized the unconstitutional and undemocratic meaning of the Smith Act.

When we returned from Atlanta in 1955, the California party was in better shape than others, and it is significant that the Smith Act cases out there were the first to be reversed by the Supreme Court.

In New York, the largest party organization, a veritable "Young Turk" movement had battled the policies of the absent state chairman, Robert Thompson; the county organizers were at the helm of this movement and they came into bitter conflict with the National Office. Much of this was reflected in the New York state

publication, *Party Voice*, very bold and refreshing compared with
the party's national magazine, *Political Affairs*. Articles appeared
here critical not only of the minority, represented by Foster and
Thompson, but of the compromises which those of us in the majority leadership had been making for years.

My wife, who was legislative director of the New York party
and well-known for her presentation of our policies at State Legislature sessions in Albany and before the New York City Council,
was one of the leaders of this "insurgent" group. I finally began
to comprehend what she had been intimating in her letters. I had
found her observations difficult to accept, since I had shared
responsibility for failing to resist the Foster grouping with suffi-
cient resoluteness and consistency.

A particular role in this crisis was played by two of the *Daily
Worker's* editors, Joseph Clark (who was our correspondent in
Moscow from 1950 to 1953) and Joseph Starobin, who had been
stationed in Paris from early 1951, and had then gone to Peking,
where he was the first American correspondent to spend a year
in the New China, and from which he also scored a "scoop" in
visiting the battlefronts of the Indo-China war on the Ho Chi
Minh side. He was the first Western correspondent to have done
so since 1946. Both of these men were party veterans, and had
held posts of confidence beyond the purely journalistic; Clark
had been a YCL organizer in Detroit, and Starobin had directed the party's peace activities in 1949–51. Each of them had
quite independently of the other reached radical conclusions
while abroad. They felt that the party had lost touch with American realities. They insisted in their letters that the international
situation was being misjudged, and they had begun to have
doubts about many Russian policies. In their view, a drastic re-
orientation away from imitations of the world Communist movement was essential, and they tried to suggest this upon their return in the summer of 1953, three years before the Khrushchev
report.

Both of them were met with suspicion and hostility by the
Foster grouping, which insisted that they remain silent. When
they refused to do so, Foster tried to oust them from the *Daily*

Worker. Starobin left the paper in protest, refused to re-register, and his relations with the party became tenuous. He had tried in his book, *Paris to Peking,* to suggest some of the things on his mind; the book was for many readers an anticipation of the crisis. Clark's memoranda on party policy became a *cause celebre* in the top leadership. Alan Max, the managing editor, and his associate, Milton Howard, refused to accede to Foster's demands that Clark be removed, feeling that his views should at least be given a hearing and not spurned out of hand.

Both Eugene Dennis and I met with these colleagues as soon as we left Atlanta. It was evident that they had been trying to say something important on the party's course and future. When Dennis and I made our political return, at a Carnegie Hall mass meeting on the *Daily Worker's* anniversary, in January 1956 (well before the Soviet XX Congress), we decided to reflect our awareness of this prevailing mood, and to foreshadow important changes. Dennis, in the main speech, drew the greatest applause, and also raised many eyebrows, when he said that the party would re-examine all its policies at the earliest opportunity including those theoretical propositions which experience had outmoded. My remarks were centered on the national significance of the struggle for democracy in the South—which had been one of my chief concentrations of study while in prison. I said that the defiance of the U.S. government by the Dixiecrat conspiracy was a threat of rebellion and constituted the chief menace to the nation.

Answering the McCarthy charge that we were "Fifth Amendment Communists," I said we were proud to be known also as "First Amendment" and "Thirteenth and Fourteenth and Fifteenth Amendment Communists"—in fact, we were "Constitutional Communists." The speech challenged the Republican Administration to enforce the Constitution, and it pledged Communist support to any government which would do so.

The speech had said nothing of the Soviet Union. Party theologians, with their keen nose for policy changes, sniffed at that, and there were suspicions about the phrase "Constitutional Communists." But both Dennis and I were determined to take the helm toward a new course, and focus on the need to root the organization in American reality.

All of this preceded the Soviet XX Congress. It also prepared us somewhat for it, although the Congress revelations came as a bombshell, and in a sense diverted us from what might have been a purely autonomous re-examination of policy. I remember remarking at a *Daily Worker* editorial board meeting that the new turn of events, this time, had not caught us entirely unawares; this time the party would not be taken by surprise. Many of my colleagues were aghast. What made me think the party was prepared? I explained that in Atlanta, ever since Stalin's death in March, 1953, we had come to the conclusions that a vast change was under way. Wasn't that obvious to every one? My co-workers disagreed. They insisted I was misreading the realities. They felt the party membership had been completely unprepared, and would be shocked and staggered. Of course, they were right and I was wrong.

Few were more shaken by the Khrushchev revelations than the *Daily Worker* staff, which had the daily responsibility of commenting on events. Alan Max spoke his mind boldly, on March 13, 1956, admitting that the Soviet Congress had jolted him: "We went overboard in defending the idea of Stalin's infallibility, in opposing any suggestion that civil liberties were not being fully respected in the Soviet Union. . . .

"Where were the present Soviet leaders during the period when they say collective leadership was lacking?" he asked. Then he broached the key question: "What about our own mistakes?"

"What do our readers think about the matter?" Max went on. The readers thought plenty. The paper received an unprecedented flood of mail, and even more unprecedented, we decided to print all the letters, regardless of viewpoint—a step which the *Daily Worker* had never taken before. The full page of letters, in our modest eight pages, soon became its liveliest and most popular feature, a permanent department entitled "Speak Your Piece." Readers spoke out as never before, pouring out the anguish of many difficult years.

It was just at this time, while the *Daily Worker* reflected this shock—with perhaps greater candor than any other Communist paper in the world—that somebody in the government chose the moment to attack it. Late in March, 1956, agents of the U.S. Treasury Department seized the premises of the paper, as well as the offices of the party itself, on the allegation of non-payment of back taxes. No notice had been given. In fact, the first bill for this so-called non-payment of taxes arrived two days after the paper had been seized. The allegation was itself fantastic, since for the past decade the paper had a deficit of $200,000 a year, made up by systematic "drives" from readers and friends.

It is still a mystery whether this fantastic assault on an American newspaper was the decision of top circles in Washington, determined to deal a body blow to the Communists as they were reeling from the shock of events abroad, or whether it was the brain-child of Donald C. Moysey, the Internal Revenue Service director of Manhattan, trying to win political promotion by his belated McCarthyism. Whoever was responsible, the move backfired. The *Daily Worker* received enormous—and free—publicity, and continued to publish from new offices, despite harassing conditions. Virtually every major newspaper denounced the seizure as a threat to the freedom of the press.

At this point, on April 2, 1956, our offices still occupied, the *Daily Worker* published an editorial regarding events in Hungary. This was the issue that would, in the next two years, dominate the battle between the diehard groups in the party leadership, and the forward-looking elements who wanted a change, and wanted to draw all the conclusions from our own history and from world events. Laszlo Rajk had been a veteran Hungarian Communist, a fighter in Spain, a leading figure in the especially cruel and difficult anti-fascist Hungarian underground. In 1949, while foreign minister, he was tried as a "spy," allegedly an agent of Marshal Tito, of Yugoslavia, and put to death. Seven years later, he was exonerated, and the Hungarian government of that time staged a garish procession in Rajk's honor, with his widow weeping at the bier, and the same government leaders who had unfairly condemned Rajk in the line of march.

Our editorial, condemning the system of frame-ups in the countries calling themselves Socialist, was unlike anything that had ever appeared in our columns. It caused a storm among our readers, and attracted world attention. Opinion in Communist ranks here was about evenly divided; some congratulated us for having saved Communist honor, and others berated us for betraying what they called "workingclass internationalism." A bitter argument developed in the paper's pages, but in those months we were still in the process of trying to present arguments and persuade each other: the irreconcilability of views had not yet crystallized.

Yet with each new revelation from abroad, the lines grew sharper. One of these was the disclosure that Yiddish-language institutions and publications had been summarily abolished in the Soviet Union in 1948—a fact which American Communists had for years denied, but which was now made public by a Communist paper in Poland. The leading Yiddish-language poets, writers and artists, those who had become so familiar to the American Jewish public during the war, had been put to death on frame-up charges. The *Daily Worker* expressed its "indignation, anger, and grief," and added its "dissatisfaction that the Soviet leaders have not offered any explanation of what took place." "What has been done to punish all those responsible?" we asked—questions which remain unanswered to this day. The Soviet government still refuses to permit the re-establishment of Yiddish language cultural institutions and publications on the spurious ground that the Jews of the Soviet Union have chosen the path of assimilation, an entirely arbitrary judgment since the Jewish people were never consulted on the matter. On the contrary, all recent visitors to the Soviet Union who have talked with Jews, report a desire to see the Yiddish language and culture continued. For centuries the Jewish question has been the acid test of the democratic-mindedness and humanity of societies and individuals; the failure on this score by the Soviet Union which rescued millions of Jews from Hitler's ovens and gas chambers, is the most shameful blot on its record. The American Communist Party knows the facts and does not dare to defend them; but its failure to protest vigorously and demand a change, reflects a moral and political bankruptcy and a lack of courage. The party has not yet learned that justice and liberty, like peace, are indivisible. Such was the atmosphere in which the party's National Committee held its first full meeting (with the absence of Robert Thompson, then in jail, and several still "unavailable") in April, 1956. It was the first such get-together in five years.

The main report by Eugene Dennis was a devastating critique of the party's policies over a whole decade. Like all reports, it was not only his own, but had been discussed and approved by the National Committee members in advance. Dennis characterized the party's policies as super-leftist and sectarian, narrow-minded and inflexible, dogmatic and unrealistic.

He singled out the crucial issue of the "war danger," and in effect, admitted that much of what the party had done since Browder's time had been based on a misreading of world and domestic realities. Though Foster's name was not mentioned, and the entire leadership was indicted, the inference was unmistakable. Dennis projected the idea of replacing the party with a "united, mass party of Socialism," whose doctrinal basis would necessarily have to be much broader than our own, and which was to be formed with many Socialist-minded Americans outside our own ranks.

Dennis carefully, and characteristically, avoided putting his finger on the basic reason for the party's failures, namely, our worshipful and imitative relationship to the Soviet Union. On the other hand, Max Weiss, the national educational director at that time, who had never been accused of undogmatic tendencies, gave the report on the XX Congress and he unmistakably concluded that our relations with the Soviet Communists had been wrong, unequal, one-sided, and harmful.

William Z. Foster was present at this decisive meeting and he vehemently opposed the reports of Dennis and Weiss. In his view, the party had been guided as well as possible, and history would vindicate his leadership. Foster was a remarkable man, a workingman who had educated himself. He had been one of America's finest labor organizers. Samuel Gompers, John L. Lewis, and Philip Murray had all paid him this tribute. The way he led the 1919 steel strike, one of the century's pioneer efforts in industrial union organization, gave many lessons to those who finally organized the mass production industries in the '30s.

The story is told (by the late John Steuben, a veteran Communist labor leader who had been close to Foster until the Hungarian events caused him to leave the party) that John L. Lewis himself once appealed to Foster to forget the Communists and devote his great talents to labor organization. But like many Americans of an earlier generation, he had developed after the Russian Revolution a fixation on all things Soviet: his common-sense realism about the American labor movement was contradicted by a romantic view that what the Russians were doing would be the "wave of the future." He saw the Russian Revolution as a model for the United States, as is plain from his volume, *Toward Soviet America*, written in 1932, although he later repudiated it.

Foster stood alone at this meeting, except for the half-hearted support of Benjamin J. Davis, the former New York councilman, who had been (with Thompson) one of the architects of the Party's debacle; Davis was the man who had said at an open-air meeting in 1949 that he "would rather be a lamppost in Moscow than president of the United States." Foster voted against the Dennis report and Davis abstained.

My own remarks at this meeting were different than any speech I had previously made. I felt it was time for the party to know of the profound differences in the leadership that had prevailed for a decade. Obviously, the Foster view was in irreconcilable opposition to the majority: it was time to let the membership know the facts honestly. Others spoke in a similar vein. Yet the opportunity was missed, and once again the facts were concealed from the membership. No doubt, this contributed greatly to the loss of confidence in the ranks, which almost immediately afterward began to thin out.

At this same meeting, I had a curious but revealing exchange with Foster. I had spoken of his many monumental works that had been eulogized by party leaders, but none of us had bothered to find why so few Americans read these books, and why they had so little influence; too often, they had simply been dumped on the lower party organizations, but were not read or sold. Someone chided me for being rude to so old a man, with so venerable a record. I went over and said I hoped he realized there was nothing personal in this criticism. To which he replied, most genially, that he was not the least bothered by it.

"Why," he exclaimed. "My books have been translated all over the world . . . into Russian, into Chinese, and many other languages." I was struck by Foster's complete divorce from interest in America. It did not seem to matter that few Americans were influenced by his work, so long as foreign Communists held him in high repute, or so he believed. He saw himself a world figure. He lived in a make-believe world of his own, and though more typically "American" than most party leaders, he was also strangely remote from his own land and people.

During this same meeting, the party's National Committee received another jolt: a letter from a friend in Britain was read which we learned later was a résumé of the secret Khrushchev report on the Stalin era. Until then this document had simply been rumored, and many thought the rumors were unfounded. Now we had the essence of the text from an unimpeachable source. One speaker after another expressed shock, and drew the obvious conclusions that our relations with the Soviet Communists had been unsound, and our grasp of the real Soviet problems very poor. I said that I could no longer consider myself a Stalinist nor accept the nice balance some tried to strike between the good and bad things Stalin did. I compared it to the case of a man who had been a fine person most of his life and loved his family but in the last years of his life murdered his wife, his children and his neighbors—such a man was a murderer and whatever else he might have done could not change that fact. I asked how we could have been so blind, since it was now clear that many people knew the truth which we had refused to believe even though for the past three years there had been many indications of the facts about Stalin. The answer, I went on, was that our philosophy of Marxism had become a closed system for us instead of the philosophy of change it was supposed to be, that we were victims of a narrow exclusivism and considered ourselves to be the sole guardians of the truth. We had developed a contempt for the views of people not in agreement with us and this insulated our minds against whatever we did not wish to hear. We had ceased to think and develop; the monolithic character of the communist movement had come to mean that whatever Stalin said became our policy. What was Marxism-Leninism? I asked, and answered that it was whatever Stalin said it was. We had to learn to think for ourselves and to make a critical assimilation of all the best thought of mankind, whether Communist, non-Communist or anti-Communist, or remain blind to essential aspects of reality.

There was no respite that spring and summer. In June, 1956, the State Department released the full text of Khrushchev's secret speech about Stalin. What had hitherto been newspaper reports, although the truth was fully known to the party leadership, was now a public document. The bitter truth was out, and there was no escaping it. As usual, the party leadership, under general secretary Eugene Dennis, was hesitant and indecisive—and silent. But the *Daily Worker* would not evade immediate comment. Its editorial the following day, and in the days thereafter, did not mince words in expressing the drastic conclusions which we drew from the revelations, not only of Soviet realities, but of our own imitations of Soviet policy.

We decided to print the text of the Khrushchev speech, despite opposition within the party councils, and the *Daily Worker* became the only Communist paper in the world to do so. We had decided at least in this respect to break with the make-believe pattern of the past. The pretense that news was only what the party press published, and that if a news event remained unreported, it had somehow never happened, had to be ended. It seemed fantastic to us not to publish such an important speech by the leading figure in the world communist movement, but this is exactly what the Soviet Union did. Khrushchev said at the end of his speech: "We cannot let this matter get out of the party, especially not to the press. It is for this reason that we are considering it here at a closed Congress session. We should know the limits; we should not give ammunition to the enemy; we should not wash our dirty linen before their eyes." I know many American Communists who curse Khrushchev to this day for "washing our dirty linen" before the eyes of the enemy. It was not Khrushchev's speech that did the damage, however, but the crimes of the Soviet leaders headed by Stalin, and the effort at continued concealment even though correction was begun, only compounded the harm. This concealment prevented the full exposure and elimination of the evil; it laid the basis for the subsequent retreat by the Soviet leaders and the upheavals in Poland and Hungary.

To be sure, our purpose in publishing the speech was to strengthen Socialism whereas the State Department hoped to weaken Socialism. That William Z. Foster and his cohorts would oppose us in the party's national committee was no surprise. But now Dennis joined with them. At this point, I handed in my resignation as editor-in-chief on the grounds that if I did not enjoy the National Committee's confidence, I could no longer edit the paper. I wished to be free to take my views to the membership. The party's leadership was fearful of the consequences of so open a clarification of the issues, and refused to accept this resignation. I withdrew it, and the paper continued to speak its mind as the majority of the editors saw the issues.

There was one phrase in Khrushchev's speech which made a deep impression, the one in which he interrupted his own recounting of the Stalin era with the remark: "We cannot say that these were the deeds of a giddy despot. He (Stalin) considered that this should be done in the interest of the Party, of the working masses, in the name of the defense of the revolution's gains. In this lies the whole tragedy!"

Here was the nub of the matter. Stalin was no madman, and his crimes could not be placed solely on his own shoulders. His co-workers had been at fault, too, in fact the party itself. Irresistibly I was led to feel that the system which he expressed and which had evolved in the Soviet Union had some deep, generic faults within it.

Murray Kempton has written, in his *Part of Our Time*, that "the Communists offer one precious, fatal boon: they take away the sense of sin." It is a perceptive insight. Communism, as the Russians have shaped it, recognizes only one sin—failure to serve the party absolutely and blindly. All else is justified in this name, and that is how crimes are committed which fail to be considered crimes. When I try to trace what happened to the wonderful idealism, the zeal and enthusiasm of my early years, I think it was this subtle, gradual, almost unnoticed change: our original ideal was to serve the people, and this had been transmuted into the idea that we must serve the party, which has been equated with the people as its leader and vanguard. But what happens when a party becomes remote from a people? What happens when men within this party strive to make it master, instead of servant of the people?

That summer of 1956 many of us still felt that we could change our own organization. Thousands of members were already leaving, among them many prominent figures.* But at that time, the leadership still held firm, and it was decided to convene a na-

---

* One of those most shaken was Howard Fast, the only literary figure of note left in the Communist Party. He was a controversial figure not only in the country generally but in the party too. A fabulously successful author before becoming known as a Communist, he had been boycotted for his political beliefs. In the Communist movement he was both idolized and cordially disliked. His forte was the popular historical novel, although he was not noted for his depth of characterization or historical scholarship. Fast had made money but he had also lost it because of his adherence to his principles, and he had gone to jail for his beliefs. Fast had stuck out his neck more than most; he had received the Stalin Prize and defended everything Communist and attacked everything capitalist in the most extravagant terms. It was to be expected that he would react to the Khrushchev revelations in a highly emotional manner, and I know of no one who went through a greater moral anguish and torture.

I told Dennis and other party leaders of Fast's deep personal crisis and implored them to talk to him, but outside of some of us on the *Daily Worker*, not a single party leader thought it important enough to talk to the one writer of national, even world-wide, reputation still in the party. Later when he announced his withdrawal and told his story, party leaders leaped on him like a pack of wolves and began that particular brand of character assassination which the Communist movement has always reserved for defectors from its ranks.

Fast's book, *The Naked God*, contains considerable truth, but it suffers from his weakness of portraying people as either good guys or bad guys. I am far from the angel he depicts and the others are not quite the devils he makes them out. The reality is more subtle, complex and contradictory. But the *Daily Worker*, to its credit, never joined in the torrent of abuse from the Left that was heaped on Fast. His reaction to his Communist experience has been highly charged with emotion, but not without cause. At the very least, as a man who had given his whole life and career to communism, Fast deserves more understanding and compassion from the Left.

tional convention for February, 1957; this would be the first convention in more than six years. In accordance with the Party's custom, a document was prepared, entitled the "Draft Resolution." It was meant to provide the basis for discussion, and embodied the ideas expressed in the Dennis report to the National Committee meeting the previous April. Members were invited to debate the issues in a special pre-convention discussion bulletin, and in the pages of *Political Affairs;* this discussion more or less supplanted the free-for-all which had been the feature of the *Daily Worker's* pages all that spring and summer.

Published in September, 1956, the Draft Resolution was in many ways a most remarkable document. It went further than the Dennis report in saying that "the roots of the Party's errors were not to be found in the events of the past ten years alone." Here lay the admission, for the first time in the party's entire history, that its mistakes were not merely current, and not simply tactical, such as all political movements inevitably make. Our problems were more fundamental and basic. It dated back to the party's inception forty years earlier.

The resolution said that the party had suffered from a "doctrinaire acceptance and mechanical application" of many of the ideas of Marx and Lenin and had to "free itself from deeply ingrained habits of dogmatism and doctrinairism." It went on to say that the party bases itself on Marxist-Leninist principles but added the key phrase "as interpreted by the Communist Party of our country," which was inserted to make clear that henceforth we would interpret Marxist theory for ourselves instead of accepting the interpretations Marxists abroad had made for us, as we had done throughout our whole history. The resolution said further that we "must extract from the rich body of this theory that which is universally valid . . . must distinguish better between the additions to Marxist theory made by Lenin which are valid for all countries and those specific aspects of Lenin's writings which reflect exclusively certain unique features of the Russian revolution or of Soviet society . . . will have to be bolder in re-examining certain Marxist-Leninist theories which, while valid in a past period, may have become outdated and rendered obso-

lete by new historical developments . . . we as well as other
Marxist parties have already discarded as obsolete Lenin's thesis
that war is inevitable under imperialism. We have long since rejected as incorrect Stalin's thesis of the alleged law of inevitable
violent proletarian revolution . . . we are making important
modifications in the theory of the state, as evidenced in our advocacy of the peaceful, constitutional path to socialism . . .
Creative Marxism is impossible without the ceaseless re-examination and reappraisal of theory in the light of ever-changing
reality."

Stating that the party "formulates its policies independently"
and "is not subject to any external allegiance or discipline either
of an organizational or political character," the resolution added
that over the years the party "held certain wrong and oversimpli-
fied concepts of what its relations should be to other Marxist
parties . . . tended to accept uncritically many views of Marxists
of other countries. Not all these views were correct; some did not
correspond to American conditions . . . [the party] also viewed
uncritically developments in the Soviet Union and other Socialist
countries . . . mistakenly thought that any public criticism of the
views or policies of the Marxist parties of these countries would
weaken the bonds of international workingclass solidarity or bring
comfort to the enemies of peace and socialism." We were therefore "entirely unprepared for, and deeply shocked by the admis-
sions of crimes, violations of socialist justice, mistreatment of
certain national minorities, and the basis for the rupture of relations with Yugoslavia—all at variance with the truly liberating
character of socialism." The correction of these wrong relations
with foreign Marxists "requires the equality and independence of
Marxist parties in the mutual discussion and resolution of common problems; the right and duty of the Communists of all countries to engage in comradely criticism of the policies and practices
of the Communists of any country whenever they feel this necessary. This will strengthen, not weaken, international solidarity. It
will advance the cause of socialism in all countries."

The resolution went on to say that "Bureaucratic concepts of
Party organization, systems of leadership and relations between

the Party and the masses have been a prime factor in contributing to our errors . . . hindered the early and timely correction . . . discouraged full and free participation of the membership in the discussion of policy . . . contributed to the weakening of inner party democracy . . . resulted in departure from the very procedures established by our own constitution . . . resulted in disciplinary actions which further inhibited expressions of disagreement." The resolution attributed this in part to our "mechanical application of certain principles of organization adopted by other Communist parties which functioned under different historical conditions." This was a reference to Lenin's organizational principles of democratic centralism and monolithic unity under which all Communist parties operate. The resolution called for "guarantees of real inner-party democracy through provision of channels for freedom of discussion, dissent and criticism within the framework of carrying out the majority will." And it said that "in the past we tended to assume that all that was worth while in other socialist currents and groupings would inevitably flow into our own organization. This assumption was always incorrect and should be replaced by serious and painstaking efforts to assist in the eventual development of the broadest possible unity of all socialist-minded elements."

Whether any other Communist movement had ever produced so devastating a self-examination I cannot say, but certainly no American political party had ever done so, the American Communist Party included. William Z. Foster was furious with this document, although at first he voted for it, with qualifications, a short time later changing his vote to outright opposition. In private, he declared that "the resolution has Gates written all over it."* This was not true, since the Draft Resolution was the prod-

* The movement for change in the Communist Party in 1956 and 1957 was a great human upheaval involving thousands of people, who wrote thousands of letters and articles and made innumerable speeches. It was not an organized movement but was largely spontaneous. Contrary to popular belief there was no organized Gates faction. I was connected with a trend of thinking which for several reasons came to bear my name. I was the most prominent representative of this trend, and the newspapers used my name as a convenient shorthand means of identification. Foster and the Soviet Communist press made me the main target, and this increased my prominence

uct of many hands, and the fact that many of my views were incorporated in this resolution simply reflected the reality that almost the entire leadership was of much the same mind as I was, and the same went for a good part of the membership. Dennis confined himself to amendments and qualifying phrases, to which he always attached such importance. He was ever on the lookout for escape-clauses from straightforwardness.

The discussion on the Draft Resolution gave everyone a chance to clarify their thinking, and put matters down black on white. Foster did so in an article for the October, 1956, *Political Affairs* in which his reservations about the Draft Resolution and his opposition to change became very plain. One phrase in his illuminating article revealed how pathetic the party had become under his leadership. He spoke of the need to "Americanize our Party," and this provided me with the jumping-off point for my own discussion article in the November, 1956, *Political Affairs*.

I spoke of this phrase as "the most damning indictment of our Party that could possibly be made. Way back in the 1880's, Engels used to entreat the German Marxists who had migrated to America to Americanize themselves, to learn the language and customs, and become part of the mainstream of the labor movement, and to apply Marxism to America creatively and not dogmatically. For us now, after 38 years of existence as an American Party, made up of Americans most of whom were born here and have no problems of language or customs, to have to admit that we must still Americanize ourselves, reveals our situation better than anything I could possibly say . . . Foster has hit upon, involuntarily perhaps, what I believe to be the heart of our problem. This tragic situation cannot be cured by a few patches here and there as we have been doing for many years. It can only be solved by drastic and basic changes."

in the United States. Actually, I was less the leader of the movement than a reflection of it. Of the 17,000 Communists who were still members in January 1956, 10,000 of them quit the party before I did. I did not lead them out, *they* led *me*. This book does not do justice to the contributions of hundreds, even thousands, to the important struggle that took place. Nor does it attempt to list the scores of state and national leaders who played a prominent part in the struggle.

My article was entitled: "Time For a Change."

The article focused on the new situation which began with the victory over fascism in 1945. "The existence of a bloc of socialist countries which is beginning to equal and will in the course of the next decades surpass the capitalist world in material strength, the growing power of the neutralist bloc, and the phenomenal growth of the labor and socialist movements in the capitalist countries, have brought about a power equilibrium which makes possible and practical the prevention of a new world war for the first time in history," I wrote. The new era was not a static one, I went on. It was marked by the continuation of the arms race "which has led to a temporary stalemate, an uneasy truce, and unstable peace." However, the emphasis in the new era was "already beginning to shift away from arms to economic and political competition." The essence of the struggle for peaceful coexistence, I continued, was to "transform the present unstable peace into a lasting one."

The new era was having "profound repercussions on our domestic scene," I wrote. Here there had also been significant changes, with the growth and unification of the labor movement and the Negro people's movement. A return to the catastrophic economic situation such as developed in 1929 was not likely, I said, because the labor movement is not inclined to be the "helpless victims if and when a depression comes" again.

The long period of peaceful coexistence would be marked by great evolutionary changes, by the coming of socialism "through the constantly successful struggle for peace, prosperity and democracy." In America, this road lay through the uniting of the people against the monopolies. While the conditions for peace provided the most favorable climate for popular progress, this would not come about "automatically or out of the goodness of the heart of capitalism; nothing can or will be achieved without struggle against Big Business."

To help effect these changes necessitated "sweeping changes in our party"; in fact, we must build a "party of a new type," I said. The party could not follow the concept which was originally geared "to a revolutionary situation, or the expectation of the rapid development of one." It could not be patterned on a party which had been built in conditions of Czarist illegality and which had been dedicated to violent revolution, but must be a "fully democratic party" that is "legal and solidly based on American reality and will be recognized and accepted by American workers as their own."

To build this kind of party, I went on, required several major changes:

The first of these was with regard to theory. We claimed to be scientific socialists. But science "is a living and not a dead thing." Science that failed to develop "loses touch with reality and ceases to become a correct guide to action." I objected to the use of the term Marxism-Leninism because "if anyone asks me whether I base myself on the principles of Marx and Lenin, I want to be able to answer which of those principles I believe in and which I do not." I also said that the term Marxism-Leninism lent itself to distortion, since the giving of the names of people to a science, even though they were "unquestioned geniuses," inevitably limited that science. To limit science "to the discoveries of any particular individual will automatically restrict its development and transform it into a lifeless dogma." Marx and Lenin "founded and brilliantly developed scientific socialism," I went on, and "it is correct in that sense to identify the science with their names, but it is also necessary to see that the science must develop and inevitably go much further than its original founders . . ." The issue was to determine what remained valid of the doctrines of Marx and Lenin, what was no longer valid or needed to be modified, or what may never have been valid. "This is a life and death necessity for us and we can accomplish it only by ceasing to regard Marxism-Leninism as something sacred, holy and inviolate." Marx himself once exclaimed, I recalled, that he was "not a Marxist."

The second change which was needed, I wrote, was in our attitude toward the Soviet Union. We had been right in recognizing the "historic role of the USSR in blazing the trail for socialism and in transforming the world situation to where lasting peace is now possible." We had been right in defending the Soviet Union as the first socialist country against its enemies who wished to overthrow it by force and our action "proved to be in the best patriotic interests of our country." However, this attitude became transformed into the concept of "Soviet infallibility" and "the idea that the Soviet Union was the only possible model for other countries." This was bound to have fatal consequences, not only because it blinded us to terrible mistakes and crimes in the Soviet Union, but it also prevented us from basing ourselves on American reality. "We Americans must guarantee that American socialism will be fully democratic socialism," I said. "We will be able to achieve that, partly as a result of the pioneering efforts and enormous sacrifices of the Soviet Union and the other socialist countries, partly because we will be on guard against repeating the mistakes of the Soviet Union if we master all the lessons, and especially because of our own more favorable circumstances and historical traditions." I had learned, I wrote, that the expansion of democracy is not automatic under socialism but must be fought for. "Socialism creates the material conditions for the fullest expansion of democracy . . . but it must be built just as socialist economy must be. Violations of democracy are not inherent in socialism but on the contrary come into conflict with it . . . but we also know now that neither is it inherent in socialism that democracy cannot be suppressed, restricted and violated. Better controls by the people over their leaders and institutions must be devised than up until now in order to make impossible any future violations of democracy."

The third big change which we must make, I wrote, was to build "a different kind of party." "To make our contribution to the achievement of the broadest type of American socialist democracy superior in every respect to our present democracy," I went on, "requires the most democratic kind of Communist Party." The present concept of the party "may have been necessary for a period in which war was inevitable and peaceful, constitutional transition [to socialism] impossible, but this is no longer the case." I said we must take a "new look at the concept of democratic centralism" which seems to result in a "semi-military type of organization." Our experience, I said, had been that there was always a tendency for this to become transformed into "maximum centralization and minimum democracy." Whether this was inherent in the concept, I said I did not know, but "the essential thing at this time is to make the party fully democratic from top to bottom." All organizations needed a certain degree of centralization, I went on, or they would cease to be organizations. But centralization must be subordinated to democratic functioning. Certainly we "must have majority rule" over our leaders and policies but we "must guarantee the right of dissent after policy has been adopted and while it is being carried out."

I declared further that we were not "a political party as the American people understand it." Political parties in America were electoral organizations primarily, I said, and "we must admit we are not that today if we are honest with ourselves." Rather we were a political pressure group, trying to influence the main political trends in the country. In keeping with the more modest role that we actually played, we should stop calling ourselves a party, I said, and become a political action association. This would "facilitate the improvement of our relations with the labor movement and other people's organizations, help to legalize our status, and enable us to play a more influential role in the affairs of the nation." I also recommended that the name of the party be changed, not with any illusions that such a change would automatically solve our problems, "but it will dramatize to the American people that our party is making profound and genuine changes." Whatever changes in name and form, and whether we were prepared to make them at the coming convention or later, "we must be a socialist working-class organization which bases itself on scientific socialism, participates in and strives to give leadership in the new ways required by the present situation to the immediate struggles of the people, and to educate for socialism on the basis of those struggles."

At the height of this discussion, while we were preparing for the February, 1957 convention, the Polish and Hungarian events rocked the entire Communist world. It seared the souls of Communists everywhere such as no single event had done. And in the United States, what had been a discussion until then now became a bitter factional battle which was to continue without let-up for the next year.

The revolutionary change in Poland, to the everlasting credit of the Polish leaders, took a positive form. Instead of replying to the strikers in Poznan with repression, the Polish government recognized that only by deep changes in their own practices could they gain the confidence of their own people and conserve what was good and durable in their building of Socialism. A train of events ensued which brought to power Wladislaw Gomulka, a veteran Communist who had stood almost alone in defying the Stalinist policies both within his own country and abroad. Fortunately, the Soviet leaders realized in time that in clashing with the Polish national revolution, they could not budge Gomulka and would turn all Poland against them.

In Hungary, the opposite thing happened. Instead of avoiding the use of force against the people, as in the Polish instance, Soviet leaders intervened in the situation on two different occasions, turning the country against them while the world stood aghast.

A stormy meeting of the American Communist Party's National officers convened just after the first Soviet intervention on October 25. Among others, I indicated my dismay and opposition to the Soviet Union's action with great heat and passion, exclaiming: "For the first time in my life, I am ashamed of being a Communist!" Many of my colleagues were shocked at this statement. Foster, who was present, denounced me as a Trotskyist, so far was he from comprehending the impact of these events not only on myself but on millions of Communists and their sympathizers. When I asked him whether he favored the shooting down of workers by a Socialist power, he had no reply.

In later weeks, he came up with the answer that the Soviet intervention had been a grim necessity. Grim it was, but was it necessary? Was it really true that the Soviet leadership could find no way of satisfying the demands of the Hungarian people and yet of keeping them as members of the Communist bloc except by brute force? Could what was happening in Hungary be explained simply by "imperialist intervention"—when every fact of history and politics pointed to the mistaken course of the

Hungarian Communists, under Soviet tutelage, as the underlying reason?

When the Soviet Union intervened for the second time, the *Daily Worker* took its stand, despite the protest of most of the party leaders. In our issue of November 5, 1957, we editorialized on the Soviet action of November 4 as follows: "The action of the Soviet troops in Hungary does not advance but retards the development of socialism because socialism cannot be imposed on a country by force; it does not help but damages the relations between socialist states; it does not strengthen but weakens the influence of the Soviet Union itself which has been playing a major role toward ending the cold war and establishing peaceful co-existence. It does not combat but plays into the hands of the hypocritical reactionaries . . . What is taking place in Hungary has two sources . . . First, there were the grave distortions of socialist principles introduced by the Soviet Communist leadership and the Rakosi group in Hungary. The second source was the continuous attempt by reactionaries in Hungary, openly supported and encouraged by Washington, to overthrow socialism. When Nagy unilaterally ended the Warsaw Pact—which came into being as an answer to NATO—and sought a condemnation of the Soviet Union in the UN, he opened up his country to right-wing reaction . . . Nagy's weakness in dealing with the resurgent reaction, sprang, in our opinion, primarily from the past Stalinist errors of both Soviet and Hungarian Communists . . . The use of force by the Soviet troops in Hungary will bring no lasting solution to that country's problems. That is why we support the Hungarian masses who sought to solve their own problems as they were settled in Poland, without violence, without foreign troop intervention and without allowing the supporters of the old fascist regime to regain power."

Reactionaries here, through radio programs beamed at Hungary, had given people there the false impression that we would give military assistance to an armed revolt, which was impossible unless we wanted to precipitate a world war. Instead of empty propaganda denunciations in the United Nations, we should have declared to the Soviet Union our readiness to negotiate a mutual

withdrawal of foreign troops from Europe. Unless we were prepared to make corresponding withdrawals of our troops from
Europe, it was completely unrealistic to expect that the Soviet
Union would withdraw theirs. As we said in our editorial: "The
withdrawal of all foreign troops throughout the world to their own
soil would open the way to solution of the most knotty problems
of world politics . . ."

That the role of the United States government—responsible for
years of intrigue, propaganda, and refusal to negotiate a settlement—was a factor in the Hungarian events, who will really deny?
No one can be proud of that role. But those of us who had been
brought up to seek out the deeper meaning of historical events, to
treat history as a science, and above all to tell the truth in politics
even when it hurt to do so, could not be satisfied with the "cops
and robbers" and "cloak and dagger" interpretation being placed
by official Communism on the Hungarian tragedy. Here lay the
parting of ways between tens of thousands of American party
members and the organization to which they had given so self-
sacrificingly. In the top leadership, the die had also been cast,
even if we did not all recognize it at the time. Until the Hungarian upheaval, the fight for a changed American Communist
movement had been gaining ground, despite opposition from the
Old Guard and despite the indecisiveness of many middle-of-the-
roaders. After that, the tide changed.

The *Daily Worker's* editorial expressed itself clearly enough—it
was the only Communist paper in the world to denounce the
Soviet action. But despite the strong stand of the *Daily Worker*,
many quit the party because the actions of the Soviet Union spoke
much louder than our brave words.

The National Committee which met immediately after the
events was so badly divided that it could only issue an "Open
Letter" to the membership, criticizing the first Soviet intervention as a mistake, and agreeing neither to "reject nor condone"
the second. The national convention, some months later, did not
even touch the issue, because the disagreement continued.

If the Hungarian issue was the dividing line in the party's
struggle, as far as the political content of two different policies

were concerned, it is also true that after Hungary, the form and tone of the battle changed. It became much harder to argue anything on its merits. Serious discussion soon degenerated into the exchange of epithets. Invective and abuse replaced reason. Foster was particularly adept at this sort of thing, and in the course of that autumn and winter, 1956, a partial list of what he called me would go as follows: "right-winger, Social-Democrat, reformist, Browderite, peoples' capitalist, Trotskyist, Titoite, Stracheyite, revisionist, anti-Leninist, anti-party element, liquidationist, white chauvinist, national Communist, American exceptionalist, Lovestoneite, Bernsteinist. . . ."

At one point, he was about to brand me "imperialist agent" but others persuaded him this was going too far and would boomerang against him. Of course, this atmosphere was not entirely of Foster's own doing. Other party leaders refused to condemn these methods, despite appeals from many quarters. Probably the worst moment of all came at the New York State convention, prior to the National Convention, when one veteran woman Communist, whose hard work I had known and respected for two decades, got up to say: "I loved the Johnny Gates who fought in Spain against Franco, but I hate the Johnny Gates who has taken the same position on Hungary as Franco."

Such was the result of several decades of mis-educating people. By the same logic, this person might have denounced the Soviet Union for having the same position on the Suez affair as Franco! How could people remain together in the same movement when the mutual regard we had once had for each other now turned to hate? Foster's methods succeeded, no doubt, in destroying the confidence of half the party's membership in me, but by the same token these same methods killed the confidence which the other half had felt in him. In this way, the prestige and authority of the entire leadership was being destroyed.

By the time the February, 1957 Convention opened, the party's membership had greatly changed, and the entire proceedings had a certain unreality. Thousands of members had left us in the preceding six months, and those who remained were not only few in number but were the least capable of change. Yet most of the leadership of that time, apart from Foster, Davis and Dennis, was still trying to make as much of a change as possible. I shared in this effort, hoping that somehow by a proper set of resolutions and decisions, and perhaps by changes in personnel, a new orientation, and a revival of the party was possible. I still disagreed with many friends—such different people as Johnny Steuben, Howard Fast, and Joseph Starobin—each of whom in their different ways had come to the conclusion some time before that this party could not be regenerated, and would have to be abandoned.

When the newspapers described the 16th National Convention as achieving a "declaration of independence from Moscow," and a "victory for Gates," they were right as far as the letter of the resolutions went. Not only had Foster made a major speech at the convention, attacking the Draft Resolution, but Jacques Duclos, the French Communist leader, once again (as 12 years before) intervened with a letter to the Convention attacking its main document as " revisionist."

Despite these attacks the Draft Resolution was adopted with minor amendments. Taken by themselves, the Resolution adopted and the new constitution were remarkable; if they could have taken on flesh and breathed life into the organization, they would have produced a much different kind of party from what we had known. But the reality was that the members had left us, and our resolutions were to remain words. The acid test lay in the selection of new leaders. A program without men and women to implement it is worthless. A bold, new program required bold, new leaders, and this would have meant the forthright removal of the old Foster-Dennis leadership, and the selection of those who were most closely identified with the new course which the convention had adopted.

The convention achieved a typical compromise. The issue was skirted by the elimination of the posts of chairman and general secretary. Foster and Dennis were not re-elected to these posts, which were abolished; and this was in a sense a rebuke to them; on the other hand, neither were the opponents of these discredited leaders allowed to try their hand at running the organization.

Virtually the same national leadership as before was re-elected. This assured the continuation of the stalemate that had existed for a decade, and doomed the new program in advance.

After February, 1957, the situation deteriorated rapidly. Members who had stayed around for the convention now decided they had had enough. The exodus received a further push when the New York State convention elected Benjamin J. Davis as chairman. His name had become anathema to thousands of those active men and women who had watched him and his associates run a powerful movement to the ground. The Foster forces refused to accept the verdict of the convention, and immediately began to try to undo it. The resolution on the form of party organization had been a compromise; the party as such was to be continued, but proposals to change the party to a political association had been ruled in order, and were tabled for further debate. Such a debate was never permitted to take place. Foster now demanded that all those who had favored a political action association prior to the convention had to be proscribed.

There was one moment in March, 1957, when I was under considerable attack from three directions. The presidents of the New York city colleges had refused to let me speak before student groups, and at the same time, the House Committee on Un-American Activities chose to haul me before it, although it was investigating a matter with which I had not the remotest connection. At that very point, Foster and Davis moved to oust me as editor-in-chief of the *Daily Worker*. I found myself in one single week trying to be heard before new audiences on behalf of the party's new program, while at the same time defying the House Committee, and fending off the attack on the party's policies from within its own top echelons. Many leaders by this time were closer to Foster's views than mine. But they feared the consequences of ousting the paper's editor who had become identified in the public mind as the protagonist of a new and independent course.

All of this was soon to come to a head in a somewhat oblique way. The first move was an effort to hamstring the paper by assigning to it Jack Stachel, an old-timer. Stachel was an expert at defending publicly policies which he said privately he did not believe in. Another was the appointment of Simon W. Gerson as executive editor. Their initial objective was to get rid of Joseph Clark, who had remained in the party despite the buffeting of all these years, and who said what he thought on international issues, even if it pained the most theological of the paper's readers. The attack on Clark was, of course, a way of getting at me.

This issue came to a climax at the July 27, 1957 meeting of the National Committee. Here, a major effort was made to remove Clark. To my way of thinking, Clark's writings were an exercise of his right to dissenting views, which the recent National Convention had guaranteed to every member. No one on the paper was trying to censor Foster's articles, and I felt that Clark should write what he pleased, even when his editors disagreed with him. Clark was under fire, obviously enough, because he spoke his mind on some of the Soviet Union's policies, which were in growing retreat from the spirit of Geneva, and from the liberalization of the XX Congress; all this was still taboo in the party despite the national Convention's decision that Soviet policies should no longer be accepted blindly and without discussion.

The real issue was not Clark's journalistic heresies, but whether the party was serious about implementing its own Convention decisions. Our failure to do so would only enable our opponents to argue, I said, that the "convention was a phoney, which is what J. Edgar Hoover says it was, that we did not mean what we said, that we're not really independent, that it was only a façade, to pull the wool over the eyes of the American public."

The atmosphere of the debates can be gleaned from an exchange between myself and the party's Indiana organizer, a particularly scholastic leader, Emanuel Blum. He had remarked that "William Z. Foster had saved the party twice, once from Browder and now from Gates." My reply was that in "saving the party from Browder in 1945, we went down from a membership of 75,000 to 17,000. Now that Foster has saved the party from Gates, we are down from 17,000 to 10,000. . . . The more we 'save the party,' the more it is disappearing."

I continued, "People are leaving the party, but the only thing that some of us think should be done is to tighten the screws. They aren't leaving fast enough, so drive them out! Let us devote some time to trying to keep people in," I appealed. "Let's not be so quick to write people off. If a comrade presents views we think wrong, let us argue them. Convince and persuade people— it's more difficult than chopping their heads off, which is easy. That's the easiest thing we've been able to do in our own party, and in the world Communist movement. We're very good head-choppers, but we haven't proved to be so good when it comes to persuasion."

The aforementioned Blum had stated that any advocate of a "political association" rather than a party was serving the cause of imperialism. I replied: "This is the way you talk to enemies, not to comrades. I find no basis for comradeship with people like Blum."

"We have serious differences here," I argued "but they are differences on how best to advance the fight against imperialism. Let us not divide the Party into those who are for imperialism, and those who are against imperialism. We had enough of that in the pre-Convention discussion, and it's time we put an end to it. How can I feel at home in an organization when I am called pro-fascist or pro-imperialist, and where the National Committee takes no public position in the matter?"

The motion to oust Clark was defeated, largely because the party's leadership did not want my resignation at that moment. The epilogue to this affair—which had literally preoccupied the party's discussions that entire summer of 1957—was a curious one, but it also illuminated the underlying issues. Having found his political life on the paper and in the party so miserable, Clark finally resigned, in September 1957, after 30 years of service. I published his letter of resignation, which was sharply critical of the party's course, and this act was itself unprecedented in party annals. Our practice had always been never to let a man explain why he was leaving our ranks, but to make the fact public in the form of our own denunciation. The party leaders were angry, and attempted to prevent Clark's letter from appearing. But it did appear, followed by my own statement taking issue with his resignation, but acknowledging that the intolerable atmosphere was one of the causes for Clark's resignation. I added that if the growing drive within the party to reverse the Convention's decision went unanswered, it would destroy the organization.

At the *Daily Worker*, we did another unprecedented thing: we gave Clark a farewell party. Our political differences were clear, but we wished to demonstrate that we were parting as friends, not enemies. We wanted to symbolize the kind of Socialist movement we hoped some day to build. Every member of the staff attended, including those who differed with Clark most sharply. The only exception was George Morris, our labor editor—embittered and vindictive, and unable to face the fact that the American labor movement had not heeded the advice he had given it for thirty years. The news of this farewell was included in my statement on Clark, and caused a storm. Elizabeth Gurley Flynn scolded me later. It was all right, she said, to have had the affair but very wrong to publicize it. . . .

Our meetings became interminable in that autumn, and their atmosphere grew more tense, more personal, more vindictive. At one of them, Bob Thompson (who was now out of jail) attacked the executive secretary of the New York state organization, George Blake Charney, challenging his "Hamlet-like doubts about the future of the party."

It was unfortunate, I replied, that people like Charney and myself could not always be as sure and decisive about everything as Thompson had been. But where had this brought him? When Thompson took over the New York organization in 1945, it had enjoyed considerable influence in the New York labor and political scene which was now completely gone. Perhaps we would have been better off if Thompson had had just a few doubts about the correctness of his policies. "Where doubt ends, stupidity begins," I reminded Thompson. But he had never bothered to read that wise old philosopher, Montaigne.

Another sore point, and an increasingly serious one, was the way foreign Communists persisted in misinforming their own public about the affairs of the American party. This was true of the Russians and the French, in particular. Foster's speech at the

Convention, for example, had been presented as though its policies had been adopted; in fact, it was a minority speech in opposition to the majority's policies. But few Russians or French Communists would know that from what they read. When Alan Max, our managing editor, wrote several articles in the *Daily Worker* quoting the record, and setting it straight, the party leadership would not back him up. It was refusing to defend its own program.

The official Soviet theoretical magazine, *Kommunist,* published a long article by one Ponomarev, shamelessly distorting my article in the pre-Convention discussion, "Time for a Change." Ponomarev said, for example, that I had wished to transform the American party into a debating society. I had said the exact opposite. His quotations were simply inventions. I proposed that the party make a public correction of these falsifications. This was refused. James Jackson, a Negro leader of the party (who had done courageous work in the South) put the matter in a nutshell when he said that we had no right to criticize the Soviet Communists—had they not just launched the Sputnik into the skies? When we had such an achievement under our belts, Jackson continued, then perhaps we would have the right to criticize the Russians.

Here was the essence of our tragedy, and our failure. The American Communist movement was not a conspiracy; it was a mental attitude, entirely voluntary, even subconscious. Our attitude had been: "The Soviet Union, right or wrong." I was now proposing a decisive qualification: "When right, to be kept right; when wrong, to be set right." But the counsel of Carl Schurz, a great American of Lincoln's day, was too much for most party leaders.

Late in November, 1957, the Ford Forum, a long-established group in Boston, invited me to defend the Communist viewpoint on the same platform with Granville Hicks, the distinguished literary critic who years before had left the movement following the Soviet-German non-aggression pact. It was an important occasion, with more than 1,000 people in attendance. In the course of my remarks, I said that "as an American I wanted to see my country take the initiative in halting the H-Bomb tests, and gain for itself the moral credit of such a step; as a Communist, I wanted to see the Soviet Union take that initiative; as a human being, interested in the preservation of the species, I wanted both countries to agree to the simultaneous cessation of tests. . . ."

Back in New York, I discovered that these remarks had created another storm, though party leaders in Boston had found them effective. Benjamin Davis asked by what right I was suggesting that the Soviet Union take the initiative in ceasing bomb tests (though half a year later it did just that!) and above all, I was criticized for implying that any distinction could be made between being a Communist and being an American! I realized that in such an atmosphere, my days in the party were numbered.

Two events decided my course. The first was the 12-Party statement at the Moscow celebration of the 40th anniversary of the Russian Revolution; it had been signed by leaders of all the Communist states, except for Yugoslavia. In content, it was a clear retreat to the rigid and dogmatic days of the unlamented Cominform. To make matters worse, Thompson, Dennis and Davis now insisted that the American Communists must endorse this declaration—despite the fact that it had been evidently restricted to those states in which the Communists held power. The purpose was to establish a new loyalty test by which to judge party members. It was an attempt to drag the party itself, by now almost a corpse, backwards to oblivion.

The second event was the decision to suspend the *Daily Worker*. This paper had survived as a daily for 34 years, and had written an important page in American journalism; it had outlived many an earlier financial crisis, and could do so again. The latest crisis had made the paper's situation worse than it had ever been. It was reduced in size to four tabloid pages and our staff and expenses were cut almost in half. The paper's circulation had gone down to 5,000 daily and 10,000 on Sunday due to the losses in party membership but also because of Foster's crusade to discredit the paper. For a time, when the paper was speaking out boldly, we had achieved a spontaneous increase in circulation. But after we began to be muzzled we lost the support of those who wanted us to speak out as we had done previously, and we continued to meet with hostility from the conservative trend in the party. The National Executive Committee of the party on December 22, 1957, voted to recommend the immediate suspension of the *Daily Worker*, to be replaced by a weekly. I voted against it and wrote an appeal to the full National Committee.

I considered this decision to be the "most fateful" and the "most harmful action" ever taken by the party, that the "country at large would consider that with the ending of the *Daily Worker*, the party, too, was ceasing to exist for all practical purposes."

I went on to say that "I do not consider the death of the *Daily Worker* inevitable . . . Substantial funds which would help to meet the paper's emergency are being deliberately withheld by a minority of comrades who are in effect waging a political strike against the program of the last Convention, against the majority of the national leadership and against the paper whose policy is in accord with that of the leadership. The national leadership must come to grips with this attempt to choke the *Daily Worker*. It must smash the boycott. The national leadership must face the fact squarely that the *Daily Worker* is not dying a natural death. It is being murdered.

"The paper is being destroyed by a small group of willful and reckless comrades in the leadership who never believed in the 16th convention program in the first place and have done everything possible to reverse it. This group has been led by Comrades Foster and Davis and in recent weeks have been joined by Comrade Dennis . . . Throughout the 34 years of its existence, the *Daily Worker* has withstood the attacks of Big Business, the McCarthyites and other reactionaries. It has taken a drive from within the party—conceived in blind factionalism and dogmatism —to do what our foes have never been able to accomplish. The party leadership must once and for all repudiate the Foster thesis, defend the paper and its political line, and seek to unite the entire party behind the paper. It must reiterate the policy of the 16th Convention with its placing of dogmatism and sectarianism as the main danger and with its call for a new course in the party's theoretical and organizational work. The national leadership must openly repudiate the opponents of the convention program."

If this is done, I concluded, "it will not be too late to save the *Daily Worker,* to save the program of the 16th National Convention, and consequently, to save the Communist Party itself for a useful and vital role in American life."

A mail vote of the National Committee was taken and the decision to suspend the *Daily Worker* was upheld overwhelmingly. This was the end of the road. The endorsement of the 12-party declaration meant that the party had returned to the same old stand that had proved so fatal in the past. The end of the *Daily Worker* in the manner it was being accomplished meant that the party did not even believe in the program it had adopted. Such a party did not deserve to live. The party really decided to commit suicide. The last issue of the *Daily Worker* was to appear on January 13, 1958, 34 years to the day since it was born. The suspension of the *Daily Worker* was the final dramatic proof of a situation that had existed for some time, that the Communist Party of the United States has ceased to exist for all practical purposes. It may persist for a time like other radical sects in American history.

On New Year's Eve, 1957, I attended an office party at the national headquarters of the Party and told Elizabeth Gurley Flynn that when the *Daily Worker* went, I would go with it. The following Monday I was called in by Dennis and other leaders of the party and asked whether it was true I was going to leave the party. I said "Probably." I was then asked "when," and I replied I would let them know when I was ready. They then passed a motion to remove me from all posts. I told them mildly that they ought to examine the new party Constitution which stated that any member of the party could resign without prejudice, and that their action was obviously unconstitutional. [I walked out of the meeting after I had the pleasure of telling everyone present that "I have the utmost contempt for every one of you, the same contempt you have shown for the party's program and constitution."]

That was Monday, January 6. Time was running out. The evening of Thursday the 9th I wrote my letter of resignation after discussing it with my wife. She had long known of my feelings and was impatient for me to draw my conclusions. I called up Si Gerson, the executive editor of the paper, informed him I had written my letter of resignation, and was calling a press conference at the Hotel Albert the following day to inform the public. I invited him to cover it for the *Daily Worker*. He said he was sorry about my decision, that he would not cover the event himself but would send another reporter. I then called Sid Stein, at that time the national secretary of party organization, read him my letter, told him about the press conference, and then I went out to mail the letter.

It read as follows: "I hereby submit my resignation from membership in the Communist Party of the United States, effective immediately. I have come to this decision, after 27 years in the Communist movement, because I feel that the Communist Party has ceased to be an effective force for democracy, peace and socialism in the United States. The isolation and decline of the Communist Party have long been apparent. I had hoped, as a result of the struggle that has been going on in the party for the last two years, that the party could be radically transformed. The program adopted by the last National Convention gave some promise that this might happen. Not only has this program never been carried out, it has been betrayed. I have come to the reluctant conclusion that the party cannot be changed from within and that the fight to do so is hopeless. The same ideals that attracted me to socialism still motivate me. I do not believe it is possible any longer to serve those ideals within the Communist Party. Obviously, under these circumstances, my continued employment as editor-in-chief of the *Daily Worker* and the *Worker* will no longer be desirable to you. Consequently, my function as such ceases as of this moment."

It had taken me only a few minutes to write this letter. How many thousands had taken this step, without writing letters! How unthinkable it had seemed to us when we joined! Yet how inescapably events had left no other course.

XI

THE END IS A NEW BEGINNING

I AM NO LONGER A COMMUNIST, BUT I AM CONVINCED THAT AMERI-
can life needs an effective and courageous radicalism. To be a
radical means to go to the "root" of things, and our country in
this third quarter of the century faces problems that cannot be
solved without getting to their roots.

Two years ago, I felt the shame of being a Communist when
a Socialist power in whom we had all placed such confidence
found no other way of rectifying its own mistakes except by the
threat of armed intervention in Poland and by full-scale warfare
in Hungary. As these lines are written comes the senseless "liqui-
dation" of the ill-fated Hungarian premier, Imre Nagy, and his
associates. Obviously, the crisis of communism has deeper roots
than the individual idiosyncrasies of a Stalin. These were exposed
by his own comrades-in-arms, who have since made some changes,
yet some of the terrible deeds for which he alone was blamed are
being repeated by his successors, and blindly applauded by Communists the world over. There is something wrong in this system.
It is the system which produces the individual, not the other way
round.

Tens of thousands of us left the American Communist Party,

which we had built and defended many long years, because its leaders insisted on imitating a political party built on semi-military lines, and conceived in conditions of illegal struggle against Czarism. I once believed that the "dictatorship of the proletariat" was only a synonym for a workers' and farmers' government, which would engage in building a socialist democracy.

This was a naive view. The "dictatorship of the proletariat" has turned out to be a very special kind of government, in truth a dictatorship and not a democracy, the rule of the few over the many, and not the rule of the people at all. It is based on the total monopoly of the Communist Party, itself dictatorially operated, over the minds and actions of men. This easily becomes socialist despotism.

Yet it is not unmitigated evil. Many Americans who never saw anything good in the Soviet Union while American Communists could see nothing bad, are now learning to their surprise of great strides there in science, education, culture and industry. These extraordinary results flow from an economic system that has abolished the private ownership of the means of production and made possible socialist planning. There are some socialists who maintain that the lack of democracy in the Soviet Union means that socialism does not exist there, but such a view, I believe, is mere semantics. There can be no doubt that capitalism has been abolished in the Communist countries. What is true is that socialism is incomplete and distorted in the Communist countries. It remains to be fulfilled.

The American Communist Party has failed, and has disintegrated. Less than 5,000 members remain, of whom no more than a third pay dues, and few carry on meaningful activities. The average age level is past 50, and for a decade there has been no recruitment of young people or new members. All of which contrasts with the 75,000 members at the close of the World War, apart from 20,000 young Communists, and it contrasts also with at least the 17,000 members when the party's crisis broke open in 1956. But all other socialist groups and parties in America have also failed. Their membership is negligible and their influence insignificant.

The reasons for the Communist failure are evident, and this book has to some degree tried to explain it. But why the lack of success of the other Socialist-minded Americans? They have surely been anti-Communist and anti-Soviet, but this has not helped them, either. They cannot compete with non-socialists on this ground alone. The Communists were dazzled by the Soviet Union to the point of blindness, but other socialists were blinded by their own hatreds.

A successful American radicalism, which is needed in this country and is yet to be built, will have to be a native one, and its chief reason for existence will not be an obsession of one kind or another with the Soviet Union.

Despite their fatal attitude toward the Soviet Union (which, at times, was even an asset) the American Communists came closer to being a successful radicalism than any other. It was because, at their heyday, they had understood better than other socialists that American radicalism has to be identified and integrated with the great popular movements of our people. It is true, as many have pointed out, that the objective realities of American life— the relative prosperity and democracy—have hindered the growth of the Socialist idea. But of itself, this does not explain our general failure. American life *does* need basic changes and there have always been plenty of problems requiring radical solutions, even in "good times."

In my view, many socialists have not understood, or have forgotten, that there is no basis for a socialist party—in the sense of an electoral party—so long as the labor movement does not accept socialist ideas, and supports candidates of the two major parties. Where socialist parties have competed for votes with labor-backed candidates of the major parties, the labor movement has inevitably looked upon this as a threat from the Left which played into the hands of reaction on the Right. This in turn has served to isolate socialists from the labor movement and even to make socialist ideas suspect. Socialists must find it possible to play a role in the present-day political activities of the labor movement and from that vantage point seek to exercise influence.

American socialists need to find their own forms of organization in order to develop socialist ideas and activities. But these forms need to be developed always with an eye to making it easier for socialists to be part of the broader labor and peoples' movements, rather than to become ever more isolated. Socialists who ignore this, or are content to preach to the workers from the outside of their ranks, or think the real situation can be by-passed, are doomed to futility and impotence. Their efforts, no matter how heroic or well-intentioned, can amount to no more than a cry in the wilderness.

The mountain is not going to Mohammed. Socialists will have to learn to be loyal parts of the existing movements, and help the people in them to learn by their own experience that Socialism is the ultimate solution, if indeed experience shows that it is. The present socialist groups have been so concerned with preserving their distinct character that they have become virtually extinct. The socialist success of the future depends on the ability to find common ground with the actual currents in the country. Only in this way can these be helped to genuine advance and influence. American Labor is bound to move to new levels of political action, and leadership in the nation, but only in the way it wishes to, and not necessarily in the way impatient socialists may propose.

I continue to believe in Socialism, but I do not propose to go from one sectarianism to another. The answer to the present splintering of the Left is not to form still another splinter, later to divide again like an amoeba. Nor would the unification of all existing socialist groups, desirable as that might be, provide the solution. If that were possible (which I doubt), all of them combined would still constitute only an infinitesimal force in American politics. The problem would still remain of working out a fruitful and effective relationship with the great currents of political and intellectual opinion.

Let me make myself as clear as I can on this point. I know there are a good many people of socialist views who feel strongly that socialist tickets are the urgent need of the hour. I respect the desires of these people, and do not doubt their intentions, nor their devotion to what they believe. There may be times and places in which a "protest" candidate can galvanize activity, and sometimes a group or a committee, even if undertaken by a small number, can exercise a great educational influence. But I cannot agree that this is the main problem in reviving a Left. Even if all these activities had a certain success, it would still leave the big problems unsolved. For the big problem remains how men and women of the Left can influence that much larger, more decisive group which is the existing labor movement, the existing Negro people's movement, the existing democratic current. In the face of this outstanding problem, the worst thing a socialist can do today is to be irrelevant.

Socialists have defined radicalism in too narrow terms, and like the Communists they have insisted that the game be played on their terms, or no dice. If radicalism were confined only to those who believe in socialism, then its future would be bleak indeed. But I can see an inherent radicalism in many phases of American life: it wells up in our churches; it is latent in the Negro people; it cries out from the protest of our scientists; it is present in all walks of life where men and women realize that the "rat-race" of their daily lives must be replaced by something more sensible, more humane, more creative.

If radicalism is conceived of as a Left-wing in the whole of American life, comprising the most forward-looking people in the existing popular movements, then it will be seen to have a substantial mass base. I think that there are key ideas which unite liberals, progressives, and socialists and these provide the basis for a modern radicalism: they are the ideas of peace with all peoples and the use of our resources for development and growth; they are the ideas of social control, public regulation, and a curb on the profit motive wherever it hurts the human being; they are the ideal of a moral and personal regeneration on the basis of participation in something bigger than oneself, for the sake of others as well as oneself; they are the ideals of brotherhood and fruitful work of hand and brain which come to us from the whole of the democratic and radical tradition.

I do not call myself today a socialist, without qualification. Bitter experience has taught us to specify that we mean *democratic socialism*. It is necessary to distinguish what we have in mind from what has been attempted in the Communist countries, i.e., public ownership without political democracy. The assumption that the abolition of private ownership of industry would automatically usher in a higher type of democracy than exists in any capitalist country has not been proven.

Democracy will have to be fought for, guarded, expanded, and never taken for granted. Eternal vigilance is the price of liberty for socialism as it was foreseen to be crucial to capitalist democracy by the Founding Fathers. The "liberty and justice for all" in our Pledge of Allegiance is the goal that remains to be achieved under socialism just as it has not been achieved under capitalism.

When the Soviet Union was newly-born, economically-backward and surrounded by more powerful enemies, bent on its destruction, there was perhaps some justification for restrictions on democracy (though not for the crimes committed). But what justifications are there for such restrictions when the Soviet Union has become so powerful as to rival the United States? Is there any excuse any longer for failing to move toward a full and ample democracy, with government responsive to the people, and with the people making a choice between alternative policies, and being guaranteed the mechanisms to choose alternative leaders? How can this be done, if not by freedom of thought and speech and press, and rich, self-confident debate? The idea of Mao Tse-tung to "let all schools of thought contend, let a hundred flowers bloom" remains a good one, and needs to be universalized, as well as applied in China itself. So long as only one school can contend, there will be dogma. And if only one flower can bloom, there will never be gardens.

War is surely no solution either for the evils of capitalism or of communism. I am just as much opposed to the violent overthrow of the Communist governments as I have been, and remain, to the violent overthrow of the United States government, if for no other reason than the fact that either would precipitate world war. Only one solution is possible today. That is the evolution of both the capitalist and the communist societies to better ones. This evolution is bound to go toward the socialization of capitalism, and the democratization of communism. In both cases, this will constitute a revolutionary transformation, and it will be the outcome of a prolonged, turbulent, but essentially peaceful struggle. The common task of all humanity, whatever its views on particulars, is to create the most favorable world atmosphere for this evolution, an atmosphere in which our mutual fears are reduced, and in which the recourse to war as an instrument of national policy is banned. In such an atmosphere, the competition of the two societies can only be beneficial to their mutual progress, each learning from the other and adapting what is best in the other. Such an atmosphere will create the best conditions for the expansion of freedom at home, and abroad in the Communist lands.

I did not quit the American Communist Party in order to embrace the ideas of John Foster Dulles, or to enlist in the cold war. For what we have to do, as a matter of defending the nation's security, is to end the cold war. The longer it continues, the worse off the country is. For the first time in history, Man possesses the capacity to destroy mankind. War is no longer the continuation of politics, as Clausewitz once said, but the end of politics, and of everything. It is no longer possible to choose war as a calculated risk. The risk is incalculable. Everything human contains some risk. But the one risk we can no longer afford is that of war.

The explosion of H-bombs, with their deadly, universal radiation, will not distinguish between Khrushchev or Eisenhower, between capitalists or communists. Both the United States and the Soviet Union now possess several times the amount of atomic weapons which could destroy civilization. What, then, is the point of continuing this arms race? The obvious thing to do is the one that has not been tried, which is to cease the H-bomb tests, arrange the simultaneous withdrawal of all troops from all lands foreign to them, and progressively reduce the stockpiles of both atomic and conventional weapons, under a system of inspections supervised by the United Nations.

Politics has been defined as "the art of the possible." John Foster Dulles has developed a foreign policy which can only be considered as the "art of the impossible." The job of a secretary of state is above all to protect the country's interests by the preservation of peace. This requires "total diplomacy" directed toward securing an agreement with the Russians and the Chinese—the two principal factors in the opposing coalition. Negotiations cannot be successful, and agreements cannot be achieved, on our own terms. Neither the Russians nor the Chinese can be treated as vanquished, when in fact they are our equals. We can neither accede to settlements on their terms, nor expect they will do so on ours. There is a world-wide stalemate of power, and "unconditional surrender" cannot resolve it. Agreement is impossible unless it is based on self-interest of both, and only as this takes place can there be mutual trust.

This has not been the Eisenhower-Dulles approach, and here lies the root of its failure. Our German policy is perhaps the prime example, and underlies all other difficulties. Who, in his right mind, can expect that the Russians, devastated twice in a lifetime by the Germans and today more powerful than the Germans, will ever agree to unifying that country on the basis of a unified Germany becoming part of the NATO alliance, equipped with atomic weapons?

Yet this is the premise and goal of our policy. The only rational conclusion to be drawn from it is that either we do not want a united Germany at all, or that we do not want a general European settlement. For what is the point of talking about encouraging trends toward the independence of eastern European countries when the re-arming of western Germany, with atomic weapons, clearly makes such independence impossible? Fear of a militarized Germany is more powerful in all parts of Europe than fear of the Russians. The failure to act on this truth puts the whole world under a pall of fear.

Our Far Eastern policy, in particular the refusal to recognize that a new China exists, is another example. Asia, like the Middle East, is traversing a vast revolution, but instead of associating with this revolutionary change and seeking those non-ideological points on which the common interest of settlement and accommodation can be found, we cling to Chiang Kai-shek and Syngman Rhee. In the Middle East, where a revolution of similar proportions is under way, we refuse to acknowledge either the aspirations of the peoples concerned, or the legitimate interest of the

Russians who border on this region. In Latin America where the social and political problems are not too far different from those of the Arab world, we disregard the democratic strivings of the people and prejudice their economic sovereignty. Then we are surprised and indignant when the President's envoy and possible successor faces anti-American demonstrations.

We are losing ground to the Soviet Union, not because its policy is so superior to ours, but because ours is so appallingly bad that theirs is made to look wise and good by comparison. The foreign policy of Mr. Dulles is a failure, a source of ridicule and danger. It will prove to be fatal, so long as it is based on the futile, negative effort to "roll back" communism, refusing to recognize the revolutionary character of the age, and obsessed by military strength rather than the bold economic and social measures, in harmony with this revolutionary age, which are needed. Mr. Dulles has been losing friends and alienating people. What is needed is a policy which makes friends and wins people. This will require not only his retirement to private life, but a drastic re-orientation of outlook which only a new political combination of forces can bring into being.

I did not, of course, quit the American Communist Party to discover the virtues of capitalism as a system. The fallacy and irrationality of this system has again been demonstrated by the current recession, the twenty-fifth in four times that many years. Periodic recessions are undoubtedly the law of capitalism, but it is not a divine law, no more than the "divine right of kings" was once thought to be. It is difficult to believe that this system represents Man's highest skill in the management of economic affairs, since at least one-fifth of the nation is poorly-fed, badly-housed, not well clothed, and most of mankind lives in abject poverty.

The root of this irrationality lies in the production of goods, sold only for the profit of the few, and not for the use of the many. When production fails to be profitable to the few, it ceases, regardless of the great human needs.

The United States of America has achieved an economy of abundance for the first time in human history. All previous societies have been economies of scarcity. Marx and Engels, the founders of modern communism, thought this could never be attained under capitalism, only in a socialist society. This is not to say that sizable islands of poverty and suffering still do not exist in our society. The fact that they exist despite an economy of abundance is both an indictment and a challenge. Economists like J. K. Galbraith are coming to the conclusion that the fallacy of our economic system lies in the fact that production is an end in itself unrelated to social and human needs. Marx pointed out a hundred years ago that the essence of capitalism is production for the sake of production. This is the result not of greed on the part of individual capitalists who may be more or less rapacious, but of the nature of the system which is based on private ownership of the means of production and the profit motive. Capitalist production must be profitable to survive, and to make profits it must expand endlessly. Production, to be placed on a rational basis, must have a social rather than a private motive; in other words goods and services must be produced not according to whether they are profitable, but whether they are needed.

It has become axiomatic that as the steel and auto industries go, so goes the nation. But the steel and auto industries are owned and controlled by a few men who make all the decisions. The whole country is affected by what a few men decide, the fate of our economy is determined by them, and the nation has no say in the matter. When industries and businesses become so big that the destiny of the nation is dependent on their status, then it seems to me that the public which is vitally interested and affected must also have a say in the matter. The profit motive of the few inevitably comes into conflict with the social needs of the many. Eventually, I think, the facilities for production will have to be socially owned and operated as the most rational and efficient way of relating production to the satisfaction of human wants rather than the private profits of the few. Socialism does not necessarily mean total state ownership, which is both unnecessary and undesirable, and not conducive to democratic functioning. It seems to me that giant industries and vital services that are nationwide in scope like steel and communications should be state-owned and operated, big enterprises on a local scale probably co-operatively owned, and I see no reason why small businesses, farms and services should not continue to be privately owned. Socialism can be said to have been established when the element of social ownership, in both its state and co-operative property forms, becomes dominant in the national economy. The evolution toward that goal, which will constitute a gigantic revolution when consummated, lies along the path of an increasing degree of public regulation and control over privately owned Big Business. The essence of democracy is the control by the majority of the people over their leaders; there is no reason why that should not apply as much to economic production as to political life. Indeed, it is a necessity if democracy is to survive and expand.

A quarter of a century has passed since the laissez-faire economic policy of Herbert Hoover proved so disastrous and was rejected by the American people. The New Deal established the principle that government must act in times of economic distress and a Full Employment Act was passed in 1946. But the Eisenhower administration seems to be following the same policy of inaction as characterized the Hoover regime of an earlier day, relying on the same bankrupt philosophy that Big Business will solve the situation by its own efforts. If ever an administration unashamedly represented the policies of Big Business, it is the Eisenhower administration, and its complete reliance on the wisdom of Big Business has brought us into this mess. Continued reliance there will probably get us in deeper or if it does get us out eventually, it will only be after much needless cost and suffering. We need an administration too that is motivated by social needs more than by profit needs, that will put human rights ahead of property rights.

The ultimate insanity, the most dangerous feature of our society, is its reliance upon increased arms production as a cure for the recession and the main prop for the economy. If capitalism cannot be harnessed to the goals of peace and cannot achieve economic stability without massive preparations for war, then nothing can justify its continued existence. There is no doubt that the fear of economic collapse is one of the chief obstacles to coming to agreement on disarmament and disengagement. That is why disarmament and disengagement must be combined with a positive economic program to replace the swollen armaments factor in our economy. There are abundant needs to satisfy at home and abroad, at least as vital to our security as armaments, to keep our economy humming and expanding for an indefinite future. Our cities, housing, educational system, health facilities are either deteriorating or lagging far behind our growth in population. We need to build housing, schools, hospitals, roads, parks, irrigation systems, and power facilities on a vast scale. We need to refurbish our transportation systems. We need to overhaul and improve and extend our unemployment and social security benefits.

As automation and technological advances become more widespread, we will need to reduce the length of our work-day and work-week, and to expand recreational, cultural, educational, entertainment and servicing facilities in order to make the most meaningful use of our additional leisure time. On an international level there is the enormous market potential provided by the great majority of mankind that still lives in the most terrible poverty. We must get over the archaic and fallacious notion that helping to industrialize the underdeveloped countries will threaten our own industries. Our best customers are the most advanced countries, western Europe, Canada, Australia, etc. We need to remove the innumerable barriers that block the great expansion of international trade. Helping to raise the standard of living of the world's population will create a tremendous new and unlimited market. All this is known, there is no secret about any aspect of such a program, but it is not being done because it runs counter to the traditional narrow outlook of the private interests that produce for profit.

I did not quit the Communist Party to embrace the Un-American Committee.

About a month after my departure, the House Committee on Un-American Activities subpoenaed me and I appeared before it in executive session. I refused to answer any questions about my political views before or after I quit the party on the grounds that Congress had no constitutional rights to pry into political beliefs.

If that was all they were interested in, I offered to sell them a copy of my pamphlet "Why I Quit the Communist Party," a compilation of my articles in the *New York Post*. They would not buy it. I stood on the First and Fifth Amendments to the Constitution and told the Committee I would use every amendment in the Bill of Rights if necessary, that the Founding Fathers had added the Bill of Rights to the Constitution to protect Americans from political inquisitions such as this Committee. When the committee asked me what ideas I had to offer on curbing subversive activities, I advised the Un-American Committee to go out of business, saying it had proved to be a greater menace to American liberties than the Communist Party had ever been. At this point Rep. Scherer of Ohio jumped up and exclaimed "That proves you are still a Communist!" and demanded that I be cited for contempt. This same Congressman said at a meeting sponsored by Aware, Inc., some weeks later that the Communist Party had a fifth column behind it of 25 million Americans. He evidently arrived at that figure by totaling the approximate number of Americans who had voted the Democratic ticket in the previous presidential election. Rep. Scherer, of course, is a Republican.

The Communists call me a traitor to the cause but the extreme Right insists I am still a Communist. It reminds me of the old *Daily Worker* cartoon of a cop beating a man over the head with his club at a demonstration. The man is protesting "But officer, I am an anti-Communist." The cop replies "I don't care what kind of Communist you are," and continues to beat him over the head.

My prediction that J. Edgar Hoover and various congressional committees would claim the Communist Party was now stronger than ever, was confirmed almost immediately. Indeed, this is the main thesis of Hoover's latest book, *Masters of Deceit*. He reaches the curious conclusion that the fewer members, the stronger and more dangerous the Communist Party becomes. By this standard, the high point of the menace of the Communist Party will come when it ceases to exist altogether. Many people must wonder whether the billions of dollars lavished by Congress on the FBI to combat communism were worthwhile if after 40 years of ceaseless FBI activity, the Party is more powerful than ever. Actually, the Communist Party of the United States has dwindled almost to the vanishing point and this alarms the FBI and certain other legislative committees whose main business has been built around the idea of a growing American Communist menace. There's no more gold in them thar red hills.

The most significant feature of the party's decline is the kind of people who have left in the last two years. These were not the Johnny-come-latelys or people on the fringes of the movement but the tried and tested cadre of the party. They went through every twist and turn of policy, veterans of 25 years standing who had dedicated their entire lives and made every conceivable sacrifice, in short, people whom the FBI called the "hard core" of the party. The fact that such people quit is proof that they were never like the picture that was painted of them but were sincere adherents of an ideal. They left because of fundamental reasons—what they once thought the party stood for could no longer be squared with reality.

The major disintegration of the party took place when the wave of McCarthyism was receding and not when it was at its height, once again proving that the most effective answer to Communism is more and not less democracy. I do not have the slightest intention of devoting myself to the destruction of the little that is left of the Communist Party because I consider there are far more important and meaningful things to do. Besides the present leaders of the party are doing a good job of driving people out; they do not require assistance from me or anyone else. I dwell on this because the myth of alleged Communist Party strength is still being perpetuated by extreme reactionaries who fear to lose a weapon against progressive and liberal causes.

Although I have profound disagreements with the Communist Party and consider that it has outlived whatever usefulness it may once have had, I am unalterably opposed to any efforts to deprive it of its constitutional rights. To do that would endanger the rights of all of us. The way to preserve democracy is to practice it, not to destroy or undermine it by thought-control laws like the Smith and McCarran Acts. Our country has rightly protested the imprisonment of Djilas in Yugoslavia and the murder of Nagy and

Maleter in Hungary. We would be on much higher moral ground in demanding justice in these cases if we also became indignant over the tortures and murders in Algeria, Cyprus, etc., but especially if the last remaining men in prison for their ideas in our own country were freed,* if laws proscribing men for their ideas were repealed or declared unconstitutional, and if witch-hunting legislative committees were abolished.

The crisis in education has broken on us with great impact. Forced into the open by the Sputniks which dramatized the enormous advances the Soviet Union has made in science, technology and education, it has nevertheless been long in the making. The causes lie deep in the values of a society which holds the making of money to be more important than the making of better men and women. A business-minded society can hardly inspire either young people or their teachers to the idealism and devotion to truth which the scientific age demands. In the long run, science is bound to revolt against making the means of destroying mankind when its true function is to liberate mankind. In fact, it is already doing so. Military obsessions and secrecy mania have succeeded neither in keeping ahead of our rivals nor in keeping scientific advances secret from anyone but ourselves. McCarthyism and the drive to conformity have only impeded the development of our own science and culture. The quest for knowledge cannot best be served by the aims and ways of business society; that is why the Eisenhower administration, spokesman for Big Business, cannot really do what has to be done to re-educate America for the space age.

The principle of public regulation of certain industries is not new in American history. Congress and state legislatures have established commissions to represent the public interest in such matters as the rates and fares charged by public utilities and carriers.. These are recognized public services which operate through governmental franchise. The principle is a valid one and needs to be extended to wider areas of industry, but above all it needs to be enforced where it already exists. The Federal Com-

---

* Gil Green and Henry Winston, convicted with me in 1949, are still in jail, serving out 8-year prison terms.

munications Commission is in the news these days with charges of favoritism. The problem of the regulatory agencies is that they come to be staffed by people who tend to represent the people they are supposed to regulate more than the public whose interests they are sworn to uphold. This is because essentially we have Big Business government as a result of which the public gets the short end of the stick. The reality of American politics is that the lobbies of the powerful private interests exercise far greater influence over the actions of the federal and state governments than the people in general. A prerequisite for significant economic and social progress is a new political advance and realignment that can bring about a more representative government than now exists.

Formidable obstacles block the path to political progress. A GOP-Dixiecrat coalition which represents the interests of a tiny but very influential minority of Americans, dominates the Congress and prevents the passage of overdue social legislation in education, housing, health. This situation exists largely because, first, we still do not possess universal suffrage, and, secondly, the suffrage which we have won is distorted by an unrepresentative and undemocratic method of apportionment. Our country was born in a revolutionary struggle which established that taxation without representation is tyranny; we fought a great Civil War as a result of which chattel slavery was abolished and the Constitution amended to give the right to vote to all regardless of race, creed or color. The right of universal suffrage has been established in law and property qualifications and discrimination against women have been abolished; nevertheless a significant section of our citizenry is deprived of the franchise. Our democratic revolution has still not been completed and tyranny still stalks the land. Negroes are no longer chattel slaves but new bonds of oppression and second-class citizenship have been fastened on them. At the root lies the unconstitutional, undemocratic and immoral denial of the right to vote to a majority of Negroes in the South, and as a consequence to millions of Southern white citizens as well. This is achieved by a combination of legalistic subterfuges and naked violence. The result is that the blocs of Southerners in Congress and in Southern state legislatures are elected by a minority of the citizenry and are generally reactionary-minded. A man like East-land could not possibly be elected to the U.S. Senate if all the people of Mississippi were allowed to vote. These Southern re-actionaries consequently enjoy almost a life tenure and, through the seniority rule in Congress, come to exercise dominant posi-tions in the committees of Congress and a power far out of pro-portion to what they really represent.

The system of apportionment on the basis of which we elect our representatives to state and federal governmental bodies came into being when the United States was still in the horse-and-buggy era and we were still a rural nation. Today when we are a great industrial power, the majority of Americans live in cities and only a small minority is engaged in agriculture, the system is weighted in favor of rural areas. Our urban population is grossly under-represented by an archaic, grotesque, undemocratic set-up. This results in a stranglehold of reactionary Republicans over many state legislatures and of reactionary Democrats over the legisla-tures in the South.

Limitations on the franchise and unrepresentative apportion-ment are the unfulfilled tasks of our American democratic revolu-tion. They have become the chief roadblocks to American eco-nomic, social and political progress. Genuine representative and popular government requires the elimination of these major ob-stacles to democratic advance.

We may be on the threshold of a new popular upheaval such as produced the New Deal. The 1960 elections may usher in a new era as did the 1932 elections. The trend now, as then, is away from Big Business government. But the coming to power of men like Lyndon Johnson and Speaker Rayburn would be no solution, only a shift from Republican to Democratic conservatism. What is re-quired is a *new* New Deal, a program that will go beyond the New Deal, for the situation is more advanced today than in the Nineteen Thirties and requires more advanced solutions. The original New Deal was led by liberal capitalists and the social forces that backed it were the small businessmen and farmers, the labor movement and the Negro people. Labor was still relatively weak and un-influential but its right to organize was won under the New Deal and industrial unions were established in the mass-production industries. The Negro people, too, began to organize and to make themselves felt as a force in American life. This represented a significant advance for labor and the Negro people but they were too weak as yet to play a major role in government. The situation is different now. Labor and the Negroes are far better organized, and this time could play a far more influential role in a new coalition government, although not yet dominant. The New Deal established the principle of government responsibility and intervention to ensure the well-being of the nation. The new New Deal will have to guarantee the genuine enforcement of this principle which today exists largely on paper and is more honored in the breach than in the observance, and will go beyond it by establishing the principle of social control of production, of public regulation of Big Business, and will put the social motive ahead of the profit motive. This will not yet be socialism, for industry will still be privately owned, but the owners will no longer have a total monopoly on the making of decisions vital to the nation and will have to share that power with the new government and the public. This will not come about easily, no more than the first New Deal did, but only through great popular struggles and conflicts.

The kind of mass popular party that will evolve in our country will probably be similar to the British Labor Party, which is a coalition party of trade unions, cooperatives, the professional and white collar classes and small businessmen. It will not, of course, be exactly like it; for example, it will not be socialist in program (although neither was the Labor Party at the outset). It is not excluded that the Democratic Party can be transformed into such a party through the elimination of the Dixiecrats and the more influential role of the trade unions, Negro organizations, scientists, educators in the affairs of the Party. If this cannot be done, then the Democratic Party will inevitably burst asunder and a new party will be formed.

These are some of the ideas—as I have touched on them in the preceding pages—that I have been thinking about, and speaking about in the last two or three years. Some of them date from the time that the fight was being conducted within the Communist Party; others have become clearer since I left the organization. They do not represent a fully-formed "system." But they are coherent elements in a re-appraisal of the problems which confront thousands of others, as they do myself.

What have I been doing since last January, 1958 when my withdrawal from the Party was announced at a press conference at the Hotel Albert, in New York? Many friends, and just curious bystanders, have asked that question. What are my plans? is another question, and one that is not easily answered. But I can sum it up in the same phrase I used in the original press announcement, namely, I have been trying to "rejoin the American people."

More fruitful, more stimulating, more exciting than perhaps any other experience—including writing for the *New York Post,* or appearing on the Mike Wallace program—has been the privilege of making contact with much younger people, mostly in the American colleges and universities.

The audiences have ranged throughout the country: at the University of Wisconsin (both the Milwaukee and Madison branches); the University of Michigan, the Harvard Law School Forum, Phillips Exeter Academy, the University of Chicago, Roosevelt College, Swarthmore, Bard, C.C.N.Y. (which might have been my Alma Mater), Brooklyn and Hunter, Southern Methodist and Baylor. There have been meetings of another kind, too—at the American Friends Service Committee high school student seminar in Washington, and a Liberal Party chapter in New York. Some meetings have been small, some averaging 400 to 500 students, and in many cases, members of the faculty have been present.

Probably the most remarkable experience of all was in Texas, my wife's home state, at Southern Methodist University, in Dallas on April 23, 1958. I had been invited there by the Student Council Forum, as one result of the Mike Wallace broadcast. As usually happens, the reactionaries overreached themselves and brought about consequences they did not intend. A women's club protested this invitation on the grounds that I was really an unregenerate Communist and an avowed atheist besides, unfit to address a Christian university.

In partial accommodation to this protest, the original idea of having me as the sole speaker was changed, and I was now to be questioned by a panel, with three university professors, and a certain Herbert Philbrick, the alleged authority on Communism who has made his living recounting horror tales, and who happened to be down that way. Ordinarily, I would not come within a ten-foot pole's distance of Philbrick. Inasmuch as the issue of free speech had been raised with respect to myself, I consented to appear on the same platform with him. I had nothing to fear from his questions. And I had quite a few of my own.

All of this produced front-page publicity in many Texas newspapers on a most unusual scale. Any kind of Communist, even an ex-Communist, is a rarity in that great state. Radio stations kept calling long-distance for telephone interviews, and the airport at Dallas was crowded with newsmen, TV photographers and radio reporters as though I were a candidate for high office. They tried in every way to get a shot of me shaking hands with Philbrick, but all they came up with was the photo of Philbrick extending his hand toward my back that was turned on him. The result was a meeting of 3,000 students, with an overflow audience of another 500.

It was a thrilling meeting, and I learned as much from these students as they from me. The *Dallas Morning News,* publishing a summary of my remarks—essentially what has gone into this book—found space for a full page of it. And its headline read: "Gates For Socialism And Against Capitalism." I dare say Socialism has rarely had so much publicity in Texas.

At the University of Texas, in Austin, the authorities forbade the meeting on the grounds of my Smith Act conviction, with the consequence that the student YMCA invited me to an off-campus debate on Marxism with a local professor. The invitation was withdrawn when it turned out that I would not represent orthodox Marxism. The *Dallas Morning News* ran the story under the amusing headline: "Gates Not Red Enough For Texas U. Y.M.C.A."

This expedition to Texas was climaxed with my appearance at a Baylor University class in Comparative Christianity and Communism. The discussion was keen, and far from revealing a silent, or shook-up, or beat generation, it showed that such generalizations can be truthfully applied only to a handful of young Americans. It was a far cry from my own days at school, but the picture I have of these young people is that they are seriously studying the issues of our day, grappling with the intellectual problems that tomorrow will present themselves as practical. There was an amusing finale when I told this class that my father, vice-president of his synagogue, had been praying for years that I leave the Communist Party. My mother-in-law, who is Catholic, had been doing the same with respect to her daughter. Each was no doubt convinced that his and her prayers had been answered.

My wife and I were not sure whether the credit goes to Jews or Catholics, I told them. After the laughter subsided, the chairman said: "Mr. Gates, I want you to know that you may have had Jews and Catholics praying for you and your wife, but after tonight there's going to be a lot of good Methodists and Baptists praying for you, too."

It is a moving thought, as much as it may sound amusing to some. Whether our problems will be solved by prayer or not, it is certain that these young men and women are the ones who must face the issues of today and tomorrow. The society they inherit from their elders is not what they had the right to expect, and they surely will remake it. They bear no responsibility for our mistakes, but they may learn from our past, with its great and meaningful moments, and its unworthy ones. These young people will continue the best in our American heritage, in terms of the present as they understand it, and the future they want. To the youth of America, in the hope that they will succeed where we did not, I dedicate this book.

INDEX

Abt, John, 55, 143
Acheson, Dean, 123
Acton, Lord, 74
Aleutian Islands, 89-90, 93
Alger, Horatio, 11
Algeria, 206
Amalgamated Association of Iron, Steel & Tin Workers, 34
Amalgamated Clothing Workers, 38, 115
Amazing Stories, 11
America First Committee, 77
American Federation of Labor, 23-25, 34, 37
American Friends Service Committee, 210
American Labor Party, 38, 147
American League Against War & Fascism, 38
American Legion, 104
American Student Union, 76
American Veterans Committee, 104
American Youth Congress, 37, 69-72, 77
American Youth for Democracy, 91
Amherst College, 105

Amter, Israel, 32-33
Anarchists, 52
Anderson, George, 149-50
Anderson, Sherwood, 26
Argosy All-Story, 11
Arista, 13
Atlanta Federal Penitentiary, 136-38, 141, 143, 146-51, 155, 158, 160-61
Attlee, Clement, 56-57
Aware, Inc., 204

Babe Ruth, 10, 13
Baldwin, Joseph Clark, 87
Bard College, 210
Barton, James, 11
Bates, Ruby, 20
Baylor University, 210, 212
Bennett, James V., 140
Beria, Lavrenti, 152-53
Berlin airlift, 134
Berry, Abner, 111
Bill of Rights, 4, 204
Bittelman, Alexander, 155
Black Belt, 106-07
Blackett, P. M. S., 96
Black, Justice, 135

Blum, Emanuel, 184-85
Bonus, Veterans, 24
Booth, Colonel, 95
Bottcher, Herman, 88
Bowers, Claude G., 46
British Battalion, 56-57
Bronx Home News, 16
Brooklyn College, 210
Brooklyn Dodgers, 91
Browder, Earl, 38, 69-70, 79, 82, 87-88, 91-93, 96-99, 102-05, 107-08, 133, 136, 152, 164, 184
Buffalo Bill, 11
Bukharin, Nikolai, 54

Cacchione, Peter V., 91, 105
Cahan, Abraham, 8
Camp Chaffee, 85, 88, 95
Camp Kilmer, 99
Camp Mackall, 94
Camp Upton, 83, 85
Camp Wolters, 88
Cantor, Eddie, 11
Capital, 22
Carey, James, 76
Carlson, Frank, 21-23, 25
Carnegie Hall, 91, 160
Carter, Nick, 11
Cash, W. J., 141
Castor Oil, 8, 39
Central Intelligence Agency, 153
Central Park, 8
Chamberlain, Neville, 57, 65
Chapman, Gerald, 149-50
Charney, George Blake, 186
Chiang Kai Shek, 132, 199
Chicago Tribune, 112
Childs, Morris, 110
China, 3, 36, 132, 197, 199

Churchill, Winston, 75, 79, 81, 91, 108, 109
CIO, 3, 23, 37, 42, 116
Civil War, U.S., 20, 56, 73, 207
Clark, Joseph, 88, 111, 159-60, 184-86
Clausewitz, 198
Cold War, 3, 198
College of the City of New York, 14, 16-17, 21, 210
Columbia University, 111
Cominform, 109, 112-13, 188
Commissar, 47
Communazis, 76
Communist International, 37-38, 74, 76, 79, 91, 106
Communist Party, 16th National Convention, 181-82, 184, 186-87, 189-91
Communist Political Association, 92-93, 98
Communist Veterans Encampment, 117
Congress, U.S., 5, 10, 145, 147, 203-04, 206-08
Constitution, U.S., 160, 207
Copic, Colonel, 56, 58, 61
Coughlin, Father, 36
Cowley, Malcolm, 26
Cromwell, Oliver, 47
Cullen, Countee, 26
Cult of the Individual, 152
Cyprus, 206
Czechoslovakia, 53, 65, 73, 78, 115, 153

Daily Worker, 4, 13, 20, 26, 79, 101, 104-05, 109-12, 121, 133, 138, 144, 155-56, 159-63, 167-70, 179-80, 183-91, 204

Daladier, Edouard, 65
Dallas Morning News, 211-12
Dallet, Joe, 29-30, 48, 50
Danbury Prison, 143-44
Dancis, Winston, 17
Darrow, Clarence, 141
Dartmouth College, 29
Davis, Benjamin J., 104-05, 109-10, 133, 142, 165, 182-83, 188-89
Debs, Eugene Victor, 136, 141
Democratic Centralism, 172, 176
Democratic Party, 11, 17, 25, 35, 37, 115-17, 123, 147, 204, 208-09
Dennis, Eugene, 74-75, 104-05, 109-10, 138-43, 147, 151-52, 155-56, 160, 164-70, 173, 182, 188-90
Department of Justice, 101, 108, 119, 135
Dewey, Thomas E., 112, 117
De Witt Clinton High School, 10, 12-13
Dictatorship of the Proletariat, 36, 72, 109, 193
District 65, Distributive Workers, 117
Dixiecrats, 160, 207, 209
Djilas, Milovan, 205
Doran, Dave, 56-58, 61
Dos Passos, John, 26
Dostoevsky, 11
Douglas, Justice, 125, 135
Douglass, Frederick, 141
D'Oyly Carte Company, 99
Draft Resolution, 170-73, 182
DuBois, W. E. B., 106, 141
Duclos, Jacques, 96-98, 182
Dulles, John Foster, 198-200
Dunbar, Malcolm, 62

Durante, Jimmy, 11
Dyer, Congressman, 138

East Berlin, 153
Eastland, Senator, 208
East Side, Manhattan, 7-8, 11
Ebro River, 57, 59-60, 62-64, 83
Eisenhower Administration, 15, 134, 198-99, 202, 206
Engels, Frederick, 72, 123, 173, 200
Enlisted Men's Reserve Corps, 100, 119
Ernst, Morris, 13

Farmer-Labor Party, 37
Fast, Howard, 169, 182
FBI, 4, 204-05
Federal Communications Commission, 206-07
Federal Jury System, 131
Feuer, Lewis, 17
Fields, W. C., 11
Fifteenth Brigade, 53, 56-57, 60
Fifth Amendment Communists, 160
Fifth Column, 54
Finnish War, 77-78
Five Year Plans, 17
Flynn, Elizabeth Gurley, 135, 186, 190
Foley Square Courthouse, 102, 119-120, 135, 144
Ford Forum, 187
Ford, James W., 26, 105
Forer, Joseph, 143
Fort Benning, 93
Fort Dix, 99
Fort Sill, 85, 93

Foster, William Z., 25-26, 35, 38-39, 70, 93, 97-98, 104-06, 109-10, 114, 119, 133, 142, 158-60, 164-66, 168, 172-73, 178, 181-84, 186, 188-89
Franco, 41, 52, 54, 66-67, 181
Frankfeld, Phil, 155
Frankfurter, Justice, 125
Frank, Waldo, 26
French Revolution, 47
Friends of Abraham Lincoln Brigade, 68-69, 74
Frontiers, 18, 24
Full Employment Act, 202

Galbraith, J. K., 201
Galileo, 141
Gardner, Virginia, 111
Garland, Mr., 10
Garvey, Marcus, 106
Gates, Lillian, 90-91, 93-94, 96-99, 103, 121, 140, 143, 154, 156, 159, 191, 212
Geneva, 184
Gerson, Simon W., 184, 191
GI Bill of Rights, 103
Gilbert and Sullivan, 99
Glasgow, Ellen, 141
Golden Book, 11
Gold, Michael, 8
Gompers, Samuel, 164
Gomulka, 109, 113, 178
GOP, 35, 70, 116, 123, 207
Gordon, Max, 17
Great Depression, 3, 14-16, 23, 35, 174
Green, Gil, 69, 80, 104, 107-08, 120, 135, 206
Green, William, 24-25

Gregory, Horace, 26
Guernica, 52

Hale, Nathan, 130
Hall, Gus, 49, 120, 122, 135, 143
Hall, Rob, 111, 144
Hand, Learned, 134
Harding, President, 136
Hart, William S., 9
Harvard, 111
Harvard Law School, 105, 210
H-Bomb, 3, 188, 198
Heard, Alexander, 141
Hearst Press, 12
Hecht, Joseph, 59
Hemingway, Ernest, 46, 60-61
Herndon, Angelo, 105
Hicks, Granville, 26, 76, 187
Higgins, Jimmy, 19
Hillman, Sidney, 37, 141
Hiroshima, 96
Hiss Case, 131
History of the Communist Party of the Soviet Union, 72
Hitler, 3, 35-38, 41, 64-66, 75, 77, 79-81, 95, 135, 163
Ho Chi Minh, 159
Hook, Sidney, 26
Hoover, Herbert, 3, 15, 18, 24-25, 202
Hoover, J. Edgar, 4, 5, 39, 46, 129-30, 146-47, 184, 204
Hotel Albert, 191, 210
Hotel & Restaurant Workers Union, 117
House Committee on Un-American Activities, 4, 183, 203-04
Howard, Milton, 111, 160
Howard, Sidney, 26
Hughes, Langston, 26

Hugo, Victor, 141
Hungary, 113, 162, 165, 168, 177-81, 192, 206
Hunger March, Ohio, 32-33
Hunger March, National, 23, 25, 32
Hunter College, 210

Indo-China War, 159
Internal Revenue Service, 162
International Brigade, 41, 44, 53, 66
International Correspondence School, 90
International Labor Defense, 21-22
International Ladies Garment Workers Union, 38
Isserman, Abraham, 143
Italian Elections, 112

Jackson, James, 187
Jackson, Justice, 130
Janney, Russell, 131
Japan, 82, 89, 95
Jewish Question, 114, 152, 163
Johnson, Lyndon, 208
Josephson, Matthew, 26, 141

Kadar, Janos, 113
Kempton, Murray, 168
Key, V. O., 141
Khrushchev, Nikita, 75, 157, 159, 161, 166-69, 198
Kommunist, 187
Korean War, 132-34, 152
Kostov, 113
Kreymborg, Alfred, 26
Labor Defender, 21
Labor Party, British, 56-57, 209

LaGuardia, Fiorello, 147
Landon, Alf, 70
Lapin, Adam, 17
Lardner, James, 65
Lardner, Ring, 65
Lash, Joseph P., 17, 76
Latin America, 200
League of Nations, 66
Leavenworth Penitentiary, 148
Leibowitz, Samuel, 20
Lenin, V. I., 17, 26, 98, 123, 170-72, 175
Lewis, John L., 37, 77, 93, 164-65
Liberal Club, 17
Liberal Party, 147, 210
Lincoln, Abraham, 187
Lincoln Brigade, 50, 56, 60, 62, 65
Lincoln, Elmo, 9
Little Steel Strike, 49
Lodge, Henry Cabot, 87
Long, Huey, 36
Loyalists, 41, 58, 60, 62-64, 66
Lubell, Samuel, 7, 141
Luce, Clare Booth, 87

MacArthur, General, 96, 132, 134
Mackenzie-Papineau Battalion, 50
Madison Square Garden, 69
Maginot Line, 79
Malenkov, Georgi, 153
Maleter, Pal, 206
Mao Tse Tung, 197
Marcantonio, Vito, 87, 140, 143, 147
Marshall Plan, 115-16
Marty, André, 112
Marxism, 96, 166, 171, 173
Marxism-Leninism, 158, 167, 170, 175

Marxist classics, 17, 69, 123, 126

Marx, Karl, 17, 22-23, 26, 69, 72, 123, 170, 175, 200-01

Masters of Deceit, 5, 46, 129, 204

Matthews, Herbert, 46, 60-63, 67

Max, Alan, 111, 144, 155, 160-61, 187

McCabe, Louis, 143

McCarran Act, 130, 142, 145, 205

McCarthyism, 102, 113, 131-35, 139-41, 157, 160, 162, 189, 205-06

Medina, Judge, 22, 40, 120, 123-26, 131

Meet the Press, 128

Menjou, Adolphe, 124

Merriman, Robert, 56, 58

Merriwell, Frank, 11

Mexico, 45

Middle East, 199

Miners Strike, 92-93

Minor, Robert, 82

Montaigne, 186

Morris, George, 111, 186

Moscow, 22, 37, 74, 109

Moscow Trials, 54

Moysey, Donald C., 162

Munich Pact, 65, 75

Mussolini, 35, 40-41, 64-66

Muste, A. J., 33, 142

Nagasaki, 96

Nagy, Imre, 179, 192, 205

Nation, 12, 140

National Association for the Advancement of Colored People, 20

National Maritime Union, 117

National Negro Congress, 38

National Recovery Act, 35, 37

National Youth Administration, 39-40

NATO, 177, 199

Negrin, Juan, 66

Negro Nation, 106-08

Nelson, Steve, 62

Newcastle Jail, 39

New Deal, 4, 31, 35, 37, 202, 208-09

Newman Club, 17

New Republic, 12, 140

New York Daily News, 121

New York Herald-Tribune, 60, 140

New York Post, 16, 128, 140, 204, 210

New York Times, 12, 60, 140, 153

New York World, 12

New York Yankees, 10, 13

Non-Aggression Pact, Soviet Union and Germany, 74-75, 77-78, 108

North, Joseph, 111

Old Vic, 99

Open Letter, 180

Orwell, George, 53, 154

Paisley, William, 146

Parachute School, 93

Parole, 139, 148, 156

Party Voice, 159

Passport Division, 43

Pearl Harbor, 81-82

Pearson, Drew, 88

Peck, Tony, 32

Penny Auctions, 30

People's Democracies, 109

People's Front, 38-40, 76

Philbrick, Herbert, 211

Phillips Exeter Academy, 210
Phoney War, 78-79
Pledge of Allegiance, 10, 82, 146, 197
Plessy v. Ferguson Decision, 106
Poland, 79, 113, 168, 177-79, 192
Political Affairs, 104, 133, 170, 173
Pollitt, Harry, 75-76
Ponomarev, 187
POUM, 52-54
Progressive Party, 115-18
Prohibition, 9, 11
P.S. 179, Manhattan, 9
P.S. 42, Bronx, 10
Public Works Administration, 39

Radek, 54
Rajk, 113, 162
Rakosi, 179
Randolph, A. Philip, 76
Ratner's Restaurant, 7
Rayburn, Speaker, 208
Raymond, Harry, 111
Recession, 15, 200
Red Army, 47, 93
Red Book, 74
Regenstreif, Sol, 26
Regents Scholarship, 13, 16, 19
Remington Case, 131
Reporter, 140
Republican Party, 11, 17, 25, 117, 123, 147, 160, 204, 208
Republic Steel Corporation, 29, 34
Reuther, Walter, 110
Revisionism, 96, 181-82
Rhee, Syngman, 132, 199
Rickey, Branch, 91
Riis, Jacob, 8

Robinson, Frederick E., 18
Robinson, Jackie, 91
Rodney, Lester, 111
Rogers, Frank, 31
Roosevelt College, 210
Roosevelt, Eleanor, 70, 77, 142
Roosevelt, Franklin D., 3, 25, 30-31, 35-36, 42, 53, 65, 70, 73, 76-79, 81, 87, 91, 95
Rosenberg Case, 131
Ross, Carl, 88
Ross, Lillian, 88-89
ROTC, 18
Rover Boys, 11
Ruhr, 95
Russian Revolution, 17, 22, 39, 165, 170, 188
Russians, 4, 22, 40, 54, 187

Sacher, Harry, 125
Salisbury, Harrison, 153
Salvation Army, 23
Sarah Lawrence College, 128
Scherer, Congressman, 204
Schlesinger, Arthur, Jr., 141
Schmuck, Peter J., 16
Schneider, Isador, 26
Schuman, Frederick L., 26
Schurz, Carl, 187
Schwellenbach, Lewis K., 117
Scottsboro Case, 20-21
Second Front, 93
Self Determination, Negroes in Black Belt, 106
Senate, U.S., 81, 208
Shakespeare, William, 99
Shaw, George Bernard, 13
Sheean, Vincent, 46, 60-61, 65, 74
Shields, Art, 111

Sinclair, Upton, 19

Slansky, Rudolph, 113

Smith Act, 22, 40, 42, 49, 78, 101-02, 108, 117-19, 123, 126-28, 130-31, 138, 141, 155, 158, 205, 211

Smith, Alfred E., 8, 11, 35, 120

Smith, Gerald L. K., 36

Sobell Case, 131

Social-Democrats, 35, 36

Social-Fascists, 36, 76

Socialist Club, 17

Socialist Workers Party, 127

Social Problems Club, 17-19, 23-24

Southern Conference for Human Welfare, 38

Southern Methodist University, 210

Southern Negro Youth Congress, 38

Soviet Union, 17-18, 36, 38, 45, 53-54, 73-81, 91, 108, 111, 115, 130, 132, 145, 160, 163, 175, 178-79, 194, 197

Spanish Civil War, 3, 30, 40-67, 71, 73, 77, 81, 83-85, 87, 162, 181

Speak Your Piece, 161

Sputnik, 187, 206

S.S. Deutschland, 42-43

S.S. Paris, 43

Stachel, Jack, 110, 143, 183-84

Stalin, Joseph, 26, 45, 54-55, 72-73, 75, 91, 98, 106, 109, 112-13, 123, 127, 134, 152-54, 157, 161, 166-69, 171, 178-79, 192

Starobin, Joseph, 13, 17, 69, 111, 159-60, 182

Stars and Stripes, 96

Stassen, Harold, 117

State Department, U.S., 42, 167-68

Steel and Metal Workers Industrial Union, 25

Steel Strike of 1919, 35, 164

Steel Workers Organizing Committee, 42

Steffens, Lincoln, 18, 26

Stein, Sid, 191

Steuben, John, 165, 182

St. Louis Post Dispatch, 82

Subversive Activities Control Board, 142, 144-45

Suez War, 181

Supreme Court, 106, 108, 122-26, 134-35

Swarthmore College, 210

Sweethearts of Servicemen, 91

Swift, Tom, 11

Taft-Hartley Law, 114

Taylor, Harold, 128

Tennessee Evolution Trial, 11

Thomas, Norman, 142

Thompson, Robert, 50, 88, 104-05, 109-10, 117, 131, 133, 135, 139, 142, 146, 155, 158-59, 163, 165, 186, 188

Titoism, 99, 109, 112-13, 153-54, 162

Trade Union Unity League, 25

Transport Workers Union, 117

Treasury Department, U.S., 161

Triangle Fire, 8

Trotskyists, 52, 99, 127, 154, 178

True Story, 11

Truman, Harry, 81, 95, 108-09, 115-17, 123, 141, 145

Twain, Mark, 49, 141

Twelve-Party Declaration, 188
Twentieth Congress, Communist
    Party of the Soviet Union,
    160, 161, 164, 184

Unemployed Council, 23, 32-34
Unemployed League, 33-34
Unemployment Insurance, 15, 17,
    23-25, 203
United Auto Workers Union, 115
United Nations, 132, 179
United Press, 101
United States Steel Corporation,
    49
University of California, 56
University of Chicago, 210
University of Manchester, 99
University of Michigan, 210
University of North Carolina, 127
University of Texas, 211
University of Wisconsin, 210

Valledor, Major, 61
V-E Day, 95
Veterans of Abraham Lincoln Bri-
    gade, 69
Veterans of Foreign Wars, 104
Vinson, Chief Justice, 134
Voorhis Law, 78

Wallace, Henry, 115-16
Wallace, Mike, 210
Waller, Fats, 91
Wall Street Crash, 14, 16
War Department, U.S., 86-87, 89
Warren, Chief Justice, 134
Warsaw Pact, 179
Washington Commonwealth Fed-
    eration, 38
Watt, George, 58-59, 83

Wechsler, James A., 128, 141
Weird Tales, 11
Weiss, Max, 17-18, 80, 164
West Street Jail, 120-21, 143
White, David McKelvey, 68
White, Pearl, 9
White Primary, 21
Wilkerson, Doxey, 107-08
Williamson, John, 110
Willoughby, General, 96
Wilson, Edmund, 14, 18, 26, 31
Winston, Henry, 69, 120, 122,
    135, 206
Winter, Carl, 120
Wolf, Milton, 62
Woodward, C. Vann, 141
Workers Alliance, 34
Workers School, 22
Works Progress Administration,
    39-40, 42, 149
World War I, 9, 16
World War II, 51-52, 59, 65, 67,
    78, 82-100

Yates Decision, 122
Young Communist League, 18-22,
    25-26, 28, 34, 37, 41, 68-73,
    77, 80-81, 83-84, 88, 90, 159
Young Communist Review, 69, 71
Young Defenders, 21-22
Young Hunger Fighters, 23
Young Men's Christian Associa-
    tion, 40, 211-12
Young Men's Hebrew Association,
    10
Young, Robert, 16
Youngstown Vindicator, 48
Young Women's Christian Asso-
    ciation, 37
Yugoslavia, 80, 112, 171, 188,
    205